Red Deer in New Zealand
A complete hunting manual

*To Dawn and [illegible]
From your old [illegible]*

[signature]

Roger Lentle and Frank Saxton

David Bateman

Dedicated to all our hunting mates who have given so freely of their companionship and knowledge. We wish you many good stalks ahead and a good stock of hunting memories if the days ever come when the hills are too high for you.

First published in 1991 by David Bateman Ltd, "Golden Heights",
32-34 View Road, Glenfield, Auckland, New Zealand
Reprinted 1991
Reprinted 1993
Reprinted 1994

Copyright © 1991 R.G. Lentle & F.L. Saxton
Copyright © 1991 David Bateman Ltd

This book is copyright. Except for the purpose of fair review, no part may be stored or transmitted in any form or by any means, electronic or mechanical, including recording or storage in any information retrieval system, without permission in writing from the publisher. No reproduction may be made, whether by photocopying or any other means, unless a licence has been obtained from the publisher or its agent.

ISBN 1-86953-037-3

Illustrations by Ray Burns, except those on
pp. 29, 88 and 173 by Lance Barnard.
Typeset by Bryan Coppersmith
Jacket design by Chris O'Brien/Pages Literary Pursuits
Printed in Hong Kong by Colorcraft

Front cover: Mature stag photographed early in the roar. (*Photos by Lance Barnard; reproduced by courtesy NZ Dept. of Conservation*)

Contents

	Introduction	4
1	Signs they leave	5
2	Their senses	30
3	What they like to eat	39
4	Effects of weather on red deer	57
5	Their regular behaviour patterns	70
6	Some hunting strategies and tactics	89
7	Dogs for deerstalking	112
8	Shooting and tracking wounded deer	123
9	From forest floor to kitchen table	135
10	Ageing: conformation, antlers and teeth	161
11	Red deer evolution: grass or tree eaters?	174
	Glossary	182
	Descriptive bibliography	188
	Index	191

Introduction

If you want to shoot more deer on your hunting trips, you have to understand them better. As you walk around the hills with a rifle you may chance upon them, but to be consistently successful, you must know and understand their behaviour.

Hunters build up knowledge from experience, and some write books and magazine articles. Scientists study in detail specific aspects of animals and then write about their findings in technical language in specialist publications. In New Zealand, the knowledge of these two groups has seldom been brought together in a way useful to a deerstalker. That is what we aim to do in this book for the stalker of red deer.

Deerstalking is the interaction of three things: the deer, the hunter and the environment. For deer, we discuss what they like to eat, their senses, their regular behaviour patterns, the signs they leave behind, their evolution, and their anatomy. For the hunter, we examine hunting strategies and tactics, the shooting and tracking of wounded deer, butchering and identification of diseased animals, and the training and correct use of deer-hunting dogs. For the environment, we look at the effect of weather and terrain on deer and deerstalking.

The information we present is not intended to enable animals to be located precisely. Deer, like all wild creatures, are not entirely predictable, and a hunter's best plans can only serve to make an encounter more likely. An element of luck is always involved — indeed it would be to the detriment of the sport if this were not so.

At the end of each chapter, we have added hunting stories drawn from our own deerstalking experiences. These stories show examples of the practical application of some of the principles we describe.

Hunting our red deer can be a rewarding pastime easily available at low cost to most town and city dwellers throughout New Zealand. We hope you find this book enjoyable and informative.

1
Signs they leave

... the boy as soon as he could walk and run, accompanied the hunters into the field. He was taught how to track the marks of the animals. Of the insects, the flight of a bird, the influence of the wind on the movements of the game. The character of the animals, how they behaved in the morning, in the noon-day, in the night. All these things were important to the hunter. Nature then in a sense was his bible and the most important writing in the bible was the spoor.

— Laurens van der Post, talking about the Bushman hunters of Africa

In the Middle Ages in Europe, men whose job it was to maintain and protect the deer herds accumulated expertise in reading deer sign. These men also provided technical skill for the lord when he hunted his deer. T.E. Donne, in his book *Red deer stalking in New Zealand*, notes that in the Middle Ages a forester was able to recognise and use 72 signs to determine the sex, size and condition of deer, just from the marks they left behind.

A lot of this know-how is still used by the present-day deerstalkers of Europe. Unfortunately, much of this European legacy has been lost by the hunters of New Zealand, probably because we had large numbers of easily hunted deer for such a long period. The commercial venison-recovery industry has so reduced the numbers of red deer that the ability to read the signs of the few that are left has again become important for successful hunting.

Print

Deer "print" is the term we will use for the footprints and other sign an animal leaves behind with its feet (overseas, the term "spoor" is often used). Some prints, such as those left in the bed of a stream, may last only a few seconds, and the splash marks on a rock at the side of a stream may last only a few minutes in summer, but footprints in a clay bank under a sheltered overhang may last for some months.

One way to estimate age is to make a similar mark next to the print in question and study it for a few minutes to see how it changes — for example, how long does a wet mark on a stone take to lose its shine, and how long does a mark in soft riverside sand take to fill up with water? Practice builds knowledge, and a high degree of skill in ageing sign can be achieved.

Foot structure

In order to understand deer print characteristics we must know how a deer's foot is constructed (see Fig. 1). Deer have a cloven foot and the two halves are called "cleaves". The "toe" is the pointed front of the cleave and the "heel" is the rounded back of the cleave. The outside of each cleave is covered in a shiny layer of horn which makes the outer rim of the print in the ground. This horny part gives grip in slippery conditions. The inner portion of each cleave is made of a soft spongy substance which is able to grip on hard surfaces.

The outwardly projecting lump of this soft substance at the back of each cleave, just at the front of each heel, is called the "ball". It is more prominent in stags. The cleaves move apart passively when the animal applies pressure and more grip is required, for example, when the animal is running, climbing a slope or is just plain heavy. Above the cleaves are the "dew claws", which are found on both forelegs and hind legs about 4 centimetres above each cleave at the back. In stags the dew claws poke out more to the side; in hinds they poke out more to the back. Because they are further up each leg, they leave marks only when a heavy animal walks on soft ground. Thus, because stags are generally heavier than hinds, stags are more likely to leave dew claw marks.

With age and wear and tear the rim of the cleaves becomes chipped in places, the toes become blunted and the inner surface of each cleave becomes worn. It changes shape from convex to concave, that is, from a bulge to a hollow (see Fig. 2). With attention to these sorts of details, and practice, you can identify even individual animals from their prints.

Soil type and the age of prints

A print that changes quickly with the passage of time is said to be "fast". For example, river sand gives very fast sign.

We will describe in detail the dynamics of print formation and ageing in sandy conditions. The same processes operate in other ground types, only more slowly.

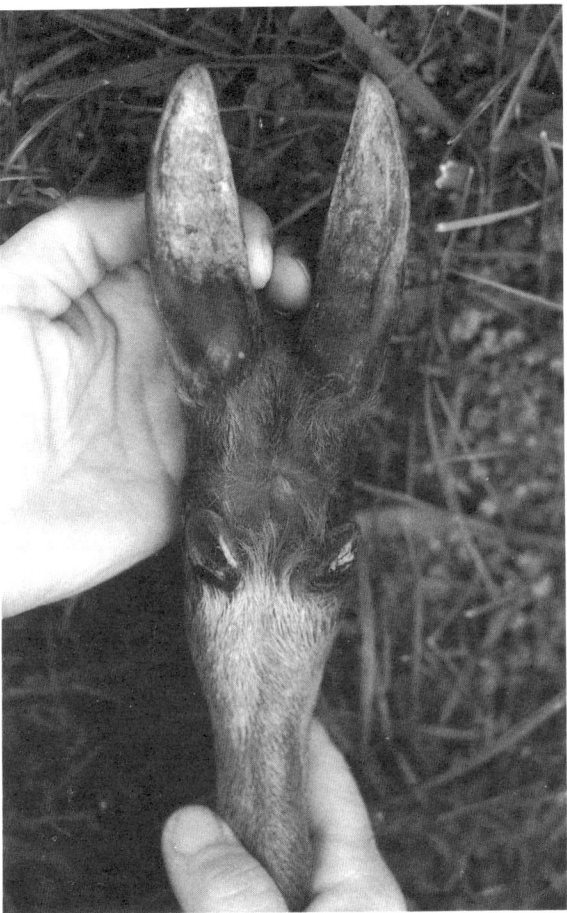

Fig. 1: Rear foot of a 4-year-old stag. The cleaves splay apart easily with pressure, giving greater traction. The separated position shown here is how they appear when the animal is cantering. Also shown are the horny rims of the cleaves and the soft inner material, a combination which gives good grip in a range of conditions.

Note also the outward bulging of the soft inner substance of the "ball" of each cleave. Stags usually have a larger, more rounded ball than is the case with the feet of hinds, and this can be used to distinguish between stags' and hinds' footprints. Also, the dew claws of stags point outwards towards the sides as much as they do towards the rear; with hinds they face more to the rear.

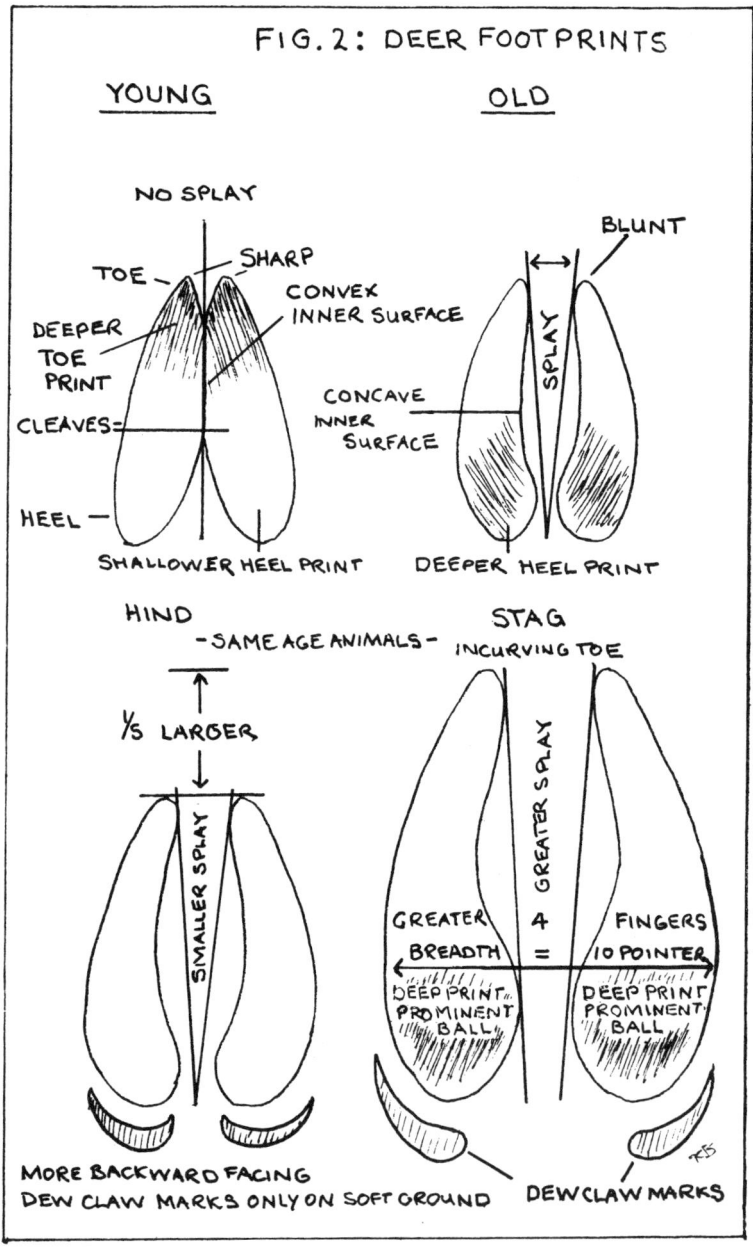

A walking deer makes steps in two stages. Firstly, it places each foot into the sand, making a clear imprint, and secondly, it applies weight to the foot. Depending on the nature of the sand, the foot will sometimes sink in deep enough to allow the dew claws to imprint.

If a deer steps into very wet sand there will be an up-welling of water on to the surface surrounding the foot as water is squeezed out. Below the surface the cleaves spread apart as the foot takes the animal's weight, and as the foot sinks a chunk of sand is forced between them. As the deer continues walking the foot is withdrawn and part of the sand between the cleaves is pulled out and flicked off the foot as it travels forward to its next placement. The sand remaining that was between the cleaves forms an upstanding ridge in the bottom of the print. The sand that is pulled out is wetter and darker coloured than the surface sand. In time it will dry out to be the same colour as surface sand.

After the withdrawal of the foot, water seeps into the hole, bringing with it a small amount of sand. This in-filling can cause a series of radiating cracks in the surrounding sand. If the sand is very wet the print can fill up with water and collapse completely, leaving only a dish-shaped impression.

In dry sand the grains fall apart and a blurred print is left. If the sand is moist its water content holds the grains together and a well defined print is created. The sharp edges of the print dry first. Studying the extent of drying is a valuable way to estimate the age of a print.

Prints made in pure clay last a long time. Clay, like sand, is made up of thousands of particles, but because they are much smaller, clay can hold more water and therefore takes longer to dry out. Even the sharp edges of a print will resist drying out and will do so only in direct sunlight. Prints made in clay will also withstand much rain, and will probably last long enough to be filled with leaves and to accommodate spider webs, and even the seedlings of forest trees.

Soils other than clay and sand are mixtures of sand and clay particles and pieces of vegetation. The time it takes a print to age in such soils will be somewhere between that for sand and clay. Where possible, follow the trail as it cuts across different ground in sunlight and in shade in order to build up a more complete picture of ageing time.

In cold conditions, water in the prints will freeze and preserve them until thawing. In rainy weather the edges of the prints are damaged by the raindrops and a lot of rain will obliterate them.

Prints left in snow disturb the reflective surface of the virgin snow.

Less sunlight is reflected from this disturbed surface, more heat is retained, and the snow in the print therefore melts faster. The prints melt from the middle outwards, making a gradually enlarging hole in the snow. The age of the prints can be difficult to judge from the size of the melted hole, because the weather can greatly affect the rate of melting.

In shallow soft snow, deer often leave a muddy trail, because the cleaves are forced through the snow and spread apart, picking up mud from the soil below in the same way as they do from sand. Not only is a mud-snow mixture thrown clear, but it also forms a dirty coating around each cleave which contaminates the snow around the next print. Warming conditions will spread a rim out over the surrounding clean snow, and in doing so the muddy colour gradually loses its strength. This colour change can often be a more useful guide to age than the melting of the prints.

The effect of a deer foot walking across grass can give a lot of information. A deer walking across grass wet by a recent shower of rain, or by dew, will cause the water to be shed, leaving the drier grass a darker green colour. This is fast sign — it doesn't last long, so your deer is not far away.

The blades of grass that are trodden on by the edge of the cleave are folded and creased in places. For the first few hours sap will exude from the damaged blades and stalks, making them a darker colour than the rest of the grass. In dry conditions the exuded sap will dry quickly and leave the damaged area a paler green than normal. After 2 days, in both wet and dry conditions, the damaged area will change from this pale green to yellow, and after another 2 days the yellow will change to brown. These changes happen only in very small areas on the leaf and will be seen only with careful scrutiny.

The projecting vertical surfaces of a clay or earth bank are good places to find long-lasting deer sign. In places where the other ground is stony or for some other reason not good at holding deer prints, sign on these vertical places may be the only evidence of the passage of deer. As deer climb a bank their cleaves separate and their sharp toes dig in to grip. Often the deer will slip and make a vertical parallel pair of gouge marks about 5 centimetres apart. (As deer go downhill they can make similar-looking paired marks with their dew claws but these are closer together.) When studying these grooves for drying look also for small amounts of material that have been scraped out and are now in piles at the bottom of the bank below the gouges.

Signs they leave

The way these piles have dried can be compared usefully with other clay at the bottom of the bank. Steep rocks can also be marked by prints either directly as scratches on the rock or by the marks left where lichens have been scraped off by the slipping cleaves. These marks on rock may last for years with little change.

Judging size, age and sex from prints

The heavier the deer, the greater the angle between the two cleave prints of each foot.

Older deer leave prints with blunter toe marks, worn edges and concave inner surfaces of the cleave prints. Younger deer tend to bear more weight near the toe, so that the front of the print is deeper than the back (see Fig. 2). Older deer tend to bear more weight towards the heel, which is one of the reasons why ball marks are more prominent in the prints of older deer.

The prints of stags and hinds differ (see Fig. 2). The cleaves of the stag are longer and more tapering in shape than those of a similar-sized hind. They have a wider heel with a more prominent ball tapering down slowly to a narrow, slightly incurved toe.

Dew claw marks are more common in stag prints than hinds owing to the greater weight of the animal. Mature stags are larger than hinds and so leave a larger print overall. (See also p. 13.)

The simplest rule is that of T.E. Donne: "Any footprint wider than four fingers laid together is a ten or twelve pointer . . . a print three fingers wide is a young stag". This rule simply describes the overall size of the animal and is not related directly to the antlers. For example, a hummel (see p. 184) could easily possess a footprint wider than four fingers, as most of them are in good condition.

Walking

A deer normally walks by moving up the hind leg on each side and placing a print almost on top of the impression left by the departing front foot on that side. This obliterates the print of the front foot except for a thin strip that remains just in front of the back footprint. This imprinting of the back print on to the front print is called "registration" (see Fig. 3).

The set of prints left by a single, walking deer, the "trail", consists of alternating right and left pairs of registered prints. Fig. 4 shows such a trail and defines the terms "stride" and "step". The length of the stride is said to equal the height of the deer at the shoulder.

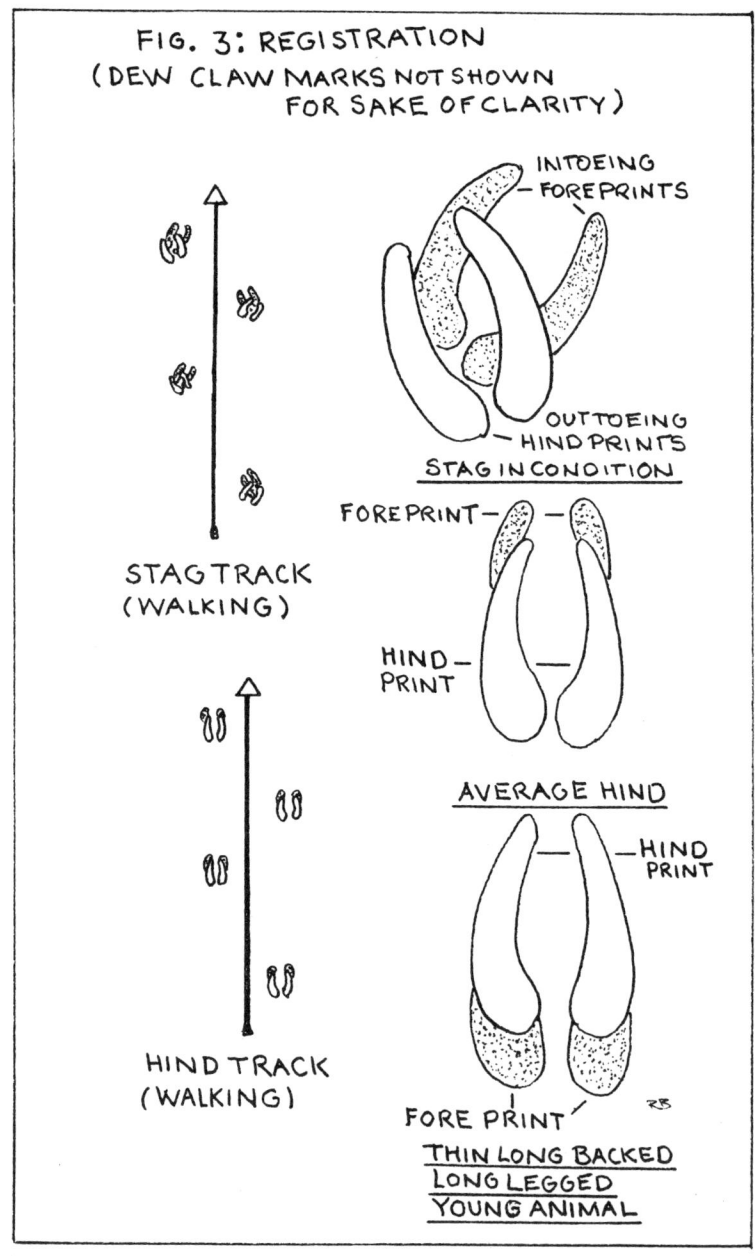

When deer run they are in fact cantering or galloping and registration does not occur. Each foot leaves its own distinct print and there is no even spacing of prints as in walking. The cleaves separate under the full power of the run, and the dew claws also begin to leave marks. There can also be a lot of slipping and consequent dragging marks in the prints of running deer, especially on steep ground. Deer often have to run up a slippery hill just to get the power needed to dig in a firm foothold. Even deer walking on hills can slip and slide about, leaving prints with widely separated cleaves as they struggle for grip.

Information on the condition and age of the animal can be obtained from the details of the registration. At the end of a good summer, stags may have a roll of fat around their hindquarters which prevents their hind legs moving as far forward as they did earlier in summer. This means the back footprint does not register as far forward on the print of the front foot and sometimes falls behind the print of the front foot, so that there is no registration. The roll of fat around the hindquarters pushes each hind leg out slightly sideways, making the hind print angle outward (see Fig. 3). A similar roll of fat pushes behind the shoulder blade and angles the forefoot inwards. Because of this, the prints of a fat stag can not only show a more rearwards registration of the back print, but can also show a back print angled outwards on top of a front print angled inwards. As the rut begins the fat stag loses condition and there is a gradual return to more normal registration with less angling of front and back prints.

The main influence on registration in both sexes is the amount the back foot is brought forward with each stride. The occasional rangy animal with long hind legs can move its hind legs so far forward that they register on the front part of the front print. A print pair is thus formed in which the remains of the front print project from the back of the rear print instead of from the front of the rear print. T.E. Donne describes a spiker that did this.

As an animal ages the amount the back foot is brought forward is progressively reduced. Thus the older the animal the less far forward the back print is registered on the front print.

Routes deer take in the bush

The course the animal takes through the bush may reveal information of its intentions. An animal wandering aimlessly will leave a trail

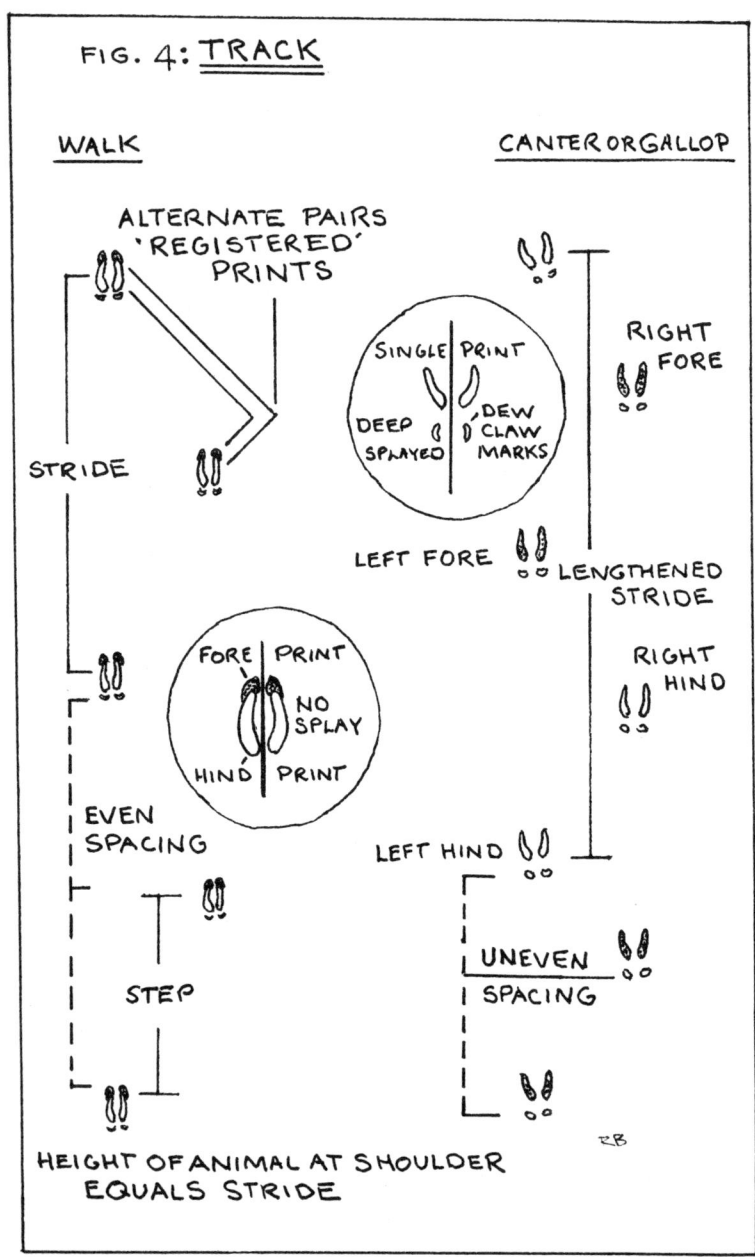

deviating from side to side as it looks for food, while a fast-moving deer intent on travel will walk purposefully in a straight line.

As deer move about they frequently use the same courses which then become established routes.

Deer make a daily journey from the cover in which they sleep to their feeding ground. The course they choose will vary according to the weather and the particular area being browsed. When deer are established in an area an interlacing network of these routes is likely.

In winter when deer are not doing much feeding they confine themselves to a smaller area which then becomes densely covered in deer routes. In North America these areas are called "yards" and the deer are said to be "yarded up". Because so many routes cross and recross one another, it is not easy to follow a fresh trail. The best way to hunt such an area is to do a careful zig-zag stalk upwind.

When deer travel longer distances than their daily feeding and bedding routine, they often create well worn routes. These traditionally used routes are often deeply trenched, where each deer has followed the trail of its predecessors exactly. Deer always take the easiest route across the landscape, usually following ridge tops and using side spurs to go down into and come up from valleys. When these routes cross from one valley to another they cross at the lowest point of a saddle. Sometimes they will follow rivers or river terraces when the valley sides are steep and broken.

These established routes will be used by deer to escape when they are disturbed. One hunting technique is to position one hunter (one who can be relied upon to *always* identify his target) overlooking the route, for example, where it crosses a saddle at the head of a valley. Another hunter walks up the valley making noise and with the wind blowing at his back.

The presence of sign on travel routes does not always indicate deer are living in the area. It may be a cold and barren place frequented only by deer en route to a better locality. By following such routes you can sometimes find out where the deer have gone. For example, if you walk along a main ridge route and find where a side route branches off to head down a spur, you should look carefully for fresh sign some little distance down the spur. You may have to explore a number of such spurs before finding the deer, or concluding that no deer are in the location.

Droppings

Deer droppings are made up mostly of the indigestible parts of the plants the animal has eaten. They also contain bile (a waste product of the liver), water and mucus (a jelly-like lubricant produced by the intestine).

By studying droppings with a microscope, scientists who have the expertise can identify the species of plants on which the deer has been feeding. This technique, however, is beyond the average hunter.

Seasonal variation

The droppings of stags vary according to the seasons (see Fig. 5). Before the "roar" (rutting season), when stags are feeding heavily, the droppings are ejected with a lot of water in them. They often make runny "pats" on the ground like small cow pats. During the roar, when stags are not feeding much, the droppings are small, hard, distinct pellets often adhering to each other. In drought conditions, hinds will also produce adherent droppings.

How to tell the age of pellets

When fresh, the warm, brown-green pellets are coated with fresh liquid mucus. The liquid mucus allows smells to escape from inside the pellet. Flies are attracted by the smells and settle on the pellets. These pellets feel heavy because of their high water content, they smell and are slippery to touch.

With time, and according to the weather conditions, the mucus dries to form a skin that holds the pellet together. In normal weather conditions the dried mucus prevents rainwater from washing away the pellet, but it does allow the moisture inside the pellet to evaporate. Over time the pellet therefore becomes lighter but otherwise remains remarkably well preserved for a long period.

In continued wet weather, rainwater gets inside the pellet and washes out the brown-green colour and the chemicals that cause smell. As various plant fibres in the dropping soak up different amounts of water, the outside of the dropping loses its smoothness. The dropping, then, slowly changes into a light-coloured, rough-surfaced pellet that when broken open has no smell. Finally it becomes a little pile of powder.

Signs they leave

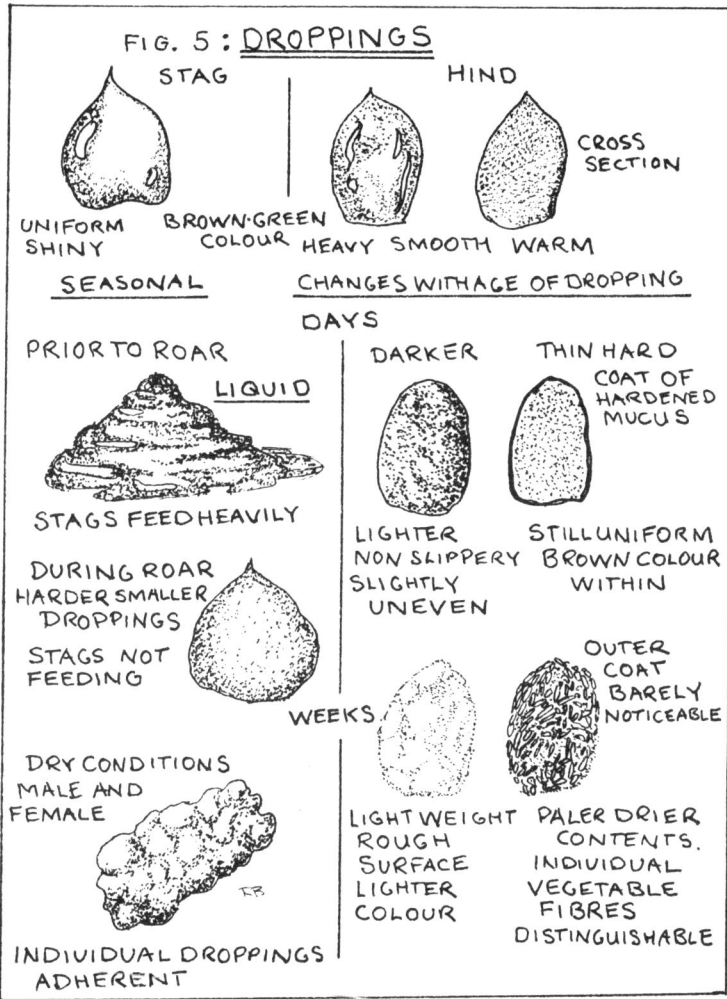

Fig. 5: DROPPINGS

Snow can preserve a pellet until the spring thaw. Frost, by freezing, will prolong the life of the pellet. If heavy rain falls before the mucus has dried, the pellet will break down quickly.

Looking underneath droppings for an indication of age can sometimes be helpful. The yellowing of any grass underneath would show they have been there at least a few days.

The bigger the dropping, the bigger the animal. In medieval

England the forester would present to his lordship a number of pellets (called "fewmets") arranged on a bouquet of leaves before the hunt. The lord could then judge the size of the stag for himself. In this ancient quote the forester claims to know that it is a ten pointer and has good eating venison.

> "Before the Queen, I come report to make
> Then hushe and Peace, for noble Trystams sake.
> and these present an leaves, by hunters law:
> and thus I say: my leige, behold and see
> An Harte of tenne, I hope he harboured bee.
> For if you marke, his Fewmets every poynt,
> You shall them finde, long round and well anoynt,
> Knottie and great, withouten prickles or eares,
> The moystness shows what venysone he beares."
>
> Book of Hunting, 1575

When estimating the size of an animal, look more at the diameter than the length of the pellet. Outside the roar a stag's droppings are normally of greater diameter but shorter than those of a similar-sized hind. Hind droppings are proportionately longer and also more barrel-shaped, curving inwards at each end. Both sexes have a dent in the back end of each pellet, and this dent is of a smaller diameter in hinds than in stags.

Scientists and keen hunters can use the number of droppings in a locality as a guide to the number of deer in an area. This is also used by animal researchers who go about counting the number of pellets per square metre. Concentrations of pellets are highest in feeding areas and lowest in bedding areas. With a little experience a hunter can easily gauge the approximate abundance of deer by observing droppings over quite a small area.

Signs of feeding

When deer eat grass, they graze, and when they eat trees or shrubs they browse. Fresh feeding sign can indicate the presence of deer and enable you to build up knowledge of the seasonal movements of deer.

When browsing, deer usually like to eat the young shoots and leaves of the tree, and to do so they reach as high as they can. When they are at the limit of their reach on four legs they will rear up on their hind legs, sometimes supporting themselves with their front legs against the tree. This manoeuvre enables larger animals to reach up to more than 3 metres above the ground.

Regular browsing can alter the shape of the trees permanently. Often trees will have no branches below the height deer can reach. At the limit of deer reach will be a zone of leaves, shoots, buds and flowers that can only be partly eaten. This is where you should look for clues.

When examining half-eaten leaves, examine the bitten edge. When first bitten off, the edge will be a fresh green colour for a few hours. After a few days the edge will take on a brown colour which will last for months. During this time the thin top and bottom skins of the leaf curl in towards each other and cover the exposed edge. When deer eat shoots and small branches the brown colour of the bitten edge is seen more easily. The bark adjacent to the bite takes about one year to grow back to cover the edge of the bitten shoot. Another good way to estimate age of browse is to find a living half-eaten leaf bud. It will have continued to grow, and what was a clean bite line through all the leaves becomes a stepladder of leaves that have grown at different rates. The amount of stepladdering is a guide to age of browse.

Bitten grass also ages in a predictable way. The severed end goes through the same changes as described above for trodden-on grass.

Stags cleaning and rubbing their antlers

Stags grow their new antlers under a soft "velvet" skin (see also Chapter 10). When the antlers mature underneath the velvet the animal feels an irritation and wipes his antlers against vegetation to get rid of the velvet. When "cleaning" or "fraying", stags prefer dense thin-stemmed foliage, which they damage.

When the velvet is gone the stag has a set of pale bone-coloured antlers which he then begins to polish against favourite "rubbing" trees. The use of different tree species in some regions gives a range of colours to the finished antlers. This variation is more between hunting grounds than between stags in the same area, although stag variation does occur. Deer prefer sturdy trees with a rough bark and they leave gouge marks, often deep ones, in the bark of the trunk and branches.

A study done in 1946 in the Lake Manapouri area found the order of preference for rubbing trees to be: beech trees (*Nothofagus*); totara (*Podocarpus*); pepper tree (*Pseudowintera*). Unless the stag inadvertently kills the tree he will probably use the same tree year after year.

Look closely at a rubbing tree to see if deer hairs are caught in the bark or lying at the foot of the tree. The exposure of fresh young bark shows where old bark has been ripped of. Recent bark stripping is revealed by sap or resin seepage from the edges of torn areas. All these sign reveal recent use.

Deer wallows

In Europe, red deer stags and hinds wallow all year round, because they are infested by ticks and biting flies that we don't have here. In New Zealand wallows are essentially things made by stags in the roar, and out-of-season wallows are rare.

The wallow is made in hind territory and always on a piece of flat ground. Often, a single rutting stag will walk a beat around a series of wallows, stirring up each one in turn; some stags will have a number of wallows that they use selectively according to weather conditions. A hunter that "still hunts" a fresh wallow will, therefore, not always see the stag.

Being able to recognise the signs of a wallow currently in use is important. With the first signs of the rut, wandering stags will begin to visit the wallows. Their fresh prints will be found in the muddy ground around the edge. The visits become more frequent until with the onset of the roar the surrounding soft ground becomes a churned mass of footprints. Then the stags begin to wallow fully, lying down in the mud, rolling on to their backs and wriggling. Plenty of sign are created. Here are the features of an actively used wallow (see Fig. 6):

- The water in the wallow becomes stirred up to a uniform brown colour.
- "Body prints" are sometimes left in the soft mud at the edge of the wallow, and body hairs may be found within the print.
- Fresh tracks are all around the wallow, and there are probably also long marks where the stag has pawed the ground with his front feet. Sometimes there are holes in the mud where the stag has dug his brow tines into the ground.
- The stag comes out of the wallow covered in thick mud and dripping muddy water, and as he walks away this wet mud drips on to leaves and ground. Also, some mud is brushed off on to the vegetation he walks past (Fig. 7). The brushed-off mud will be found on the underside of leaves and branches and so can survive a lot of rain.

- The stag urinates frequently into the water of the wallow, imparting a strong stag odour to the water and general area.

Fig. 6: A fresh wallow with a lot of "fast" sign. Only at the edge of the wallow is there any sign that the mud is settling. Fresh, wet mud has been trailed out of the wallow; for example, the small stick near the water's edge of the far side had two large splashes of darker-coloured, wet mud adjacent to the lighter-coloured, dry mud. Fern leaves overhanging the wallow also have splashes of mud. Since it had rained the night before, this splashing must have happened during the day.

Fig. 7: A few metres from the wallow in Fig. 6. The vegetation shows fresh sign where the drips have been exposed to full sunlight and then dried. This sign was estimated to be only an hour old.

Fig. 8: Taken just 5 minutes after Fig. 7. While following the trail away from the wallow Roger heard a twig snap. He stood still and this spiker walked through the bush, probably heading for the wallow. This animal hasn't got wallow mud on him so there was still a more active, rutting stag left at that location.

Ageing a wallow

The drips are good fast sign. Drips dry from the outside rim of the droplet. When dry, the drips will survive a few showers of rain before being washed off, leaving a ring-shaped mud mark on the leaf.

After the wallow has been used, the sediment in the water gradually settles out, and the depth of clear water progressively increases. This zone of clear water is seen first in the shallow edges of the wallow.

Because the water in a stag's wallow contains a lot of stirred-up mud, urine and other organic material washed off the animal, deer never drink from an active wallow — it is a foul brew. When the stag deserts the wallow, the mud and debris will settle out and in time the water will become completely clear. This can take can take 2 or 3 weeks in heavy clay soils, but less time in lighter soils. With the clearing of the water, sunlight penetrates its depths and algae start to bloom in the rich water-urine mixture. The bloom will take at least a month to develop into a submerged green scum.

The smell of deer

Deer are better at smelling hunters than hunters are at smelling deer. Nevertheless, deer have a distinctive wild-game smell that signals their recent presence. Stalking upwind you can often smell a deer before seeing it, especially if you don't smoke. When you startle a deer it emits a sudden surge of smell as it departs, which in still air becomes a localised high concentration of odour. The deer may still be close, uncertain about the danger.

Weather conditions will affect your ability to smell deer, just as they affect the deer's scenting ability (see Chapter 4).

Deer also leave their scent on other sign such as rubbing trees, deer beds and around wallows. Fresh blood from a wounded animal may be smeared on to your fingertips and smelt carefully. A "deer smell" is a sure sign of a gut-shot animal.

Deer beds

Deer spend a portion of their day resting, often using the same spot repeatedly. Such a spot becomes formed into a "bed". These beds are the shape of a bath, with a rim composed of vegetation pushed out from the centre as the deer get in and out. The centre is flattened grass, leaves or dirt. Sometimes the earthy centre has become slightly hollowed out. Recently used beds often have deer hairs and a definite deer smell. Because deer may have a number of beds which are used according to weather conditions, one empty bed does not always mean that no deer are bedded in the area.

Things that fall off deer

Deer hair is an important indication of the age of rub sign, bed sign and wallow. It also gets snagged on barbed wire, gates and the like. During the spring moult season it comes out so freely that it can be found on bushes and other vegetation, indicating a recent passage of deer. The weather quickly disperses it from these places.

A shed antler means a stag has been that way, but both cast antlers of a set are not often found. Deer are great eaters of shed antler, especially in areas where calcium is deficient. Lactating hinds have a big need for calcium, as do stags as they grow new antlers. Deer may also chew any available animal bones for calcium.

The everyday sounds deer make

Red deer make a surprising amount of noise as they are feeding and walking around in the bush: the snapping of a small twig, the brushing against branches and leaves, the biting and chewing of vegetation, the hollow fall of a foot on hard ground. The sound of a large four-footed animal moving about in the bush has a distinctive rhythm, which you should try to imitate when stalking, as part of the camouflage. This way of walking can be more successful than a stealthy creeping style, which often seems to alert deer.

You should frequently stop to listen, often for quite long periods, to hear deer. Some exciting hunting happens when you, in dense cover, hear but cannot see an animal. The animal may be browsing, grazing or lying down chewing its cud.

Unfortunately, humans have a much poorer sense of hearing than deer. Falling rain and high humidity further dampen down the passage of sound, and wind creates other distracting sounds. Only a very astute hunter can hear deer at distances greater than 25 metres, except in the roar.

A variety of "family sounds" are made by red deer but are seldom heard by a hunter. Hinds and fawns often make a series of quiet grunts to each other. Young fawns commonly make a high-pitched bleating noise when distressed. This sound will bring back the fawn's mother and can also call up the assistance of other hinds. Calling devices have been available to hunters that are claimed to make this sound and attract hinds in the fawning season. There is said to be a "calving bellow" given by hinds at the birth of a fawn and also when she returns to her newly born or "clamped" fawn.

Deer can trigger off other sounds such as the strident sound of paradise ducks alarmed by deer crossing a river or traversing river flats. Deer crossing slips may dislodge stones which roll down, generating noise and so alerting a hunter.

Roaring

Stags "roar" principally in the rut — only very rarely have they been heard to roar at other times of the year. At the start of the rut a stag will give occasional single grunts similar to a loud bark. After a week or so the barks develop into short resonant roars. As the rut progresses the individual roars become longer and strung together in runs often followed by one or two deep grunts. By this stage the stag is in the full heat of the rut and is likely to come towards a hunter who roars at him (see also Chapter 6).

Barking

This sound is not unlike the bark of a dog but has a more resonant quality. The resonance often makes it difficult for the hunter to tell from whence the bark has come. Deer bark when they are alerted. Usually, the animal has heard or seen something but is not fully sure what it is. If the deer could smell the hunter it would be sure of danger and not stand around barking.

Sometimes, if you return the bark the animal will be reassured, stand still, or even approach you. Usually, however, the animal barks as it walks away from the source of disturbance, making it difficult for you to make contact with the animal while maintaining a careful walk of deer-like tempo. Often, you will end up following the deer at the same distance for miles, the infuriating barking always just ahead. Usually the drama ends when you incautiously quicken your pace and thoroughly alarm the deer.

Apart from alarm barking, stags during the roar will also bark at smaller deer to which they are clearly superior. This is a sort of "no contest" signal to the smaller animal, which results in its rapid departure. You should therefore abstain from barking at spikers in the season of the roar unless you want them to vacate the area.

You should not bark or roar at an animal which is in such a position that when attracted towards you, will probably approach from a direction downwind of you. This may sound obvious, but in fact considerable skill may be required to avoid this happening, particularly with older, more cunning animals. Such animals will often deliberately avoid travelling directly to the source of noise but veer off and around to cut the wind of the area from which the noise is emanating. The same thing can happen in the vertical perspective — for example, a stag will often climb above you to cut your ascending scent line (see catabatic winds in Chapter 4).

In the early seventies there were still a good few deer about on the vast clearings and massive beech slopes of the Arawhata. In spite of the constantly marauding helicopter hunters, we could still emerge at the bridge after a good weekend, our craft piled high with carcasses. Now in the eighties the situation had changed. The bulk of the helicopter hunters had moved from their Mussel Point lair — they had taken most of the deer. The few that remained in this vast watershed were skittish and kept well clear of the tussock tops and river flats. This was now bush-stalking country.

Across the river from our traditional first night's camp and slightly upstream from it, the Thompson Creek entered the main river. This little catchment always seemed to hold deer, a fact that had not gone unrecognised by the locals who in earlier years had erected numerous deer traps in the vicinity. The mesh wire fences remained, unused now, but still the deer frequented the spot. In spring they would still occasionally come out on the shingle-strewn flats almost to the main river's edge. During the roar they would retreat to the place where the beech-clad river terraces met the steep rock walls of the valley. However, we were here in early September and I was not sure where they would be.

The reason for the trip was twofold. Firstly, and as always, we were short of meat at home. Secondly, I wanted another try for an Arawhata head. Why, you may ask, did I not plan my trip for the roar? The locals who live in the hamlet at the river mouth would soon tell you — at that time of the year the river is alive with jet boats and hunters, causing the timid herds to head for more peaceful pastures. Coming at this time, I was counting on an unduly early spring having switched on the stags' appetites before their antlers were shed. A short sharp frosty period, a week before our departure, had firmed my resolve to come. I was hoping that the growth would have slowed as a result and the deer become desperately hungry.

I was going over this logic as I quietly eased my new craft over the main river just before dawn the following morning. My call of the tossed coin had failed and earned me the doubtful privilege of stalking the flats whilst my fellow hunter had the task of exploring the valley sides. I expected that I would merely function as an involuntary beater, driving the game up to him. I figured they would have only just descended to the very edges of the flats where I could not venture, it being too close to my cobber's territory. The wind was blowing down the main valley, but I had little doubt that with the rising of the sun, it would change direction, swirling all around the flats as the currents from the main and side valleys blended, and so carrying my scent everywhere and prompting a mass exodus of the deer population.

My mate headed downstream along the main river, intending to cut inwards later, bringing him up on the first spur of the down-river wall of the Thompson valley. I, for my part, sneaked along the very edges of the river flat as it abutted the main Arawhata river, heading upstream, past the old meat-hunter's hut, and on, until I judged myself to be almost midway between the two valley sides of the Thompson. Then I, too, turned and headed away from the main Arawhata flow, working my way in the half light slowly across the first upstream flat at the mouth of the Thomas. I had not gone 20 metres when my pessimism changed. There, on the first few grassy islands that dotted the shingle braids, was red-hot sign. The low-angled light of the rising dawn had made the sign obvious. There had been a heavy dew on this upraised area, so much so that the coarse grass blades were each loaded with frozen droplets, giving the islands a hoary white coat. Inscribed on this were clear deer tracks in which the white coating had been brushed aside, leaving the dark green blades poking through.

I slowed right down, examining the tracks in detail. There were no dew claw marks, but that was probably because the frozen earth did not allow even the heaviest-laden foot to sink in. The print dimensions were large however, a good four fingers' breadth, and were well splayed. As the tracks were fresh and the wind still in my favour, I decided to follow them. The animal had obviously been grazing; his course wandered aimlessly from flat to flat, almost doubling back on itself at one point. The track was easy to follow where it was on the frost-dusted grass, but more difficult where it crossed the gravel runs. Here the prints were interspersed with numerous others, probably left over from the preceding day. I distinguished a smaller print as well as the big job and "hooray!", they both had dew claw marks, presumably made in the gravel when it was not frozen.

I fought back the rising buck fever that was revealed by a slight shake in my rifle-carrying hand. Although I was undoubtedly close to my quarry, I knew it would not be long until the wind changed, probably only minutes. I struggled to cover the ground silently but swiftly. A stone rattled in the distance. I scanned the area from which the sound had emanated, but saw nothing other than the rising mist. Then the realisation. There was no mist other than one little plume. Another look, a stag looking at me 70 metres away! Just visible between two stands of coprosma, his frosted breath rising in the cold air. Up came my rifle. The animal was standing chest on. I could dimly make out twin bulky antlers as I centred on his body. The rifle roared away the silence of the morning. The stag turned and started to bound towards the bush edge. I centred on his hilar kill area. It was still almost too dark to see. The rifle roared again and suddenly I couldn't see the stag's outline. Then I heard a faint repeating rhythm of scraping gravel. I walked up to see the dark bulk of a stag lying on its side, the forefeet still pacing the gravel in dying imitation of an escaping run.

I examined the head, a solid, well-timbered ten pointer, the typical Arawhata deep maroon brown. By historical standards, not a good head for this catchment, but by today's standards it was at least worth the trouble to take out. Gutting the beast where it was warmed the life back into my frozen hands. It was the task of only a few moments to drag the carcass to the main river's edge to a convenient place for pick-up by jet boat. I sat and dozed by the still warm remains, savouring the morning. An hour later my reverie was interrupted by the approach of my hunting mate. He had traversed the first mile of ridge without seeing a single indication of fresh sign. In disgust he had returned to the boat and then followed my tracks up the main river until he reached me. The animals I had struck must have been living in the middle of the flat undisturbed for quite some time.

We spent another three days hunting from various points along the river but did not strike any further sign. Perhaps on the one hand my plan had worked to a degree, and we had encountered a couple of the first deer to come out of the bush that spring. Perhaps, on the other, it was just plain "tin-arsed" good luck! — *R.L.*

2

Their senses

Above all things let not the devil tempt you to trifle with a deer's nose. You may cross his sight, walk up to him in a grey coat, or if standing against a tree or rock near your own colour, wait till he walks up to you, but you cannot cross his nose even at an incredible distance, but he will feel the tainted air. Colours and forms may be deceptive or alike; there are grey, brown and green rocks and stocks as well as man — and all these things may be equivocal — but there is one scent of man that he never doubts or mistakes; that is filled with danger and terror; one whiff of its poison at a mile off — his nose to the wind and the next moment his antlers turn and he is away to the hill or wood — and he may not be seen on the same side of the forest for a month.

J. Sobieski and C. Stuart *Lays of the Deer Forest* 1848

Red deer have the senses of smell, hearing, sight, touch and taste. The three they use principally to detect the hunter are those of smell, hearing and sight. As the quote above emphasises, in the charm of antiquated English, the sense of smell is paramount. Sight is the least powerful of the senses.

Fig. 9 shows the relative importance of these three senses. If a deer detects potential danger with a subservient sense, such as sight, it will remain uncertain and endeavour to bring a further sense to bear to confirm its suspicions before taking flight. Again, if a deer hears a hunter it will endeavour at least to see the danger before deciding whether to leave the area. However, if a deer at any time *smells* the human scent the animal is instantly alarmed and will, relying on this sense alone, depart immediately. Even during the roar, when the stalker is doing a grand job imitating the roar of a challenging stag, one whiff of the hunter will fill the beast with terror, and the stag is away.

Their senses

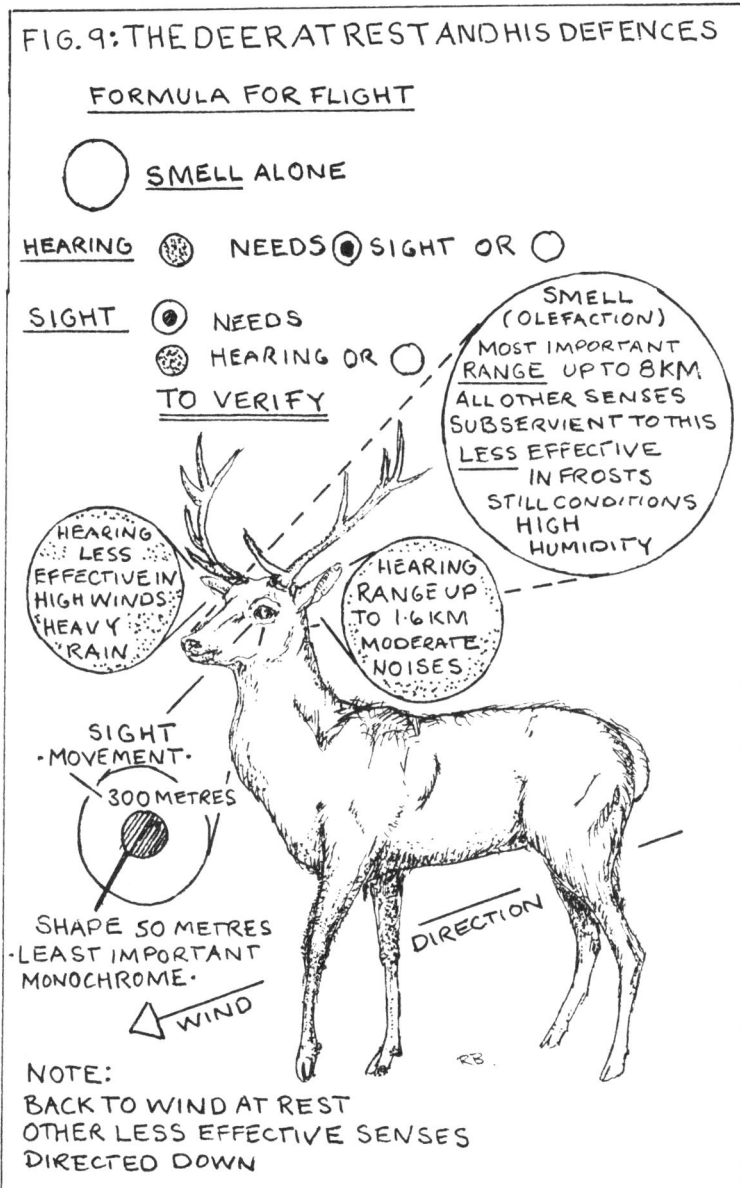

Smell

As we have seen, information from the nose takes precedence over information from all the other senses. F.F. Darling describes an incident where a stag company one-and-a-half kilometres away across open country smelt his presence. Deer have evolved large nasal passages and the parts of their brain used for evaluating smell are well developed.

A grazing deer is less able to smell a human being than one with head held high. Odours emanate from the herbs the animal is eating and mask the human scent, and near the ground there is much less wind movement to carry scent to the deer (see Chapter 4 for effects of weather on smell). Grazing deer regularly lift their heads and look about, and they test the wind for signs of danger. Typically they graze with their backs to the wind and direct their eyes downwind. In areas not much disturbed by hunting, deer seem not to lift their heads as often, perhaps making them more easily approached.

Are deer able to smell the scent left on the ground by a passing human? Tracker dogs can, of course, follow a human scent quite easily by "ground scenting". Most hunters think of pigs as ground scenters and deer as air scenters. Sometimes deer seem to pick up ground scents but at other times they walk straight over them. F.F. Darling describes conditions where very hungry deer in winter were able to follow his tracks with their noses to find the corn he was regularly leaving for them.

The reason deer sometimes fail to find ground scent may simply be because their noses are high above the ground when they are walking. F.F. Darling was lying down one day and a deer crossed downwind of him without picking up his scent. He believes this was because his scent was being blown along the ground and not rising up to the height of the deer's nose. Likewise, deer probably notice ground scent only where the scent is rising from the ground to the height of the animal's nose. The conditions that cause ground scent to rise are probably uncommon.

A fire releases into the air an enormous amount of chemicals for the deer's sensitive nose to detect. Wild animals associate fire with danger, and we are sure that in New Zealand deer have learnt to also associate fire with the presence of hunters. This is why we do not light fires on most of our hunting trips, except perhaps at the end of the trip.

Apart from detecting the scents of danger, deer have evolved a system of communication by scents. Each deer produces its own cocktail of scent from a number of sources, resulting in a smell as unique as human fingerprints.

Red deer produce scent with musk glands. These are found in two sites in the red deer. One set, the pre-orbital glands, are situated at the front angle of each eye. They are used notably in a sexual role, the stag marking his territory by rubbing his secretion on to trees and bushes. Stags seem to be able to tell when a hind is ovulating by sniffing her pre-orbital glands. The other musk glands are found on the underside of the tail in both male and female. These glands may play a part in scenting the urine, although some scientists believe that other scent-producing chemicals are contained in the urine. Certainly, red deer are sensitive to the smells of urine. Stags have been shown to be able to detect ovulation by the smell of the urine of an ovulating hind. Also, rutting stags deliberately urinate into wallows and then bathe in them, so spreading the musk over their entire bodies.

Many deer hunters in New Zealand in the roar rub themselves with the underbellies of freshly killed stags or cut off the "soil patches" and hang them on their belts. This technique was even recommended by the gentlemanly T.E. Donne in 1929. Although possibly attractive to hinds, this scent has not been found to be so alluring to hunters' wives and girlfriends!

Hearing

Deer are good at determining accurately the direction of sound by swivelling their ears around in a co-ordinated way. A deer will therefore usually have no difficulty in pinpointing a noisy hunter.

Inside the big external ears of the deer are a number of coarse hairs which are believed to be able to filter out unwanted background noise. The hairs are thought to also allow the deer to hear ultra-low frequency sounds by creating a resonance within the ear.

Deer quickly get used to sounds repeated regularly, including unusual sounds such as the daily workings of chainsaws or trains. Deer are herd animals and so learn to ignore the sounds made by other herd members as they walk about and browse. The quiet sneaking approach of a hunter is more likely to be noticed than a rhythmic approach that has the characteristics of another deer's walk.

Deer are much alarmed by sounds that have a quality foreign to the wilderness. They particularly dislike high frequency metallic sounds such as the closing of a rifle bolt. Thunder also disturbs deer. The sudden sound of a single rifle shot will disturb any deer hearing it. The deer will stop whatever it is doing and listen intently for a few minutes, but because of the short duration of the noise, it will be unable to determine from where the sound came. If there are no further shots the deer will return to browsing. A bedded animal will stand in its bed at the sound and hunker down again if no further disturbances occur. The alerted deer will be able to locate accurately the origin of further shot after which there is often a mass exodus of deer from the locale.

Therefore, there is a great advantage in one-shot kills. If a single shot misses a deer, other animals nearby may remain relatively undisturbed. Hunters should resist the desire to check the accuracy of their rifles at the hut and, except for humane finishing-off shots, be reluctant to fire more often than is necessary.

Air currents influence the way sound travels. A moderate wind will stop a sound travelling far upwind and will carry it a long way downwind. Wind also generates sound of its own by rattling trees, rustling leaves and grasses. In strong winds the deer are unable to filter out these background noises and they become on edge, generally restless and easily alarmed.

Humidity can influence the travel of sound. An increase in humidity dampens the passage of sound waves and so reduces the distance sound can travel. On clear frosty mornings humidity is extremely low and sound can travel for a long distance to be picked up by the sensitive ears of the deer.

Alarm is not the only reaction of deer to strange sounds — they will often become curious. In the old books it is even said that deer enjoy music! Of more practical use to the modern hunter is the observation that red deer can often be stopped in their tracks when running away by a short sharp yell or an imitation of a bark of a hind, even if the latter is not done well.

Vision

Deer are colour blind and not good at identifying the shape of objects. You should dress in neutral colours of a similar tone to that of the surrounding forest. If you dress in clothes that do not contrast with your surroundings and of a pattern that breaks up your outline (for example a camouflage suit), you may be able to stand stock still at 25 metres and still not be seen by a deer.

Deer, however, are particularly good at distinguishing movement, quickly becoming alerted to very small movements, even at great distances. Because their eyes are on the sides of their heads, they have a wide field of vision.

Deer are less likely to see danger approaching from above than below, and they are often oblivious to hunters on foot who are above them. Whether the structure of a deer's eye prevents their seeing upwards, or whether their habit is to expect danger to come only from below, is subject to some debate. F. Buckland, who did some research on the structure of the deer's eye, concluded that it would be physically difficult for deer to gaze upwards. The inability of deer to see danger from above is much used in Europe by mounting hunting platforms in trees; deer will often walk directly under a platform without noticing a hunter perched on it. To be able to hunt down towards deer from above is certainly an advantage, in the open or in the bush.

The Cobb Valley at the top of the South Island is a hanging valley that has a road up into it; the valley floor at the road-end is at an altitude of 800 metres. There are extensive tussock and grass river flats but large numbers of trampers use the valley floor and in doing so disturb grazing deer. There is a fallow herd in the valley and they are better able than the reds to tolerate this disturbance. The bush reaches part way up the valley sides with extensive open tops above. The forest is pure beech and is particularly lacking an edible understorey. I believe many red deer leave the Cobb after the rut and travel over the tops to winter down in the headwaters rivers of the Karamea watershed where they can descend to a lower altitude and where the broadleaf forest provides more understorey feed in the bush. The Cobb has been a Recreational Hunting Area since 1982. No helicopters are allowed to hunt the area and there is a rule that no hinds may be shot. During the mid summer all that part of the valley below the bush line is closed to hunting (to avoid conflict with trampers), and for some years not many hunters have gone hunting on the tops.

These factors probably all contribute to the large amount of time the deer herd spends grazing the open tops during the summer, especially if they haven't been recently disturbed by hunters.

I was hunting the Cobb, along with Warren Plum and Eric Hall, one weekend in late January 1988. Eric and I left our tent camp on the valley floor at 4 a.m., with a torch each, and headed for the tops on the northern side.

We reached the bush edge before daylight, and waited a short while for enough light to come before loading our magazines and walking out on to a concealed lookout point above the bush edge that we regularly use. We saw no deer and Eric and I parted company to enable us to cover more ground. I hunted along to the right while Eric went left.

I was the first back at camp, empty handed. I had heard rifle shots from both my companions and sure enough Eric and Warren came back with a deer each. We each told our stories.

This was Eric's morning. Shortly after leaving me he saw a hind group of four animals way above the bushline. He had a 30X spotting scope and by using it was able to identify a small spiker in the group. (In late January, a spiker in a hind group is peculiar.) Using the lie of the land, and with the early morning catabatic wind still blowing downslope, he stalked around towards them. Above him in a steep gut, only about 4 metres away, he startled a hind and a yearling, and the hind barked a few times as the two animals made off uphill, probably without getting his scent. The barking agitated the hind group he was stalking, so he lay low for a time and they settled down. He continued his stalk and approached to within 50 metres of the spiker, which he bagged with one shot. It had small thick "bumps", 7 or 8 centimetres long, on its head.

Warren had also walked up through the bush but on the opposite side of the valley. In the dark, he had got on to the wrong spur and now was in unfamiliar country. The sun rose above the eastern horizon and lit up a finger of bush across a shallow basin opposite. Out walked two deer. They were a long way off and Warren thought they were a hind and a fawn. He stalked in with his camera, ready to take a photo, and when the big deer gave the little one a jab in the guts, he realised he was looking at a stag company. The big deer was a mature stag, and Warren could see it had a single, velveted antler. The jostling and attacking ritual repeated itself a number of times as Warren quickly stalked in closer with his rifle, the camera having been hurriedly thrown back into his day pack. He got to within 250 metres and then saw the small deer wasn't so small after all — it was a six-point stag. The wind was beginning its catabatic shift and causing the hunter some concern. The big stag was back in the bush and out of sight when at 200 metres Warren decided he was close enough and found a rest to lie over and lined up the smaller animal in his sights. He completely shattered the peace of the early morning with three shots of his .270, before the stag lay still. After the shooting he could hear some crashing in the bush below as the big stag made good his escape.

The deer were obviously up on the tops and I wanted to get back up there again. In the mid afternoon all three of us left the tent behind and with light packs (a sleeping bag and a little food) walked together back up to the tops again, into a valley on the southern side. Before reaching the bushline we lay down for a rest, awaiting the time for an evening shot. Cautiously we stalked out, but there were no deer to be seen. Slowly we climbed up to the ridge top to look over the other side. It was a long climb and we were already tired from the morning's work.

We looked over into the first basin and we saw nothing. Further along the ridge we found another basin and gazed down into it. It held a stag.

It was late in the evening and the sun was low in the sky, casting a flood of golden colour over the tussock hollow in which he was. The wind was still blowing upslope and so Eric and I stalked down, sliding and stooping in our walk, trying to stay below the tall tussocks and so out of sight of the animal. It was my turn to shoot a deer but when I got close enough for a shot he was gone. We had a look through the bush where we thought he had entered, but there was little sign and no deer. It was disappointing and a hard climb back up to Warren on the ridge top. Warren was able to confirm that the animal had walked, still unaware of us, around the side of the basin into the bush. A most unusual behaviour at that time of day one might think. Warren, however, thought the deer had sidled around below us through the bush to come out in the first gully we'd looked into. Off we went back to the basin previously searched. We hurried as fast as we could and there in the failing light, almost as soon as we began searching, a stag was seen, then another. The 30X spotting scope made them clearly visible about 800 metres away. It was at least 9.30 at night and no time was to be lost in any fancy stalks. The uphill wind was beginning to lose its direction and strength now the sun had set.

Eric and I ran down. It was a race against time by two fatigued hunters suddenly energised. Soft shingle to start with and then spongy damp, along a creek bed. It was a surprise attack from above. Eric was sometimes alongside me, sometimes behind or in front as we raced along.

We saw what might have been a hind. Damn it! The deer came into view standing side-on in a hollow 100 metres away, then 75. We veered away from her, but we weren't stopping. She barked alarm. Warren later said she barked 30 or 40 times. He couldn't see any more, it was too dark. He could hear us crashing along at full gallop and the animal barking.

On we ran, down towards a small commanding knob below. I was in front. Eric called out "there's one!", I saw a stag 50 metres across a steep gully, aimed off the shoulder, "boomfa" went the .270, dazzling me with muzzle flash, and the stag collapsed. It all seemed to happen at once. Suddenly our whole darkening world erupted with running stags — four of them. In our haste we had almost run past them. One galloped flat out along a creek bed directly below the bank I was standing on, another three went alternately running and stopping on the steep face opposite. Eric shot and hit the closest one but they all ran faster. I put another bullet into it and it fell. I called out "two's enough, two's enough, we can't carry any more", and the remaining animals clattered off up their mountainside as peace and darkness quickly fell all around. We'd had fun.

It was 11 p.m. when we made it back to the ridge top — the three of us, with huge loads of meat and bad torches. We lay down. It was a Saturday night, not a breath of wind, a moonless night surrounded us, as if we were inside it. The stars were clear and sharp and we watched a satellite arc across. — *F.S.*

3
What they like to eat

As we discuss more fully in Chapter 11, red deer belong to the Cervidae family, which is related closely to the Bovidae family to which cattle and antelopes belong. An important difference between the two families is the type of food they eat. The Cervidae have teeth that are generally better designed for pulling off leaves of shrubs and trees and biting through small twigs than for grazing long grass, and the red deer prefer shrubs and trees. The Bovidae, on the other hand, prefer to graze grass and herbs.

Red deer evolved in Europe's deciduous forests, but after liberation in New Zealand they soon adapted to the native evergreen bush. Red deer have developed a New Zealand diet of different native trees and shrubs, preferring some species to others.

In the first two compartments of a red deer's stomach (the rumen and reticulum) the food is mixed with bacteria and other small creatures called protozoans. These organisms help to break down the leaves into basic chemicals so that they can be absorbed into the bloodstream. Some toxic chemical substances found in plants can stop these digestive organisms working. The toxic chemicals (called toxins) are present in higher concentrations in some plants than others, and deer are able to avoid eating these plants simply because they find them distasteful. A good example is the pepperwood. As the seasons change the amount of toxin contained in the leaves of different plants alters. As a general rule, the new growth of spring contains less toxin than the old growth of winter.

To obtain the correct amount of protein, carbohydrate and calcium needed for the changing requirements of their bodies throughout the year (hinds need more calcium in the spring, for example), deer vary the types of foliage and grasses they eat from one season to the next. The result is rather like a recipe that must not only feed the animal correctly but must also be acceptable to its digestive organisms.

To develop the ability to identify all the plants in our native forests would take years. Nevertheless, you should be able to identify the commonly occurring plants that deer prefer. Armed with such knowledge you will be better able to identify feed areas.

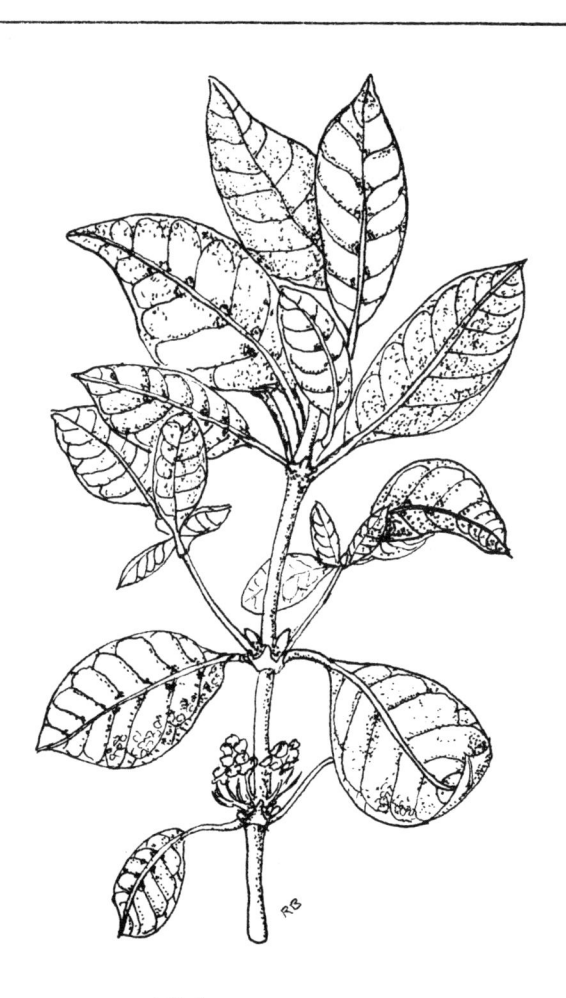

FIG. 10: KARAMU (COPROSMA ROBUSTA).
SHRUB REACHING 5 METRES. LEAVES 5-12 CM.
SHINING DARK GREEN, THICK.
UNDERSIDE LIGHT GREEN MATT.
FRUIT YELLOWISH-RED, 6-8 MM LONG.

What they like to eat

We have reduced the list of preferred browse down to the five most important species of understorey trees and shrubs. Some ferns and grasses are also important food sources, but considerable skill is needed to differentiate one fern or grass from another, and such fine discrimination is beyond the scope of us, this book and most hunters.

The species of browse we describe are listed in decreasing order of preference. The order we have here is based on our own experience and follows the order given by V.D. Zotov who studied the Tararua Forest in 1939.

Karamu *(Coprosma robusta)(Fig. 10)*

This coprosma species is highly favoured by red deer and appears at the top of all researched preference lists. Deer will, on occasion, eat its bark as well as the leaves. The tree often begins life as an epiphyte on the trunk of a tree fern. Other less commonly occurring broad-leaved coprosma species such as taupata (*Coprosma repens*) and kanono (*Coprosma grandifolia*) are also highly preferred browse. All these coprosma species are upmarket five-star tucker to deer.

Sevenfinger *(Schefflera digitata)* *(Fig. 11); Maori name: pate*

Found throughout New Zealand, including Stewart Island, but not as common as fivefinger, with which it can be confused; the length of the bare leaf stalks at the base of the leaves is much shorter than in fivefinger, the leaves are thinner and less shiny and they always appear to be limp. Deer will eat all the leaves and strip the bark from this tree, yet, in conditions of plenty it is common to see where only the younger leaves have been eaten. This is a highly favoured food for deer and appears near the very top of most lists. Still five-star tucker.

Fivefinger *(Pseudopanax arboreus)* *(Fig. 12); Maori name: puahou*

This is a common tree, although where deer numbers have been heavy it is now much less common. Points of identification include the serrated leaf edges, thick and leathery leaves, and a significant length of bare leaf-stalk at the base of each leaf. It usually appears on browse lists below the species listed above. Deer will eat all the leaves and also the bark in times of food shortage, but they usually eat only the small young soft leaves which are lighter in colour than the adult leaves, probably because of a build-up of toxins in the older leaves. Three-star tucker.

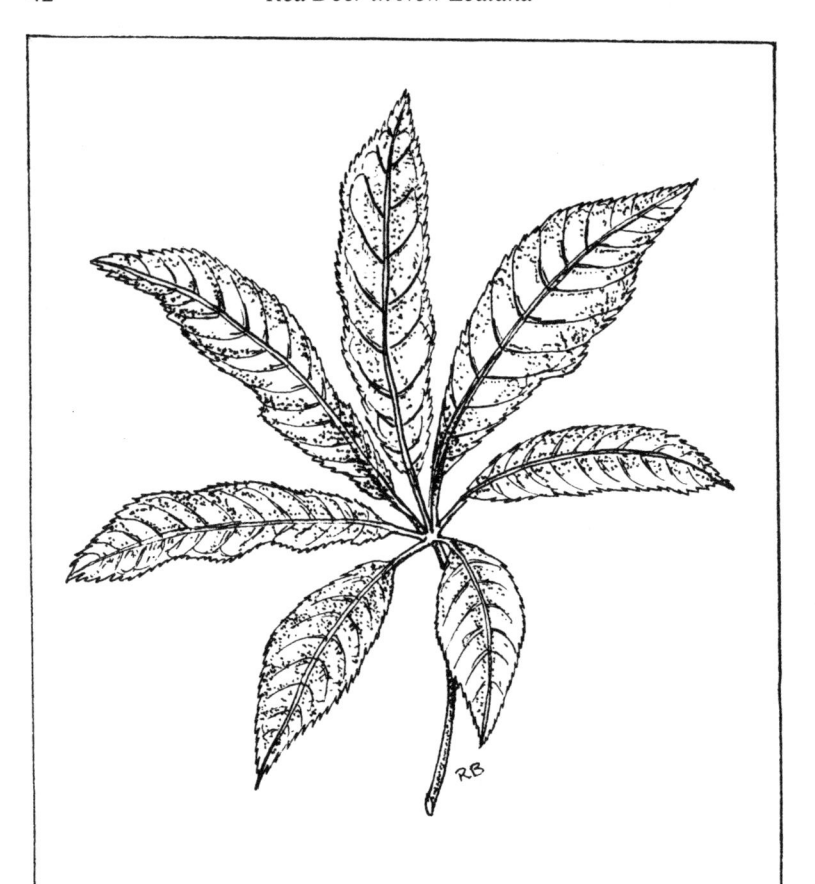

FIG. 11: SEVENFINGER OR PATE.
(SCHEFFLERA DIGITATA).

TREE UP TO 8 METRES. LEAVES COMPOSED OF SEVEN SERRATED, ELONGATED, OVAL LEAFLETS EACH JOINED BY A SHORT STALK. EACH LEAFLET 7-18 CM LONG, THIN AND FINELY TOOTHED. LIGHT GREEN MIDRIB AND BROWNISH VEINS. UNDERSIDE OF THE LEAVES PALE GREEN, MATT. LEAVES ALWAYS APPEAR LIMP.

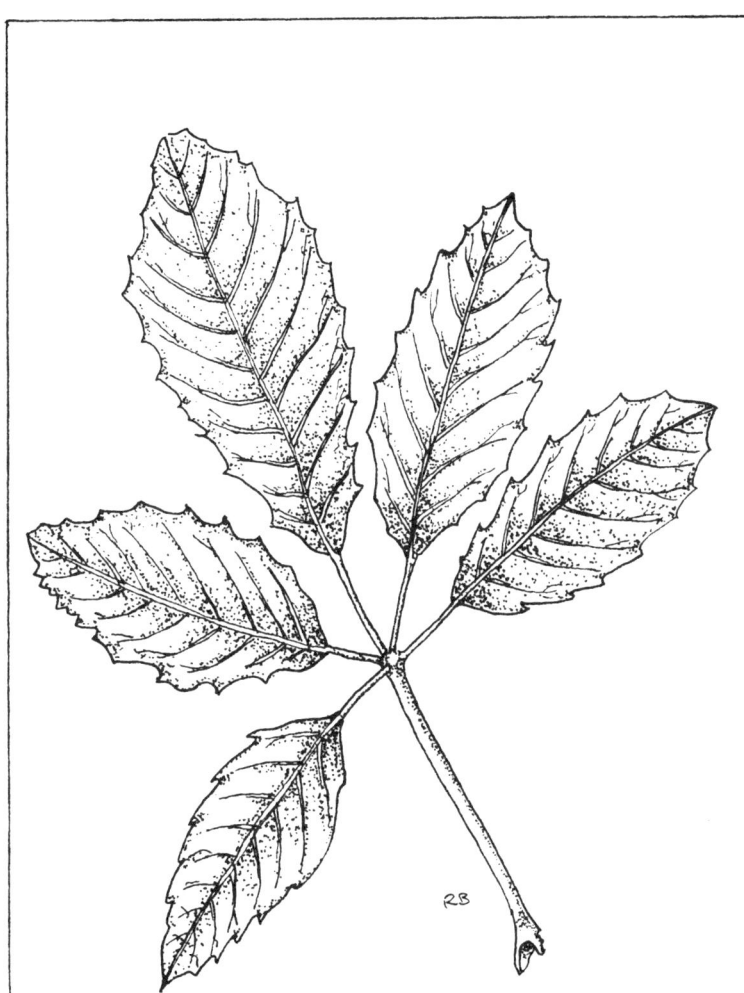

FIG. 12: FIVE FINGER OR PUAHOU.
(PSEUDOPANAX ARBOREUS).
TREE UP TO 8 METRES. LEAVES MADE UP OF 3–7 FINGER-LIKE LEAFLETS EACH 7–20 CM LONG. STALKED, TOOTHED, DARK GREEN GLOSSY LEAVES. MIDRIB AND VEINS LIGHT GREEN. FRUITS 6–8 MM, BLACK.

FIG. 13: BROADLEAF ALSO PAPAUMA OR PUKA.
(GRISELINIA LITTORALIS).

SHRUB OR TREE REACHING UP TO 17 METRES. LEAVES SHINING DARK GREEN. UNDERSIDE LIGHT GREEN MATT. EDGES SMOOTH, SLIGHTLY WAVED, THICK AND LEATHERY, 2-10 CM LONG. BERRY 8 MM LONG, DARK PURPLE.

Broadleaf *(Griselinia littoralis/lucida)*
(Fig. 13); Maori name: puka or papauma

There are two closely related species that are known as broadleaf. Puka is the smaller of the two species (*lucida*), which often starts life as an epiphyte (it grows on another tree and gradually takes it over). Puka grows to about 8 metres high. Papauma is the larger, more common species (*littoralis*), which grows to a height of 15 metres. Broadleaf is well distributed throughout the country from sea level upwards and is often found as a small tree growing in sub-alpine forests. Because broadleaf is still common in many areas where other preferred species have been browsed out, it is an extremely important plant for deer, especially in beech forest where all understorey browse species are in short supply. Often, broadleaf trees are browsed as high as deer can reach and kept in a trimmed state by continual nibbling. Dead leaves that fall from the tree are a uniform yellow. Deer will commonly eat these fallen leaves, something they seldom do with the leaves of other species. Still good tucker but relatively common food — two stars?

Whiteywood *(Melicytus ramiflorus)*
(Fig. 14); Maori name: mahoe

This tree is found in both the North and South Islands and is particularly common in secondary-growth bush and coastal forest. Decaying leaves on the ground often form a perfect skeleton. Whiteywood is rather an ordinary food for deer. We are down to one star here.

Forest types and their browse species

The type of native forest growing throughout New Zealand varies greatly. A forest is dominated by big canopy trees growing overhead, which determine the "type" of forest. More and more regional vegetation maps are now being produced, which show the distribution of forest types and which can be most useful when planning a trip. *The vegetative cover of New Zealand,* by P.F.J. Newsome (National Soil and Water Conservation Authority) gives a detailed account of forest types and a New Zealand map showing the classifications and occurrence of all forests.

FIG. 14: WHITEYWOOD OR MAHOE.
(MELICYTUS RAMIFLORUS).
SHRUB OR SMALL TREE REACHING 10 METRES.
BARK WHITE. LEAVES ATTACHED TO BRANCHES
ALTERNATELY RATHER THAN OPPOSITE,
5-12 CM LONG, SMOOTH, DARK GREEN.
UNDERSIDE SMOOTH LIGHT GREEN.
BERRIES VIOLET BLUE.

Beech forest

The most common forest type is beech (*Nothofagus* spp.) Almost half the remaining native bush in New Zealand is beech, which is found growing from the foothills to high altitudes. When seen from the air, beech forests appear a smooth, uniform green. The green colour varies, depending on which species is predominant. There are five species of beech and, typically, the predominant species changes with increasing altitude. The understorey of a beech forest is usually open and contains only scattered groups of browse species such as broadleaf, fivefinger, coprosma and olearia. Normally the ground is bare, which makes walking through the forest easy, but at times there can be coverings of ground ferns such as crown fern and prickly shield fern. At low altitudes mature beech trees grow as high as 35 metres but at high altitudes they often only reach only 10 metres and grow closer together, so reducing your visibility. Deer often prefer the more dense conditions at high altitude to the open lower slopes where it is often possible to see 100 metres in any direction.

Bush changes to open tussock where the average summer temperature is 10°C. This occurs in the far south at 900 metres above sea level, but in the north at up to 1400 metres. Beech forests usually have a clean break (without any difficult alpine scrub) between stunted beech trees and the open tussock. Deer find it is easy to spend the day concealed inside the beech forest and venture out into the open at night to feed. Often, when hunting the tussock slopes above, you will be able to walk along a sharply demarcated bush edge and remain well concealed by the bush.

Beech forest has the least amount of preferred understorey browse species of all the forest types, and when short of feed the deer will eat shoots and leaves from beech trees. This browse is more accessible on the stunted trees growing at high altitude. When browsing beech trees deer prefer silver beech, then mountain beech, red beech and finally hard beech.

The shortage of feed puts pressure on deer to graze the open tussock tops and river flats and to travel greater distances through the forest between food sources. Numbers of deer in a beech forest are often low, but because of the open nature of the forest, the greater mobility of the deer and their tendency to feed the open, some good hunting can be had.

Broadleaf forest

The use of the term "broadleaf" for a forest type can cause confusion because it is also used as the name of a species that has no direct connection with this forest type.

Broadleaf forests are dominated by the hardwood tree species, of which there are a number. In the south of the country, kamahi, quintinia and southern rata predominate. The southern rata gives a splendid red colour to the forest in early summer. In the North Island kamahi, hinau, towai, mangeao, tawa and rewarewa occur, with pohutukawa in coastal areas.

When seen from the air, broadleaf forests form a dense canopy which is more uneven in texture and colour than that of beech forests. The understorey of a broadleaf forest is more dense than in a beech forest, which will make your travelling more difficult. The understorey is likely to have an abundance of coprosma species, fivefinger and broadleaf, which means numbers of deer living there may be high. The deer are likely to have little pressure on them to travel for food and little need to feed in the open areas of tussock and river flats, making them difficult to hunt.

At the upper bush edge there is typically a broad band of dense sub-alpine scrub which makes for arduous travelling for both deer and hunters. Deer often form well used trails up through the scrub which usually follow ridge lines. Nevertheless, finding these trails may be difficult because they are often hidden underneath a covering of leatherwoods or other resilient species that spring back to cover the trail after the passage of the animal. Because the sub-alpine scrub makes a ragged edge to the bushline, it is not possible to hunt along the margin concealed by the scrub and look over the tussock, as in the beech forest. Often the best way is to sit in a well concealed spot high in the tussock and look down at the bush edge.

The lower levels of the broadleaf forest are often well clothed with lowland scrub which makes hunting the river flats equally difficult. Often you must walk in the river to move from one river flat to the next.

Some research has been done on browse preference in the broadleaf forests of the Arahura catchment in Westland. The results may not be particularly relevant to the broadleaf forests of the North Island, where some differences in the species composition of the forest is likely, but these were the main findings:

Most palatable: all the five described earlier plus kamahi, southern rata, wineberry, ribbonwood, native broom, and hen and chicken fern.

Moderately palatable: many of the small-leaved coprosmas, including stinkwood; bush lawyer, tree daisies and the mangrove-leaved akeake.

Least palatable: hook grass, Prince of Wales fern, filmy ferns, crown fern, rice grass, pepperwood and all species of podocarp.

Podocarp forest

This forest is found in both islands but only locally in its pure form. It occurs principally at low altitudes on river terraces in South Westland and on volcanic deposits in the North Island. The trees in this forest type are all conifers (they have seed cones) and foresters refer to them as softwoods. The predominant species is normally rimu but miro, matai, totara and kahikatea also occur. Seen from the air the forest usually has a spiky appearance, as the rimu trees tower some 35 metres from the forest floor and project above the lower canopy.

Podocarp forest has a complex structure. Below the dominant trees is a layer of subdominant trees such as kamahi and tawa. Beneath these trees is the understorey of coprosma, fivefinger and broadleaf, and vines such as supplejack. The forest floor is covered in ferns and mosses. It can be an extremely difficult environment in which to hunt, but the deer love the protection the forest gives them and its abundance of browse.

The coastal strip from Hokitika to Jacksons Bay is mostly podocarp forest and large numbers of deer have been taken from here by helicopter hunting in the recent past. To stalk it on foot can be a nightmare, with the thick understorey and frequent swamps where the kahikatea grow. Much feed is available for the deer, which makes it difficult to work out their location — and, in flat areas, yours too for that matter, frequent climbing of trees often being called for in order to plot a route around the next swamp! Nevertheless, joking aside, if you learn a small area well, some fine hunting can be enjoyed in a forest that is likely to be well stocked with deer.

We are unaware of any published data on the browse preferences of deer in podocarp forest. The podocarp species themselves appear as "least preferred" on the list in the study done in the broadleaf forest, and deer living in podocarp forest probably rely completely on the plentiful understorey species for food.

Mixed podocarp-broadleaf

Pure podocarp forest is not common, but podocarp forest mixed with broadleaf forest is. The forest's actual composition varies according to the relative proportion of the two components. It can be distinguished from the air by its "ruffled" appearance, with wide variation of tree height, colour and form. This mixed forest type has been extensively logged and most patches that remain are on ground too difficult to work with logging machinery. It is usually an arduous forest in which to hunt, especially cut-over areas, but with good local knowledge it can produce a lot of deer.

Mixed beech-broadleaf

This forest type occurs throughout the country and covers an extensive area in the south western part of Fiordland. It has an understorey part way between that of very open beech forest and more dense broadleaf forest. There is usually good growth of preferred browse shrubs and a ground cover of ferns but without much entangling vine growth. It offers excellent bush stalking.

Mixed podocarp-broadleaf-beech forest

As the name suggests, this forest type is a bit of everything. Rather surprisingly, it is not common, occurring only in Northwest Nelson and western Fiordland. Where we have stalked in this forest type the dense understorey has made hunting difficult, but the beasts were there.

An extensive study was done on the browse inclinations of deer in this forest type in western Southland in 1950 by J.T. Hollaway. He gave a list of preferences in order from the most to the least preferred:

large-leaved coprosmas
sevenfinger
fivefinger
broadleaf
single-leaved fivefinger
red matipo
stinkwood
marble leaf or putaputaweta
small-leaved coprosmas
southern rata
kamahi
bush lawyer

prickly shield fern
silver beech
fuchsia
wineberry
bush rice grass
hook grass
totara
miro
grass trees (dracophyllums)

Species that were never browsed were: pepperwood; manuka; crown fern; rimu; and celery pine.

This list was compiled when deer populations were high. Deer now seldom need to browse species near the bottom of the list, but the order of preference among the species still has validity.

Careful study of this list yields a lot of information useful to the deerstalker. For example, the beech species are well down the list, below the broadleaf species, rata and kamahi. In an area of mixed forest types, with a shortage of food in the understorey deer can be expected to move from areas of mostly beech to areas of mostly broadleaf tree species. Likewise, owing to the low ranking of the podocarp species (miro, totara), deer are likely to leave the podocarp areas if understorey browse is deficient, although podocarp forests usually have a plentiful understorey.

Why deer eat grass in spring

Later, in Chapter 11, we examine why deer should be thought of as principally browsers of trees and shrubs and not eaters of grass, but we have found it intriguing to seek reasons why deer occasionally desert their preference for browse and resort to grass as a food source.

In late September and October, deer typically eat a lot of grass — they are to be found on grassy river flats, in grass clearings and on the tussock at the bushline. They are said to be "flushing". This flushing happens even in forest areas where plenty of good browsing appears to be available. Come summer, however, and even where grass is still plentiful, the herds, particularly the hind groups, are back browsing mostly in the bush.

One theory that explains why deer eat grass in the spring is based on the belief that toxins accumulate in the leaves of browse trees in the winter. With the start of spring the animals become hungry, and because there is a shortage of toxin-free leaves in the bush, the deer are forced to emerge on to the grass until the spring warmth encourages the growth of adequate supplies of fresh young, toxin-free leaves in the bush.

Another explanation lies in the need for hinds to consume extra protein and calcium at this time of year, to meet the needs of their rapidly growing unborn fawns. Buds and growing shoots are high in protein and calcium, and grass produces the most new growing shoots at this time of the year. Stags are also thought to need more protein and calcium in their diet at this time in order to fuel the development of their velvet, and they, too, emerge from the bush to graze. This need in the two sexes does not quite coincide, which may explain why the stags linger longer on grass.

Some recent work has been done on the mechanisms that regulate the appetite of deer. During winter it is cold and food is short. Deer have to work hard to find enough to eat and they have to digest it in cold conditions, which requires extra energy. Therefore, deer will probably burn more energy in feeding activity in winter than they will gain from the food they have eaten. To reduce this energy loss deer have an internal regulatory mechanism that reduces their appetite in winter, so that they lose weight but do not feel hungry. The consequent reduction in the constant quest for food enables deer to live during the winter in quite small areas. Typically, these are warm, sheltered, away from hunting pressure, and often have no adjacent browsing areas. Winter hunting can be very rewarding if one of these hideaways can be found.

With the onset of spring, deer develop a ravenous appetite and move to areas of plentiful food; in early spring this means the areas of most sunlight. They will browse what new growth there is on the bush edges, then move out on to the grass.

In hunting grounds with a low deer population, deer may be able to find enough newly grown browse in the bush without resorting to grass. In some areas there will be enough broadleaf to sustain the deer without the need for grass, as broadleaf leaves do not accumulate toxins and are edible even after they have fallen from the tree. Areas that have a lot of broadleaf and a low deer population are therefore likely to be good hunting in spring.

Spring weather is New Zealand is usually variable. Deer begin eating in quantity after the first one or two weeks of warm weather,

What they like to eat

when the plants first begin to produce new spring growth. Once deer have started their spring eating they are unable to stop, even if plant growth is stopped or slowed by cold conditions. Deer may then become incautious in their desperate search for food. A hunter who watches the weather in the spring can exploit these conditions and find some easy hunting.

The hungry pregnant hinds are the first to come on to the grass in spring and they are usually the first to leave. In November when the hinds return to their territories in the bush, the stags linger a little longer. The strict pecking order within stag companies commonly results in the more mature stags occupying the safer grazing grounds, putting pressure on the younger ones to use the more dangerous grassy areas. Because these young animals are growing the most and need the most protein, they need to stay on the grass longer. Spikers that do not belong to a stag company can be found at this time of the year travelling great distances with a carelessness born of inexperience. December is the month of the "silly spiker".

Influence of altitude on browse patterns

For every 1000 metres increase in altitude, the air becomes about 6°C cooler, and so the spring growth surge appears later at the high altitudes.

In a long river valley that slowly gains altitude, the surge in spring growth will progress up the valley. A hunter aware of this can gradually shift up valley, keeping pace with the surge and the consequent zone of increased deer activity.

Hinds in a lower valley are not likely to follow the zone far up river, as they are inclined to ascend the valley sides, within their territories, to progressively higher altitudes of browsing inside the bush as the season advances. On the other hand, stags, especially spikers, are more likely to follow the surge zone up the valley for long distances. Spikers will sometimes follow the zone along the entire valley length, grazing and simultaneously looking for a stag company to join.

Lake Hauroko is aptly named. Meaning "sounding wind", the word gives clue to the fact that the lake's normally peaceful waters can be transformed rapidly to chaos, driven by the frequent northerly or southerly gales. It was thus only after careful perusal of the weather forecast that I would commit myself to the long drive from Central Otago, pausing only to pick up a permit at the Clifden ranger station, that ended at the Clifden road end. Not that I intended to embark upon the treacherous lake. Traversing its northward sinuous curves towards the Unknown River, or even heading southward into the Waitutu, were more than weekend undertakings. I was off to hunt the front country, a gently undulating surprisingly extensive area, extending north-eastwards from the thin ridge of hills that formed the eastern wall of the lake to the headwaters of the Lilburn that formed its eastern boundary. I finally pulled into the little rest area at eleven that Friday night.

An hour before dawn I was staring into the steamy depths of a half-drained mug of char contemplating the day's stalk. The wind was from the north, a light breeze, but steady. I would be able to tramp directly into the wind northwards from the road edge to reach my hunting area. Had it been a southerly I would have had to walk the few remaining kilometres to the lake, head northwards to Look-out Bluff, traverse the thin band of beech forest that clothed the ridge and drop down eastwards into the lowland mixed forest that formed my stalking ground. Officially described as "lowland podocarp broadleaf beech forest", the true nature of the ground was not a haphazard admixture as the name would suggest. Indeed, it was quite unusual. The higher undulations were clothed in beech, where exposed, and podocarp broadleaf mixture, where sheltered, both having a clear understorey carpeted with hard fern. The lower regions were different. Large areas of podocarp broadleaf forest ringed small patches of scrub. Some of these were dense "pole thickets" of seedling beech, but others were well spaced groups of coprosma and broadleaf. These latter seemed to occur mainly on clayey ground and were always densely marked by deer prints. It had taken me a few trips to work out that the deer were using these as nocturnal feeding areas, bedding in the beech-clad slopes during the day where the crown fern gave clear warning of an approaching hunter. Hence the early start, to catch the deer on their feeding grounds or at least in transit to their bedding areas.

I headed off down the road towards the lake in semi-darkness. Concentrating on the northerly side of it, I flicked my torch beam along its edge until my beam picked out a large rock with three

What they like to eat

prominent lines I had previously scratched. I took out my compass, and after forcing my way through the thin strip of scrub that bounded the road, headed off into the still silent forest on a compass bearing. Numerous previous trips had taught me the location of a number of the feeding areas and I was heading for the largest of them.

As I stealthily traversed the forest, stopping at intervals to check my bearing, the light came up. The day was overcast and dull but the dawn chorus of birdsong gradually swelled into life around me. I reached the edge of the feeding area, checked the wind and slowed my pace. The signs were unmistakable — first a set of tracks empty of water in the boggy ground, then a small pile of glistening droppings. Listening intently, step by step, I went deeper into the feeding ground. Just as I took the tenth step, I was aware of a faint sound, that of the leaves on a branch rustling violently when the branch was shaken. The sound repeated itself at intervals of 10 to 20 seconds. Fortunately the sound was coming from downwind, and I was able to stalk slowly and inexorably closer. The only noise problem was the soft clayey ground sucking at my feet when I lifted them. In order to more gently break the vacuum, I was forced to tilt each foot sideways a little as I withdrew it from the sticky suction.

I had gained another 10 metres in this manner and by now could hear a soft but distinct chewing after each episode of leaf rattling. Why couldn't I see the animal? The visibility was good, widely spaced broadleaf shrubs surrounded me and I could see 15 metres easily. My eyes strained in the growing light. Suddenly there he was, not 20 metres in front of me, a young stag, possibly a spiker, with barely discernible knobs of velvet. I marvelled that I had not seen him before, as he was fully in the open, standing quarter-on to the left, browsing an especially juicy looking broadleaf branch. One minute my eyes had failed to register him, the next they had unscrambled the confusion of optical data, to reveal him just standing there. Sadly for him I was hunting for the pot. I consoled myself that he had probably been the most incautious of his company, the rest returning to their beech-lined fastness well before the broadening of the light. Not wanting to spoil the shoulder meat, as he was close, I lined up on his neck and squeezed off the shot. He fell where he stood, and the shot reverberated away across the wakening bush.

Walking up to the silent reddish bulk of the carcass, I admired his fallen frame, feeling as always that moment of triumph tinged with regret after the hunter has made his kill. — *R.L.*

4
Effects of weather on red deer

Cold fronts and anticyclones parade across the Tasman Sea on to New Zealand. The seasons change from one to another in a never-ending cycle. The weather and the seasons bring variations in temperature, wind, humidity, sunlight and rain which affect the behaviour of red deer. An understanding of these effects and the animal's reactions to them is an important part of a hunter's knowledge.

Sunlight

The seasonal variations of animal behaviour are induced usually by changes in the duration of sunlight as the length of each day changes through the seasons. The length of time for which the sun's rays strike the earth during a 24-hour period, the "photoperiod", changes from season to season. These changes in the photoperiod are responsible for changes in the hormonal status of deer.

In autumn the length of the day quickly shortens. This change brings the hormonal cycles of both stags and hinds simultaneously into the rutting phase. Frost and low temperatures are, we believe, important factors to the final triggering of the roar but only after the deer have been brought to a state of readiness as a consequence of the photoperiod. F.F.Darling's detailed observations of deer in the rut bear this out. He describes how a period of overcast weather has delayed the onset of the roar even when temperature conditions were cold and snowy. The deer's perception of the changing photoperiod had, he believed, been confused by the overcast weather, and as they were not yet in the rutting phase, the roar could not be triggered by the cold weather. Even if the roar has started, a period of heavy overcast weather is likely to reduce sexual and rutting behaviour.

Sunlight is a source of warmth for deer and, except for the two hottest months, deer actively seek out sunlight. For example, in spring after their night-time feeding on grass, deer normally bed down in sunny sheltered spots for long periods. In winter, after a cold night, they will stand in full sun on open faces in the bush to get the warmth from the sunshine.

In the full heat of the summer deer actively avoid the sun. They will shift to feeding in dark shaded gullies and bed down only in deeply shaded places. They often have multiple beds and they move from one to another as the sun changes in the sky and erodes their shade. These beds can often be identified by the hair that has been shed from their moulting winter coat. Deer are difficult to hunt at this time as they lie out of sight in the shade for the greater part of the day, but knowledge of a good bedding area can sometimes enable you to sit quietly waiting for a deer to show as it changes beds.

Wind

Deer don't like strong wind, which removes the warm air from between the hollow hairs of their coats and makes them cold. It also makes a lot of noise, for example the rattling of branches, creaking of limbs, rustlings of leaves, which makes it more difficult for the deer to hear the threatening noises of danger approaching. In compensation, they are more alert and thus more difficult to stalk.

In strong winds you should look for places where the deer will shelter. For example, on a north-facing slope the deer will gain the sun but in a northerly wind they will also be exposed to the wind. They may travel downslope in these conditions in search of calmer air, or they may cross over the ridge top and drop down the sheltered south-facing slope, where they will be in the shade, unless the sun is high in the sky. Sometimes, to avoid travelling any distance, they may simply seek the small indentation in a terrace where they can bed and be out of the wind. In this way deer from quite a large area may become concentrated in a small sheltered place.

Conversely, deer favour light winds. Gentle breezes efficiently carry scent of potential danger. For this reason, deer will sometimes move from a place of no wind to one of light winds. Similarly, during the roar stags appreciate a light to moderate wind as it carries their roars further.

Winds caused by sun-induced temperature variation (catabatic winds)

The sun warms the earth during the day. The earth, in turn, warms the air above it which then rises. At night the heat radiates away from the earth into the night sky and thus the earth cools and, in turn, cools the air above it. On the side of a hill the cold denser air formed in this way rolls down the hillside into the valleys. With the return of the sun the warm rising air sucks air up out of the valleys. In this manner an air current is formed which comes downhill at night and uphill during the day. When a large valley abuts a mountain this up-and-down movement of air is converted into an up-valley wind during the day and a down-valley wind at night. The winds so created on a small local scale are called "catabatic winds", and every hunter should know about them.

Catabatic winds are particularly evident in the morning and evening. Being light, they are easily cancelled out by stronger, weather winds. The change from the night-time downslope wind to a day-time up-slope wind happens about 2 hours after sunrise and the change in the other direction happens after sunset. The exact timings vary according to local situations; if there is a calm period between the change it is usually only short.

An event called "thermal inversion" is associated with the catabatic effect. Sometimes, when the night has been very cold, the air that has fallen downhill becomes pooled in basins and steep-sided valleys. Because these places are often shaded from the early morning sun, the cold dense air remains puddled in them, resisting being drawn upslope. The air on the tops above the dense pooled air becomes warmed by the sun and often a layer of mist forms at the junction of the higher warm and the lower cold zones, alerting a hunter to the inversion.

On the tops there is typically a frost on the tussocks, a blue sky and a clarity of air through which the sun shines and you can see for ever. The adjacent peaks stand tall in the red of the rising sun and down in the valley stretches out a huge lake of motionless purple mist. It is one of the great sights of the mountains: one to live for and to remember.

Apart from being a visual spectacle there can be a reward for you in this situation. Deer are likely to move upslope out of the cold air puddle and into the zone of warmer air. You may encounter one of them doing this as you hunt along, just above the mistline. Be quick, it is not likely to last long, for when the sun rises and penetrates the lower valleys the inversion will disappear.

Temperature

The more deer travel in their daily routines, the more likely you will encounter them. In undisturbed places, deer generally do not travel much. Changes in temperature, however, can cause deer to move about. F.F. Darling found that the greater the variation in the daily temperature, the more deer are inclined to move. A knowledge of the daily variation in temperature can enable deer movements to be predicted. It is a complex subject but we have formulated these general rules:

1. On sunny days in winter, temperature will vary a lot as very cold frosty nights change to warmer days. In seeking to avoid the chill of the night and to catch the warmth of the sun during the day, deer usually need to travel long distances.

2. On overcast winter days the daily variation will be small. The weather is cold by day and night. Deer will move little, staying in warm places up from the valley floor.

3. In hot sunny weather in mid summer, daily variation will be large, from cool early mornings to very hot days. Deer will move to escape the sun; they will stay on the cool high ground at night and descend into the deeply shaded valleys in the day. This is the reverse of what happens in the winter, but the end product is still the same — a large daily movement.

4. Spring and autumn are seasons of transition with a variety of days, some on which the temperature varies a lot and some on which it does not. Days of winter-like cold weather can alternate with warm summery conditions. Thermal inversion, which as we have seen transforms the normal relationship of temperature and altitude, is most likely during these seasons. Spring and autumn are times when deer may move a great deal to cope with changing temperature, which when added to travel induced by the demands of their appetite, means good hunting.

Humidity

Humidity is a measure of the amount of invisible water content in the air. Warm air can hold more water than cold air. Human beings are sensitive to humidity. Those clear crisp days when it feels great to be alive and even better to be in the bush are sure to be days of extremely low humidity. All living things respond to such days with movement, feeding and play, and on such days it is common to find deer everywhere.

Humidity is important for a hunter because of the close relationship between humidity and the sense of smell. The sense of smell is the most important of the deer's senses (see Chapter 2) for identifying danger. Deer like to travel upwind, always studying with their nose what lies ahead.

Two things affect the sense of smell in deer. The first and most important is humidity. In very dry air the film of water on the cells of the deer's nose dries out and the chemicals of scent are more likely to pass through the nose without being dissolved and thus detected. With moist air the scent chemicals mostly become dissolved in the air's water vapour before reaching the deer's nose. They are easily mixed into the moisture on the nose cells and readily detected by them. Yet in wet air (such as fog or mist) there is so much water about that a deer's nose becomes runny. Many of the scent chemicals run out of the nose in the water without being detected. Like a human with a cold in the nose, the deer cannot detect smell well and, to a large extent, lose their sense of smell.

The second factor is what scientists call "fatiguing" of the senses. For example, you may notice a strange smell in a room when you first go in but after a while you become accustomed to it — you are experiencing fatiguing of your sense of smell. Such fatiguing also affects the deer's senses.

When humidity is high deer are bombarded with scent chemicals and they become used to having a lot to deal with. If the humidity in the air drops, deer for a time lose some of their sense of smell until they adjust to the lower amount of scent. This is a good time to be hunting them.

The opposite also occurs when deer have been exposed to dry air and so become extra sensitive to scent. When the air first becomes wetter they are more alert to all scents, including the scent of danger, and thus become difficult to hunt.

Relationship between frost and humidity

As the air gets colder on the night of a frost its relative humidity rises until it can hold no more water. This is the dew point and the water in the air then begins to settle out as dew, which will then freeze. During the night the long period of high humidity fatigues the sense of smell of deer, and frosty air further blunts their ability to smell. Come morning there is a bright sun, air rapidly warms, and the humidity falls sharply (much of the water from the air is on the ground as frost). Because the deer's sense of smell is slow to adjust, they are for a time rather unaware of scent in the air and their attitude is placid. The morning after a frost can be a good time for a hunter.

F.F. Darling studied the effect of humidity on deer and his general findings were:

1. During periods of low humidity there is usually beautiful clear weather. Deer movement is considerable and they are easily approached.

2. In periods when humidity changes from high to low and back again the deer don't move much but they are very irritable and easily disturbed. When they are disturbed they scatter over a wide area.

3. In periods of constant high humidity mist forms and the animals again become placid, easily approached and move only small distances.

Rain

The effect of rain on deer behaviour varies according to the intensity of the rain.

Light "misty" rain

These conditions are encountered in cloud and heavy mist, or when rain is only very light. The humidity is high, which lowers the deer's scenting ability, but if the air temperature is warm and there is no strong wind, deer seem to love browsing and grazing. In spring they prefer these conditions above all others, coming out and grazing on the tops and grassy clearings. They probably like the dressing of moisture on their "salad".

Moderate rain

An occasional deer will still graze the open, but most will be browsing in the bush which provides some protection from the rain. However, the animals are generally restless and easily disturbed, because they don't like the persistent background noise of the falling rain on the leaves and the big drops falling on to the forest floor.

Heavy rain

Heavy rain penetrates the forest canopy and there is much dripping in the interior of the bush. It is rare for deer to be in the open and even in the bush they generally stop feeding. The animals usually seek a sheltered, concealed bed and wait out the rain storm. Stalking is difficult, because besides being wet and missing the warm dry camp, a hunter will find the heavy rain blankets his sense of hearing and smell. Also, the deer are likely to be in their well-sheltered and well-concealed beds where they will be seen only at the last moment, if at all.

Snow

Deer seem to have the ability to predict the onset of snow. In the old days, when deer lived on the tops, they would descend to the security of the forest below just before it snowed, and a well-positioned hunter could wait on the major routes in ambush. Unfortunately, this tactic is not much use to the modern hunter.

When the spring snows begin to melt, the edges of the snow patches hold a particular appeal to grazing deer. These are places where grass recently covered in snow is exposed. Recent scientific work has found that when grass has been covered with snow for a few days or longer, the grass blades have a higher concentration of sugar and other high energy carbohydrates, which must be why the deer like it so much.

In very heavy winter snow, deer can become trapped in valley heads and in some situations they can be easily approached.

Following deer tracks in anything but virgin snow is seldom profitable. If the tracks lead under trees they will rapidly become obliterated by drips of melt water and lumps of snow falling out of the branches. For this reason, snow trails are worth following in the bush only where a fresh snowfall is immediately followed by a stiff frost, which holds and prevents the virgin snow in the trees falling on to the animal tracks.

Moonlight

A strong moon on a clear night enables deer to feed more effectively than on a black moonless night. They can see their way about and browse a greater area. At dawn after such a night there are likely to be fewer deer out of cover available for a morning shot, because the creatures have had plenty of time to browse their fill by moonlight and don't need to hang around at daybreak. Cloud cover diminishes the effect of the moonlight, so a night of a full moon and a heavy cloud cover is of little benefit to the animals.

Deer move about and feed on very dark nights, but their feeding is apparently much less efficient then and they move less distance. Dark nights are the most effective for hunting deer with spotlights, the deer tending to stand in the light rather than run out of it. Shooting deer at night is illegal on public lands and the practice is outside the ethics of the New Zealand Deerstalkers Association. It is a dangerous activity because of difficulties of target identification.

Equipment for measuring the weather

If you live close to your hunting ground, consider purchasing and using a simple set of instruments to keep track of changes in the weather. In this way you can identify and possibly exploit those excellent but often brief spells of ideal weather for hunting.

Maximum and minimum thermometer

This device shows the current temperature of the air and also can record the highest and the lowest temperature since it was last inspected. For example, you can wake up late in the morning and find out how cold it was last night, and the start of frosts (0°C) for the autumn roar can be pinpointed. The difference in altitude between the thermometer and the hunting ground enables the temperature at the deer's position to be estimated (for each 1000 metres of altitude the air temperature is 6°C cooler).

Hygrometer

This device uses two thermometers, one of which is kept wet and the other one dry. It enables the relative humidity (the amount of water in the air compared with the maximum amount of water the air can hold at that particular temperature) to be calculated. If your home and the hunting ground are some distance apart, this information, unfortunately, is likely to have little relevance.

Both the hygrometer and the maximum and minimum thermometer should be kept outside in a well ventilated place out of the wind and direct sunlight.

Barometer

This device measures the atmospheric pressure of the moment. Changes in pressure are not known to have any direct effect on deer. Nevertheless, our weather is dominated by depressions and anticyclones, and as these pass over the country there are big changes in atmospheric pressure. Changes in the barometer predict changes in the weather.

> In late summer we were camped in the Sabine hut, at the edge of Lake Rotoroa in the Nelson Lakes National Park. After a hot day of being annoyed by sandflies and poking around in the bush without success, we got keen on a trip to the tops, 600 metres above. At 3 a.m. the next morning two unwilling bodies struggled uphill, illuminating the forest with one inadequate torch. We wanted to catch an early morning deer in the open above.
>
> We got there, and about an hour after daylight we were sidling close to the bushline to minimise the damage of our scent travelling downslope with the night-time wind still flowing downhill. Nevertheless, the sun was becoming established on the mountain tops above and we could see it would be shining on us soon. We were looking for deer close to the bush edge. After half an hour or so Warren suddenly saw a small hind group of two deer way up high above us in the sun. We crouched down, thinking they may be walking downslope towards the bush edge and us. But they were very uncertain about what to do. Above them the tussock ran out into steep rock; it was chamois-only looking country up there.
>
> Warren began a stalk uphill, hidden in a stream bed, while I stayed within their sight. The catabatic wind was shifting from down to up and they got a good whiff of us I'm sure. I was quite a way above the bush edge at this stage, higher than I had expected to find deer, and the deer were about 600 metres above me and edging higher, with Warren out of sight between us somewhere. The shooting started. I began a hurried race across to cut them off from the bush below, but I soon realised they were just going higher and Warren was having a bad morning with his accuracy. I was up near Warren when he called out, saying he was out of ammo — we were not carrying a lot. I had a few shots standing up above the tall tussock and one animal fell over.

It was not a very clean piece of hunting at all. We were both very tired from the climb up from the lake below and now all this extra climbing, about 300 metres of it. I was on my own, climbing after one deer heading for the rocks above with the wind, now well established, blowing uphill. With the lead hind dead, it was a bewildered yearling ahead of me and I was feeling sorry for her. She did not know how to handle the unfamiliar rocks above. She died high on a beautiful morning to one of my last bullets at close range. There was a huge pool of mist in the valley below. We were pleased with the two heavy loads of venison, but there wasn't much else to be pleased with about the hunt. The rapidly changing wind direction on the night-to-daytime switch around had caused our scent to be all over the place. — *F.S.*

The red deer of the Central Otago tussock-clad uplands were plundered by the commercial venison recovery industry when it was still in its infancy, and during the live capture boom the few animals that remained were hunted down and darted or netted. The hunters of the tussock tops saw the hunting grounds of their childhood hammered, never to recover their former glory.

The red deer is, however, a remarkably adaptable beast and within a few short years of the onslaught many high country farmers were again, at mustering time, noticing the occasional animal. How they had escaped was difficult to say. Perhaps they crawled into the scant cover of a few briars when the dreaded rotary-wing sound had been heard — experienced hunters reported them doing this. On the other hand, perhaps other deer had travelled from the distant bush of Fiordland and the West Coast. At all events, the survivors were super-cunning, requiring great skill to hunt.

From time to time I would hear of lone animals and spend often fruitless weekends driving the miles of old tracks that criss-crossed the region, glassing the sunny uplands until my eyes ached.

One Friday evening I received an excited call from Duncan Henderson, a farmer friend who lived in Bannockburn, close under the Old Woman Range, at a little settlement that rejoiced in the name of Happy Valley. It was late autumn and whilst mustering his sheep he had seen not one but three stags in the head-waters of Duffers Creek.

At first light the following morning I was gently coasting along the first few yards of the track that led off the Bannockburn to Hawksburn road high on the northern shoulder of the steep-sided Duffers Creek valley. Barely half a mile along this track we came to a gate. My student companion, who had never seen a deer, disembarked eagerly to open it, but in his haste he slammed the thin metal door of the Suzuki I was driving. The sound reverberated across the steep little valley and I made a mental note to warn him not to do this when we got on to "hotter" territory. At the gate the student suddenly lost interest in the latch and started yelling and pointing. Just 600 metres from the road on the opposite side of the valley, going hell for leather for the high tops, were three stags. I was not a happy man, doubly so when I saw through my glasses that the leading animal bore at least one fork on each antler crown. We turned straight round and went home.

I rang Duncan the next day and told him of our disaster. I wanted to come back again in a couple of weeks and have another look, but he was a keen hunter himself and suggested that we could go up over the Nevis road and hunt an area on the other side of the range. The head-waters of the northern branch of Coal Creek were almost opposite those of the Duffers Creek and the animals we had so thoroughly alarmed would have probably headed for this valley. There was just one problem — the Nevis road. Barely navigable in summer, it became completely impassable with the coming of the winter snows — and the snows arrived the next weekend.

Not until November did Duncan think we could get over.

The trip over took twice as long as it would have in the summer, because of the slippery mud left by the receding snow. I hoped we could get back. Duncan and I drove to the beginning of Coal Creek and, leaving the vehicle, headed up into the valley. It wasn't long before we encountered problems. The valley was quite wide, its sides not steep, but an impenetrable cloak of briar and matagouri extended 30 metres up either side from the creek and we were thus forced upwards on to the crest of the ridge that formed the true left bank. Here we encountered yet more snow, this time deeper than on the summit crossing because mountains to the north shaded the ridge from the sun.

An hour later we were barely a mile up the valley and exhausted from tramping through knee-high snowfields. From where we sat, nibbling at scroggin and trying to keep warm, we could judge that there was sufficient snow to completely prevent the escape of any deer from the higher reaches of the valley. Any deer concealed in the strip of scrub that lay below us would have to run either downwards along the valley floor or out and down over the bounding ridges. Either way we would be within shooting range. The problem was to spot them. We had no dog to help us and spent a good half hour glassing the scrub intently with no result. Finally, in disgust, I fired two shots, their reports echoing away down the Nevis valley behind us. Silence. We glassed again, searching for any movement. Nothing.

Finally, we wearily retraced our steps, too tired to punch higher through the deep snow. We had been travelling about 10 minutes when we came to a place where three sets of large tracks had crossed our incoming trail. The animals had been heading out from the valley over the spur towards the main Nevis River. The tracks were so fresh that the earth thrown up with each step had not yet stained the snow on which it had fallen, but we had missed them — they had escaped.

It was autumn before Duncan and I walked up that spur again. The wind was blowing down the creek as we again climbed the spur looking down on the scrub. This time, we had more luck. At the edge of the scrub where the briar gave way to tussock was the single clear trail of a large stag. Better still, he was living here. We found two typical adherent "clumped together" roar-style stag droppings between the tussocks as we stealthily followed the trail. On and on we went, tense, excited, waiting for the inevitable. A mile further on we were getting doubtful. Another mile and we were sure we had walked past him. Sadly we retraced our steps out of the gully for the second time, fully expecting to see, as before, a fresh trail crossing ours. Then a sharp blow on my back, my fellow stalker urgently imploring my attention. There below us, standing in the middle of the scrub, was the same royal that I had seen heading out of Duffers Creek nearly 12 months ago. By a piece of extraordinary luck he had not winded us as we stalked past him, our wind eddying upwards over the ridge into the Nevis and not down into his domain. We fired simultaneously, the animal falling threshing into the briar. His head was a good solid timbered royal and it sits to this day not a mile from the place that I first saw it: in pride of place on the living-room wall of Duncan's farmhouse. — *R.L.*

5
Their regular behaviour patterns

General behaviour patterns

Deer are vegetarians. Because vegetable matter is low in energy content, deer have to eat a large quantity in order to extract enough energy for their needs. Typically, many hours of the day are spent eating and digesting.

Deer are ruminants, which means they chew their cud in the same way that cows do. They tear off vegetation with their incisor teeth and swallow it. It then enters the rumen, the first part of their four-part stomach. The rumen is essentially a simple muscular bag which acts as a storage organ for the torn-off vegetation. Later, when the deer are at rest, they regurgitate this food a mouthful at a time and chew it fully by grinding it down with their specially ridged molar and pre-molar teeth. This activity is called "cudding". The food becomes mixed with saliva and is then swallowed again, travelling down to the second part of their stomach, the reticulum. From here it goes to the final two parts of the stomach, the omasum and the abomasum, where digestion begins (see Fig. 15).

Scientists have estimated that the average time taken by deer to fill their rumen with vegetation is about one hour. Two hours are then required to effectively cud it. At least three rumen-fulls are needed every 24 hours in order to yield enough energy for the animal just to maintain its body weight. So deer spend most of their time browsing on the feeding grounds and chewing the cud. Cudding usually takes place away from the feeding grounds when the animal is resting on a deer bed.

Deer beds are chosen carefully, for the animal needs to be effectively camouflaged, yet have a good view of approaching danger. Beds will be in sites sheltered from rain and wind and, in the heat of summer, they will be well shaded. Favourite places are above small hillside terraces and in shrub-filled gullies. In settled weather and where they are undisturbed by hunters, deer will bed in the same area day after day.

While in their beds, deer usually sit with their backs to the wind, their legs tucked up underneath. The head is raised with eyes and

FIG. 15:

THE STOMACH OF RUMINANTS

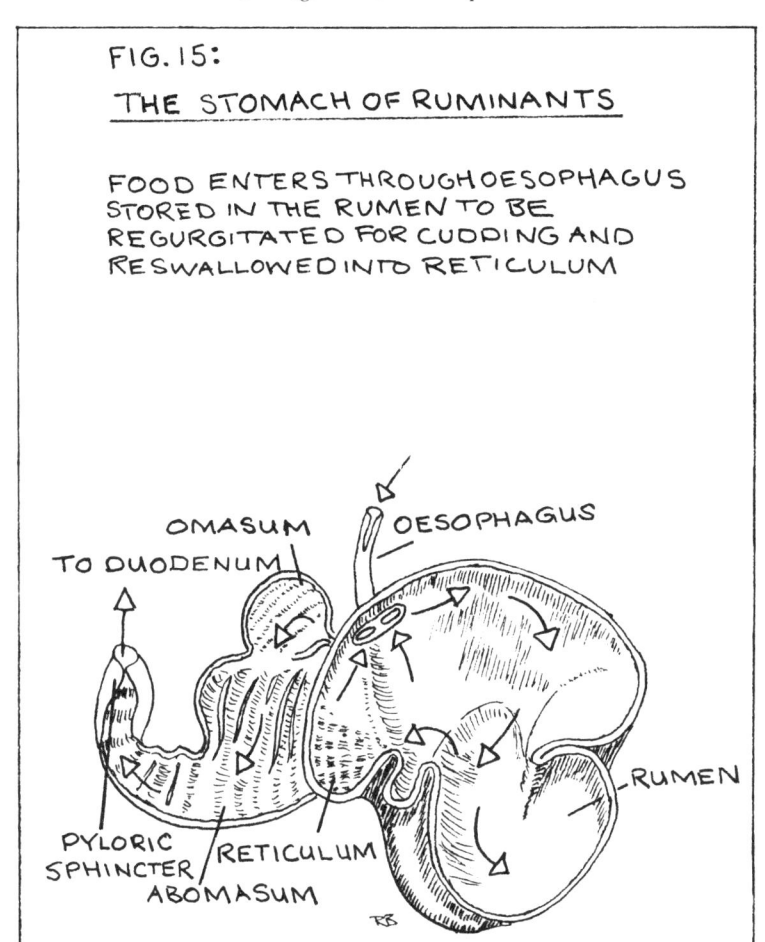

FOOD ENTERS THROUGH OESOPHAGUS STORED IN THE RUMEN TO BE REGURGITATED FOR CUDDING AND RESWALLOWED INTO RETICULUM

OMASUM
TO DUODENUM
OESOPHAGUS
RUMEN
PYLORIC SPHINCTER
RETICULUM
ABOMASUM

ears constantly scanning to the front and the sides for danger. The nose will detect the scent of any danger approaching from behind. The tucked-in legs enable the deer to stand quickly and silently if danger approaches. The lead hind in a hind group is particularly active in providing surveillance. She will occupy the most strategically placed bed and she will often get up and walk around to check all is well.

Because at least three journeys each day are needed between the feeding grounds and the bedding areas, deer like to bed as close as possible to where they feed. When no hunting pressure exists, deer will often bed only a few metres away from where they have been feeding, but when under hunting pressure, they will travel longer distances to bed in a more secure area. At some point the length of travel between the two places uses more energy than is gained from the food eaten. Deer are then likely to move to a new feeding location.

Sometimes deer develop two bedding areas, one near the browsing area, to which individual deer will retire while the rest of the group feed, and a second, safer area some distance away, to which the whole herd will retire when no longer feeding. This pattern is seen, for example, when deer come out of the bush during the night to feed on farmland. At night the herd will graze the paddocks and individual animals return at intervals to bed just inside the bush edge. With the coming of dawn the whole group stops feeding and returns to its daytime laying-up area well inside the bush.

If you are aware of the alternate patterns of feeding, travelling and laying-up, you can plan your hunting to encounter an animal during any one of these three phases.

Like all living things, deer need water. A large part of the vegetation a deer eats is the sap of plants, which contains a great deal of water. Deer do much of their browsing in late evening and early morning when their food may be covered in dew. For these reasons, deer seldom need to drink from streams, except in dry summer conditions or in parts of New Zealand that are particularly dry.

When deer become thirsty and are living in an area subject to heavy hunting pressure, they typically bed during the day and descend to drink in the late afternoon just before they start feeding. Hunting along stream beds at this time can be worthwhile.

Except in the heat of summer, deer prefer warmer places in which to live. In mountainous country, north-facing slopes get more sun than south-facing ones. North-facing slopes high up have more sun than lower down because they are shaded less from adjacent mountain tops. Deer favour these places for their warmth, particularly during winter. Places that get more sun also grow more vegetation, making such localities even more desirable to deer.

The higher the altitude, the lower the air temperature, and the cooling effect of the air is much increased if a wind is blowing. Deer have a thick coat of hollow hairs which trap a layer of warm, insulating air. Wind can blow out this air and the deer can easily get cold in strong wind. Deer therefore seek out places sheltered from the wind, especially during winter.

Their regular behaviour patterns

In determining the altitude frequented by deer on a mountain slope, both the sun and the wind have to be taken into account. The herd will change its altitude according to these two environmental factors — for example, in spring and autumn when winds are stronger, the animals will tend to bed in lower situations.

Social structure of herds

Red deer are herd animals. The helicopter hunters have demolished the big herds that once lived in our mountains, but the basic social dynamics of the herd still exist in groups of only two or three members. There are a lot of advantages in being part of a group. For example, one animal can keep watch while the others feed.

The position of herd groups within their territory will vary with the seasons. Knowledge of these migrations can help you plan a stalking strategy.

The basic division of the red-deer herd is by sex. The hinds form "hind groups" and the stags form "stag companies". (See Fig. 16.) The two sexes come together only during the rut, when stags fight for possession of hind groups, victorious stags holding such groups until worn out or beaten off by another stag. While being held by a stag the hind group still maintains its social structure with the dominant hind as its leader. The dominant hind organises a lookout and leads them all into an escape at the approach of any danger.

Hind groups

A hind gives birth to a fawn, which she suckles, protects and teaches how to survive in a hazardous world. She is a true solo mum — the stag is no help at all. Female offspring stay with their mother usually for 2 years, young males only one. The basic family unit, the hind, fawn and often a yearling hind, is said to be "matrilineal".

When the territories of two or more family groups overlap they sometimes aggregate to form a larger hind group. One hind, invariably the oldest, will become dominant, and she will hold her position for life. The dominant hind controls her inferiors by rearing up and kicking with her front legs, striking blows with the sharp front points of her cleaves — deer farmers know all about the power of these kicks. The dominant hind is particularly watchful. When danger threatens she always leads the group away by the safest route. The old-time government foot shooters had a strategy of shooting the

FIG. 16: SOCIAL STRUCTURE OF HERDS

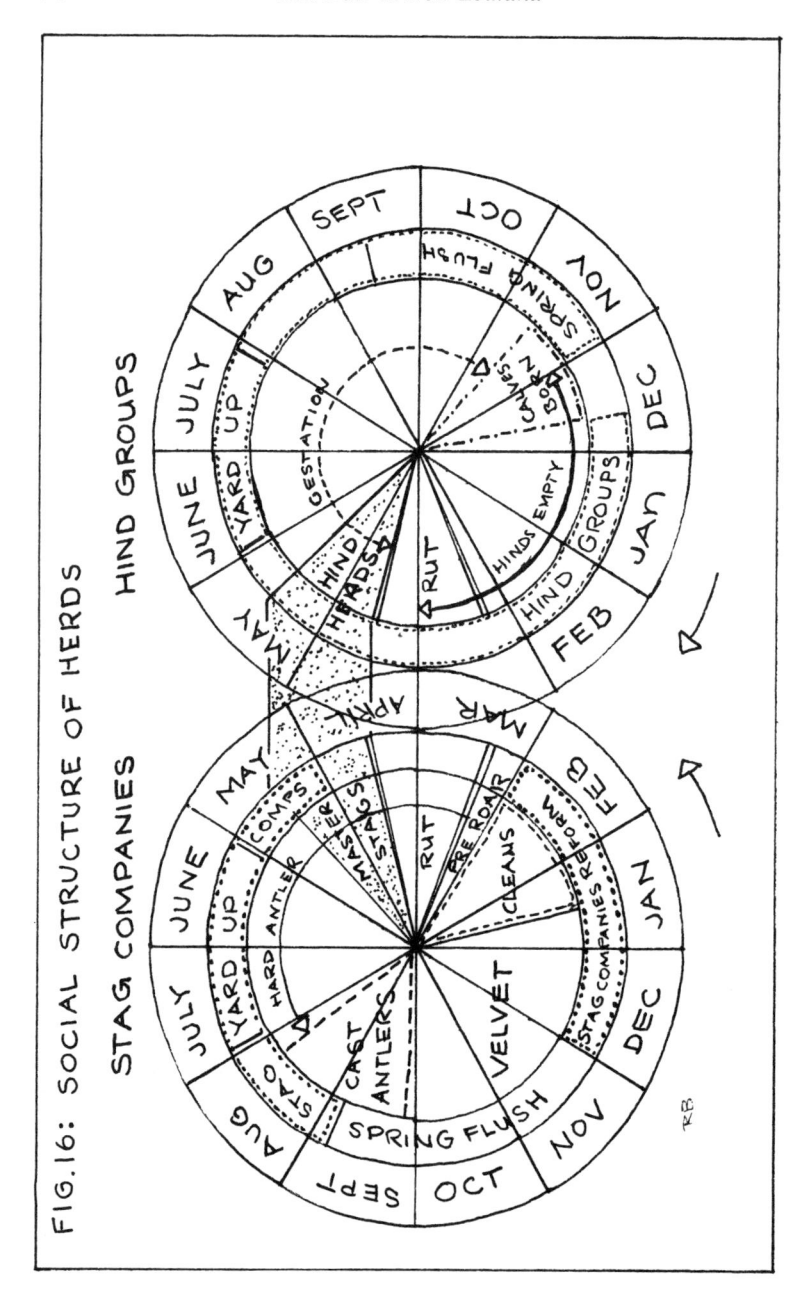

dominant hind first — without a leader the whole group became confused and were slower to make an escape.

F.F. Darling, who studied the highland deer in Scotland in the 1930s, described the existence in large hind groups of a "second-in-command" hind. Her position in an escape from danger was at the rear. When the lead hind was out of sight of the danger, the second-in-command would slow down or stop to keep the peril in sight until the lead hind, having emerged from the obstruction, could again keep it under her eye. This basic pattern is seen even in small groups of hinds. A single hind at the front and a single one at the rear, with the others in a group in the middle, gives a distinctive lozenge shape to a fleeing hind group. An alarmed stag company by contrast has an unstructured, every-man-for-himself form.

Hind groups claim the best territories for themselves — those with the best shelter, sunlight and food. Hind groups are much less mobile than stag companies, occupying smaller and more compact home ranges.

Between 1968 and 1974, R.H. Taylor, working for the DSIR in Nelson, studied the movements of red deer in the Nelson Lakes area. He used the snare system, which attached a collar to the deer's neck before allowing it to escape and roam free. A study of collars recovered from dead deer enabled measurement of the animal's movement since being snared (see Fig. 17). Some animals ended up wearing more than one collar, indeed one deer ended up wearing six. The data showed that stags often travelled considerable distances but hinds had much shorter ranges. Young stags showed the greatest movement. All the deer that moved more than 8 kilometres were young males, one of them travelling 32 kilometres.

Rather surprisingly, there was little movement between the zone of the lower forest area and the alpine zone. Only two (both males) out of the 142 tagged deer recovered had moved up onto the tops from the lower regions where they were tagged. No deer that were tagged on the tops were shot in the lower country. Taylor says the probable explanation is that red deer need forest margin in their territory, as we shall see later. When the study was carried out animal densities were higher and their herd ranges were correspondingly smaller than today. Thus an individual herd, having taken possession of a valued area of forest margin, would be less likely to move far from it.

On the Island of Rhum in Scotland the territories of hind groups have been studied extensively. By painstakingly observing the

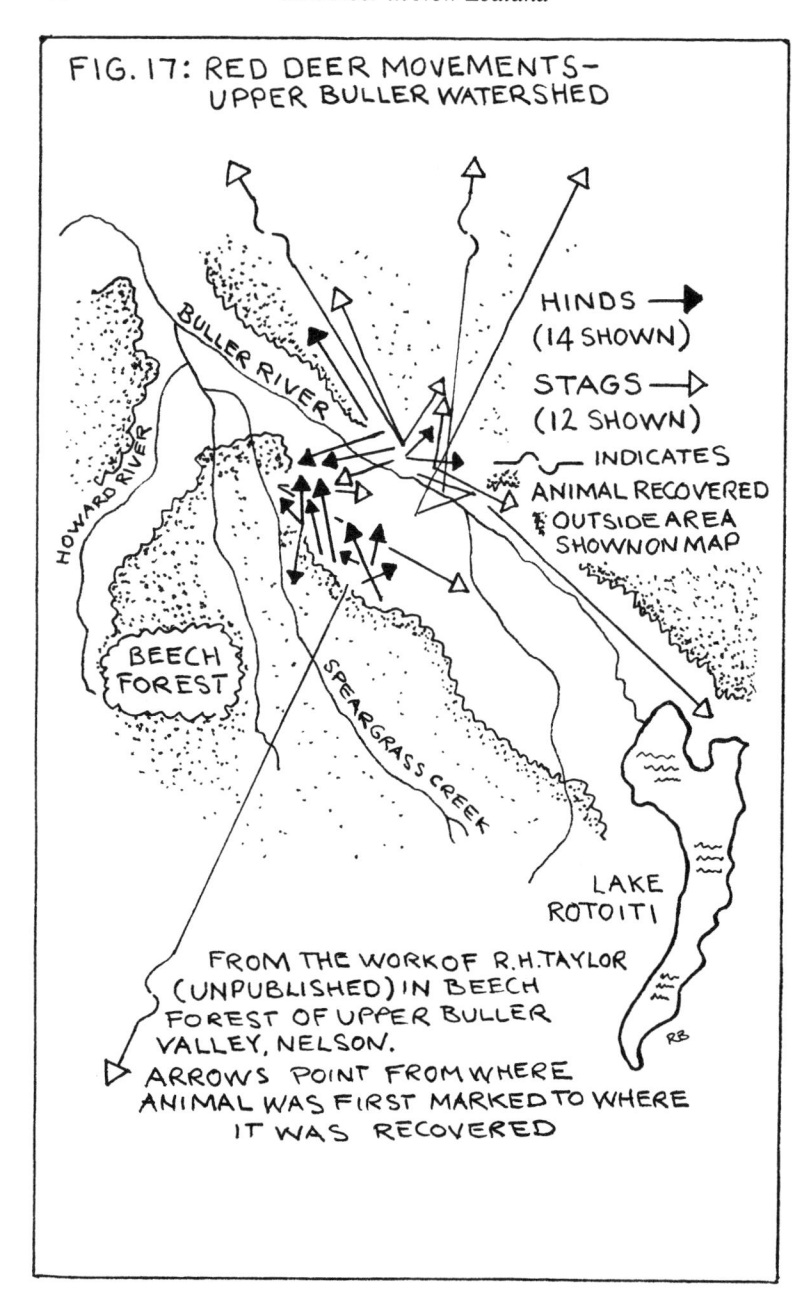

FIG. 17: RED DEER MOVEMENTS – UPPER BULLER WATERSHED

HINDS → (14 SHOWN)
STAGS ▷ (12 SHOWN)
⌇ INDICATES ANIMAL RECOVERED OUTSIDE AREA SHOWN ON MAP

BULLER RIVER
HOWARD RIVER
BEECH FOREST
SPEARGRASS CREEK
LAKE ROTOITI

FROM THE WORK OF R.H. TAYLOR (UNPUBLISHED) IN BEECH FOREST OF UPPER BULLER VALLEY, NELSON. ARROWS POINT FROM WHERE ANIMAL WAS FIRST MARKED TO WHERE IT WAS RECOVERED.

location of individual animals from day to day, researchers were able to build up maps of ranges occupied by individual hind groups. The hind groups were, as is usual, matrilineal. Such a hind group could consist merely of mother and daughter or comprise an extended family group of great-grandmother, grandmother, mother and daughter. These matrilineal family groups stick together and move together throughout the year. There is no reason to suppose that the same does not apply here, particularly as the work of Taylor in Nelson showed the same thing, only in less detail.

For the deerstalker, this means that a hind in a particular spot is likely to be accompanied by other hinds of the matrilineal group. The territories of a large number of different hind groups often overlap, producing the "hot spots" that hunters yearn for — and do their best to keep secret! Importantly, hot spots are much more likely to occur with hind groups than stag companies, because hind groups have smaller territories.

We will now look in detail at the behaviour of a hind group through the seasons.

Winter

The group will be yarded up in its winter ground, usually in the bush high enough up from the valley floor to miss most of the frosts and to catch the maximum amount of winter sun. The spot is likely to be on a north-facing slope in the head of a small gully, sheltered from the wind and with browse provided by low shrubs. On warm sunny days, especially after a hard frost or persistent rain, the animals will sun themselves on a slip or ridge top. The deer won't move far and the area becomes churned up with footprints.

Spring

The first sustained warm weather of spring brings with it new spring growth and a surge in appetite. The hind group moves off its winter ground and vigorously browses the preferred shrubs. When supplies are depleted they move on to the less preferred grass of bush-edge clearings and river flats, feeding on these dangerous areas mostly during night, particularly moonlit nights, but you may find them there in the early morning or late evening.

The yearling males, now young spikers, are driven out of the hind group by their mothers in early November, in preparation for the birth of their new fawns. These spikers are not good at looking after themselves and are vulnerable to hunters until they join up with a stag company. Yearling hinds are also driven off by their mothers but they do not leave the protection of the hind group. After the mother has had her new fawn she appears to relent and allows the female yearling close again. Darling reports that it is not unusual to see both the yearling and the fawn suckling from the maternal hind.

Fawns are born from late November to mid December, after a gestation period of 8 months. Birth and rearing take place at nursery sites that are used year after year. Birth starts with the hind becoming restless and moving a small distance away from the group to drop her fawn. As the fawn is born, the hind will give a "calving bellow". The fawn is able to stand within three-quarters of an hour and it soon begins to drink milk from its mother. Before long, both animals return to the hind group. While the hind is feeding, the fawn will "clamp", that is, remain lying still in a well-hidden position without moving until its mother calls it.

Because a hind may be fertile only for 48 hours during her hormone cycle, she may miss being impregnated during this time and have to wait a further period of weeks before she is again fertile. For this reason not all fawns arrive at the same time, the fawning period being spread over 4 weeks. Wild red deer in New Zealand seem to regularly have one fawn a year; twinning is rare and so are mature barren hinds (yeld hinds). Because good feed is available in New Zealand, hinds often give birth to their first fawn when only 2 years old.

Summer

The summer produces an abundance of food, and the hind groups are no longer forced to graze the dangerous open areas. They return to the more favoured bush areas in which growth is burgeoning. The hind groups travel slowly through their territory, feeding intensively until the onset of autumn.

Autumn

The hind groups are still in their territory but begin congregating at the traditional rutting sites where the stags are also showing up. Feeding continues for the group but less intensively. The hinds are brought into condition for mating by the shortening of the length of the day (the photoperiod). The stags' roaring probably triggers the final stage in the process of ovulation. Hinds in the best physical condition come into heat first followed by the less fit.

During her short fertile period, the hind is receptive and allows herself to be mounted. The basic attitude of the hinds during the rut is one of unconcern, but she may make overtures such as nuzzling or rubbing herself against the stag. It is almost as though they are bored by the drama of the stag conflict being played out around them. The dominant stag spends a lot of energy and time rounding up hinds from his group that have wandered off to graze. By sniffing the pre-orbital glands and urine of the hinds, he is able to identify which hinds are about to ovulate. It has been estimated that in a hind group of 30 animals, only two will be ovulating at any one time. The hinds continue to keep a watch for danger, and if it appears the hind group is soon led away by the dominant hind with the stag usually following. After the roar the hinds feed intensively until the onset of winter.

Stag companies

The smallest company of stags is that of two animals, often a dominant mature stag and a younger stag, usually a spiker. The advantage to the spiker (called a "fag" in Britain), is that he can continue the learning that ended when he was expelled from the hind group. The advantage to the dominant stag is that he can use his inferior to explore risky situations while he stays in the background, until he is sure all is well. Often hunters will shoot a spiker and then see a bigger stag escaping.

In areas of higher deer populations, the size of stag companies increases beyond two and can become very large in undisturbed regions. The order of dominance within the company is strict. Dominance is related to animal size, weight and fitness and is established by displays of intimidation and fighting. New entrants enter at the bottom ranking and from there work to improve their status. The way they fight for position is different from how they fight during the roar, and the dominance they achieve has nothing to do with what happens in the roar. Stags fighting for power usually, and especially when carrying velvet, rear up on their hind legs and "box" with their forelegs. This type of fighting does not occur in the roar. Once the pecking order is established, fighting is much reduced and minor gestures are often all that is required to indicate dominance. As stags grow old and weaker they leave the company and live out their lives in solitude.

The stag company does not provide as much care for its members as does the hind group. The boss stag is the most alert to danger, but when danger does comes he vacates the area with no regard for the other members of the company. Each stag leaves by his own route. This lack of welfare is why they are called a company rather than a group. The company is less cautious than the hind group, perhaps because as youngsters they had twelve months less training than the hinds.

Because the food stags eat is less concentrated than that of hinds, they spend more time grazing, and they range over larger distances, that is, they have bigger territories.

Winter

The company occupies its winter ground, feeding little and yarding up in bad weather. They regard their yarding ground more as shelter than a home, and even in winter the stag company follows the general rule of occupying a larger territory and travelling more than hinds. The stags continue to carry their antlers throughout the winter.

Spring

The spring brings the hungry time and the stags are driven to eating anything available. Stags are more mobile than hinds, particularly in early spring when they can be found even on the tops looking for food. Under the pressure of hunger and a shortage of feed, stag companies are likely to break up to some extent during the early spring.

Late spring and early summer is the time of the "silly spikers", the one-year-old males that have been ejected from their hind group by their mother when the new fawn was born. They are bewildered and inexperienced in the ways of the world, they are feeling very hungry after the winter fasting and their young growing bodies are continually demanding energy. The hunter is likely to find them feeding in the open without much caution, particularly in December and also on in early January. Feeding as they go, they will cover great distances looking for a group to join up with, but in heavily hunted areas many of them are shot before they do. The survivors eventually join up with at least one older stag to find relative security in a stag company.

The end of September (earlier for older stags) is the time of antler shedding. The end of spring sees the grey-brown winter coat replaced by the red-brown coat of summer in both stags and hinds. The new coat grows underneath and the old one is shed off in a patchy manner, often giving the animals a scruffy appearance for a time.

Summer

By December older stags have significant new growth of soft and very tender velvet antler. Companies led by older stags move into areas of bush with an open understorey or seek open places such as bush edges so that they can avoid damage to their velvet. In areas where calcium is deficient, stags will gnaw cast antlers and favour calcium-rich vegetation.

From mid January to late February, depending on the age of the stag, the velvet covering the new antlers hardens, becomes itchy and is stripped off by the animal as he thrashes his antlers against thin-stemmed dense foliage. These stags are sometimes said to be "hanging out the washing", as they may be seen with festoons of frayed velvet hanging around their antlers.

By early February those stag companies that split up in the spring have reformed. By early March all stags have antlers clean of velvet and are now polishing them on rubbing trees. Feeding on the plentiful growth of summer continues apace as the stags build up condition and body weight for the rut ahead.

Autumn

Mid March sees the stags in a disturbed state. Their daily movements generally increase. Their predominant gait is a high stepping trot instead of the usual walk. Stag companies break up and stags travel long distances, quitting their territories to head for their traditional rutting grounds which are in hind territory. These movements often take place at night. The old hierarchy of the stag company is lost — stags regard the rutting ground as neutral territory where all rights will be recontested. The stags begin to open up the old wallows with a few pawing motions of their forefeet.

By the end of May the bulk of the rutting activity is over and stags return to their territories and re-establish their companies ready for the coming winter. They feed intensively until the onset of winter.

Some depleted stags are unable to put on enough condition to survive the winter.

Behaviour of stags during the rut

The activity of red deer stags during the roar has been much studied and a pattern of behaviour has been identified.

As the time of the rut approaches, stags become more fractious, and by the time they reach the traditional roaring grounds each stag is systematically picking fights with other stags of similar status. These fights are simple sparring encounters which take place in the absence of hinds and do not progress to the more formal engagements of brute strength that occur later.

Each stag begins to announce his availability and strength to the hinds and potential adversaries in the district, which he does by using smell and sound.

Each stag has an individual scent by which hinds and other stags can recognise him. One component of this scent is produced by the pre-orbital gland. The stag wipes the contents of this gland on to prominent trees and the ends of sticks within his territory. The stag will also use urine to garnish areas where he has wiped his pre-orbital scent glands. He will rub his forehead and dig his brow and bez tines into areas of soft ground adjacent to wallows, then urinate on this ploughed-up area. He will thrash small shrubs with his head and antlers and again follow this by urinating.

A stag alternately urinates into a wallow and then rubs himself in it to enhance his body smell — wherever he walks is a strong stream of scent in the air proclaiming his presence.

Stags also announce their presence by the sound of their roaring. At the start of the season they give single grunts which later increase to a run of two to ten short roars all made on the same outwards breath. The frequency of roaring indicates the size of the stag. Stags roar best on quiet still days and they especially love frosty mornings when their roars will carry a long distance. Stags often have favourite "roaring stands" from which they roar; these spots have special topographical features which amplify the sound, so carrying the stag's roar a greater distance.

By using these techniques a stag hopes to attract hinds and thus become a master stag holding a harem. The objectives of a master stag during the roar are to maintain control of his harem by repelling encroaching stags, to keep the maximum number of hinds contained, to detect their readiness for impregnation, and to mount them when they are ready.

The most exhausting of the stag's duties during the roar is herding the hinds. The stag behaves similar to a "heading" sheep dog — he endeavours to keep his females in a tight group by running after any hinds that wander away. While he is chasing the hinds like this he holds his head in a distinctive way: his neck is held almost straight out in front of his body, the head chin up.

Another task is that of "chivvying" the hinds, the objective of which is to test the hind to see if she is ready for mounting. Stags chivvy by chasing a hind for a short distance with his neck and head held in the same posture as for herding. If the hind runs away the stag breaks off immediately and loses interest; the hind is ready only when she stands her ground.

"Sniffing and licking" is another way the harem-holding stag tests a hind's readiness for impregnation. The stag looks for hormonal scents by sniffing and licking the hind around the head and neck, especially around the pre-orbital glands near the eyes. A stag will often "show flehmen" after sniffing and licking a hind, by curling back his upper lip as though about to sneeze.

Besides his duties towards his hinds, the stag with a harem must repel other stags who contest his position. Before two stags lock antlers in a set-piece battle they go through an extensive ritual to ensure only closely matched stags need to fight. The ritual often obviates the need to fight; for example, during the rut a harem-holding stag will on occasion bark at an obviously inferior stag such as a spiker. This sharp reminder signals undoubted superiority to the minor rival and combat does not ensue.

Mature stags that haven't yet viewed each other are able to gauge one another's relative size from the rate of the roar, as indicated by the number of times the animal roars over a given time. A challenging stag is likely to approach only a harem-holding stag of a similar or lesser roaring rate. When the challenging stag moves to within about 100 metres a prolonged bout of roaring exchanges begins, the so called "roar contest". Clutton-Brock studied 33 such roaring contests and in 16 the contest ended the encounter. A challenging stag is apparently able to judge from the roaring rate that he is up against a superior opponent and withdraws at this early stage.

The next phase in the challenge is the "parallel walk". After the roaring contest the two stags approach one another and walk along side by side, carefully sizing up each other's body shape and size. If there is an obvious mismatch the weaker stag can withdraw. Clutton-Brock observed 24 parallel walks (some parallel walks happened without a preceding roaring contest) which resulted in only 13 pairs of stags proceeding to a fight.

The actual fight has also been divided into phases. The first phase, "initiating", occurs when one stag lowers his head and invites contact. The next phase is "locking" — the invitation is accepted and the two stags interlock their antlers. "Pushing", the real heart of the contest, then occurs. The contest is essentially one of brute strength, to see which stag has the most power and stamina. An experienced stag, however, does have some scope to show skill and cunning by steering his opponent. This steering is achieved by pushing more on one side than the other, coupled with a bit of fancy footwork and neck bending. In this way the experienced stag will steer his opponent around and use the terrain to make sure he is pushing downhill whenever he can.

Two fighting stags can quickly and nimbly lock antlers, push and disengage to lock and push again. The contest continues until one animal senses he is weaker than his opponent, withdraws and rapidly quits the scene of the combat. If after a fight the weaker stag is foolish enough to hang around, particularly with his flank exposed, the other stag may run on to him and spear him, sometimes fatally, with his brow and bez tines.

The older stags begin the ritual of the rut first. They are almost continually active, holding their hind groups, fighting off challenging stags and servicing hinds as they come into heat. They masturbate frequently. As the master stag weakens he may be beaten outright in a challenge by a previously lesser rival or have his hinds surreptitiously stolen from him without combat. He may retire for a brief rest and then return again to try to reclaim his harem. As the older stags become worn out, having lost a lot of their weight and vigour, they are forced to depart and their places are taken by younger stags who have developed full sexual maturity. By now, however, most of the fertile hinds have been serviced and the hinds are becoming increasingly restless about being confined to the roaring grounds. They begin to leave and the rutting season tapers to an end.

The Hackett is a short river flowing into the Tasman Sea between Milford Sound and Jacksons Bay. It is a long way south of the road-end at the Cascade and the only practical way to get there is by helicopter. I arrived there, with Warren and Eric, in the last week of March 1988 and set up a simple tent camp on a boulder-strewn river flat surrounded by low hills clothed in beech forest.

The first day of hunting began with Eric hunting downriver, searching for river terraces and spurs above the river that would

Their regular behaviour patterns

hold deer. Warren and I walked up the Hackett River, with the wind behind us, to its junction with a side stream, then climbed a short spur 350 metres to a bush ridge. Our mission was to see if the deer were on the bush ridges.

As we easily ascended the spur through open beech understorey the westerly wind was blowing on our backs, from the sea, up valley. We didn't see much sign of deer.

As we went up Warren gave the occasional "roar", directing the sound down off the spur, using a piece of PVC tubing with which he was able to produce a loud clear rutting sound. I had an old radiator hose constructed with two 90° bends. I gave fewer roars, not as loud as Warren's but with a deeper, more authoritative sound, or so we thought.

We found ourselves on a flat hilltop with a steep drop on the far side down to the Ryan River below. The ridge ran north-south, so for the first time that day the west wind was no longer blowing directly from behind. Warren gave a roar and immediately a stag replied from close by. Then another roared and another. Three separate stags, all to the north of us and not far away.

It was my turn to hunt and I set off along the ridge towards the roaring stags while Warren stayed back on the hilltop, giving the occasional roar which always met an enthusiastic response, especially from a stag that seemed to be on the ridge top. There was a stag with a deeper-toned roar down off the ridge to the west, which only sometimes replied to Warren. The third stag had a higher tone and he appeared the furthest away.

Once down off the hilltop, I could in the main hear only one stag roaring from directly ahead and coming towards me. Nevertheless, Warren on the hilltop would count over 60 roars during my 15-minute stalk.

I didn't roar at all, but just kept stalking towards the approaching stag, at a steady pace with the wind blowing across my line of travel. As I got closer the roaring was louder and my attention became rivetted on the animal's sound and the movement of the wind. I heard heavy and laboured breathing before another even closer fog-horn-like blast. Abruptly, I saw a big black stag looking straight down at me from between the trees, three tines on the top of one antler. The cross-hairs searched for a way between the tree trunks . . .

Twenty tons to the square inch of hot occluded gas thundered through the forest — the big animal fell right where he stood. I cautiously approached the beast to count 12 points. The stag had a very fresh wound to his head, probably from a brow tine of an opponent.

The stag with the deepest roar, although upwind, had become silent shortly after the shot. Warren walked down to me, while the higher-toned stag continued to roar. The animal was down off the steep side of the ridge to the east and so in danger of catching our scent.

Warren stalked off down the hill in a large semi-circle to come upwind of the roaring beast, while I began to headskin the shot stag, stopping occasionally to roar and so assist Warren who was hunting silently.

However, the roaring stag came up the hill and stood among some understorey down the steep bank, about 40 metres from me. The stag's neck and head were visible — he was a small 6-pointer. From this position he roared several times until he must have cut my scent, as he left abruptly. Warren came back without seeing him.

It was now Warren's turn to shoot and he led. We frequently looked at our map and checked our compass bearings in this remote untracked hill country, clothed in forest, as we navigated from one main ridge down to reach another to take us westward back towards camp. We had planned our day's stalk to take advantage of the prevailing westerly wind. At one place, we found a small hind group but no sign of a stag, an indication that the roar was only in its early phase.

By mid afternoon we had just crossed to a new ridge and were walking westwards, directly into the wind. Suddenly a stag, close and upwind, answered one of our questing roars.

Warren unslung his day pack and set off towards the animal. Shortly after dropping out of my sight, Warren heard a lot of crashing of bushes — the stag was rapidly coming in towards my roars.

Warren stood behind a tree, thinking the stag was going to come right up. I gave another couple of roars and the stag immediately replied with a couple of good rip-roaring tree shakers. Warren waited, the stag crashed about, knocking the scrub around just out of sight but no longer moving in, probably standing his ground there to engage in a roaring contest with me. Warren frequently checked a wisp of cotton tied to the tip of his rifle barrel. The wind shifted a little, the cotton responded and Warren became concerned.

He moved forward to approach the stationary animal. Ahead was a long flat bench of forest floor and the stag. Warren dropped off the edge of the bench, to better keep the fickle wind in his favour. However, the stag must have heard Warren moving and he too dropped off the bench to directly approach the hunter. By chance, I chose this moment to roar again and immediately the stag, a scant 30 metres away from Warren, roared back, heightening the tension.

Warren was standing on a deer track at one end of a small ridge just below the bench when the stag walked into clear view at the other. The animal was slightly below him, about 18 metres away and through his 2.5 power scope sights looked huge and even closer.

The stag was covered in wallow mud and appeared belligerent, not a majestic sight, a raw, even mean-looking beast in a cantankerous mood spoiling for a fight. The big animal walked straight ahead down into a small hollow on the ridge. Because the stag was so very close, front on, and lower than Warren, he presented no vital aiming point. With the stag walking only 10 metres away now, at the bottom of the small hollow, Warren had to do something to avoid being walked over — and quickly. Without stopping, the stag lifted his head to roar. Warren could see the whole animal from his cleaves to the top of his antlers but still had no heart or hilar kill shot in view. As the cross-hairs wavered and then steadied between the stag's eyes Warren pulled the trigger. The stag's four legs flew outwards, the body crashed to the ground shaking and quivering.

The once-proud beast lay dead, a 9-pointer but bigger than my 12-pointer. We quickly head-skinned it and hurried back to reach camp by nightfall. The 9-point antlers were later measured at 33 x 30 inches and 218 on the Douglas score whilst my 12-point antlers measured 33 x 30 inches and scored 198 Douglas.

Eric had seen a total of 11 deer that day, more deer than we had, but the hinds and stags were still separate. The biggest stag he saw was a small 8-pointer.

It had been an enthralling day of hunting at the very start of the rut. That night in camp we talked about the day's hunt and of the exciting prospects for the week that lay ahead. — *F.L.*

The pointed, triangular pattern of hair on this stag's face, the high carriage of the neck and poor shoulder bulk all indicate an animal 3–4 years old (see Chapter 10). *Lance Barnard*

Knowledge of vantage points from which you can glass large areas of likely country is essential. Ideally, routes to and from these points should be easily accessible in the dark, so you can easily get to and from them before daybreak and after nightfall. Here Roger Lentle glasses likely slips in the Northern Ruahines just after first light.

Above: A well-trained dog is particularly valuable when tracking wounded deer. Here Pat, a German Wire-haired Pointer, has tracked and bailed a wounded stag. *Martin Brenstrum* **Left:** "Haversacking" a deer (see pp. 145–6). Coloured plastic or a "blaze" on the carcass is essential insurance against trigger-happy shooters. **Opposite, above:** Helicopters can save a lot of meat packing. This stag was recovered from dense bush after a short drag to a handy flat.

High tops stalking the easy way: a short helicopter ride can save hours of toil, enabling you to conserve energy for the hunt. Even under today's conditions deer will often venture well out on to the tussock tops. *Norm Anderson*

Left: First deer for a young hunter. A successful stalk often owes more to patience, careful planning and good teaching rather than fitness and age. *Stuart Mirfin.* **Below:** A rare picture of a stag marking the edge of his territory during the roaring season (see Chapter 5). He does this by wiping scent from his pre-orbital glands on to a prominent tree. *Lance Barnard*

6
Some hunting strategies and tactics

He had much delite in huntinge. Many times he would go into the forest and set up there his tent with great provision of viteles.

Biography of Sir Thomas Warley, 1623.

What we hope to do in this chapter is examine and make recommendations on strategy and tactics for the stalker of red deer in New Zealand. It is said there are many ways to kill a cat other than choking it with butter. Likewise, there are many ways to hunt deer, but we do not know all of them. We invite you to take whatever you may find of value from this chapter and add to it your own experience.

Safety aspects of a hunting area

A hunter should at least know the area in the same way as a tramper — the location of the major tracks, routes, huts, river crossings, the major landmarks, emergency routes out of the area in bad weather, and so on. Yet, unlike a tramper, a hunter spends most of his time off the track and so needs to have a plan for finding his way back to a track and camp at the end of a hunt.

In big-valley mountain country there is a definite navigational logic to the landscape. "Down" means you are heading for a river valley and "up" means you are heading for open tops. Difficulties in finding directions are more likely in flat areas or broken bush-covered hilly country, which can become quite confusing once one is well within it. Fortunately, in most areas there are tracks on the ridges or in the valleys from which to work. A compass bearing can be taken showing the general direction of the track. When leaving this track you should be aware of your heading with respect to its direction so that you can, after stalking, reverse your heading and again cut the track.

The track must be clearly marked for it to be found again by this procedure.

Sometimes overgrown tracks may need to be remarked or new tracks made. For example, hunters who have just been dropped into an isolated clearing in a remote bush area may wish to mark some trails radiating out from their new campsite to help locate camp on the return from hunting trips. The traditional way to mark tracks is by slash marks on tree trunks. However, in our more environmentally sensitive age other ways need to be found. Brightly coloured plastic bags can be cut into strips and tied to trees. These markers can also be usefully left at strategic locations when hunting unfamiliar country — the fork in the river where you went up the right branch, or at the bushline where you emerged on to the tops. These plastic markers should be removed as you come back along the route.

Where to look for deer

Your first reference is a topographical map produced by the Department of Survey and Land Information in Wellington. These maps have a system of brown contour lines showing the shape of the landscape (the relief). The maps also show the manmade features of huts and tracks as well as the areas of bush, scrub, open country and so on. Some maps are available which show forest type. Draw on the map the direction of the prevailing wind so that the sheltered places for deer as well as the north-facing sunny spots become clear.

To find out more detail about the type of vegetative cover, you will need the aerial photographs used to produce the topographical maps. These are also available in colour and black and white from the Department of Survey and Land Information. Take in your map and show them the area you want covered.

When an aircraft flies over an area, each place on the ground is photographed twice along the aircraft's flight path, each photograph being taken from a slightly different angle. Two adjacent photographs of the same spot form a stereoscopic pair, which can be viewed through a stereoscope. The result is an amazingly real three-dimensional view of the hunting ground, especially when seen in colour. Features not noticed on a single photograph stand out as though they are being seen from a helicopter.

Colour is more expensive than black and white, but the expense is worthwhile for an area regularly hunted. To identify from the photographs the species of trees in the forest, an expert, or somebody with detailed local knowledge, is necessary. The district forester or ranger from the Department of Conservation may help you informally.

Knowledge of the traditional territories of deer is valuable — their fawning areas, spring feeding grounds, rutting grounds and so on. Fellow hunters are usually reluctant to divulge this hard-won local knowledge. However, these places have often been used by deer for generations, and some old-time hunters may be able to mark on your map where they used to find their deer. Unless the conditions in the area have been drastically altered, the deer will still be there. Some staff of the Department of Conservation may be able to help, especially if they have done pellet counts in the area. In all these discussions be aware of the seasons, as observations made in one season will apply again only in that same season.

For those with the money, overflying the area by helicopter is a fast way to learn an area. Take along a map and pen and get the pilot to fly slowly and low to enable you to look for deer routes. Look also for clearings that may be visible only from the air, and look at ridge tops and river valleys you intend to use for travel to see how good they appear, although even then you won't really know until you have walked them. Note features of the landscape which will assist you to find your way back on foot to the interesting places identified from the air. Ask the pilot where he thinks the best spots are, because if he has hunted the area with his machine he will know. Unfortunately, good places for helicopter hunting are not always easy to foot shoot.

If you have followed our theoretical plan so far, you will now have a map on which are marked sheltered warm areas, areas of favoured vegetation and locally known traditional areas for deer. We now suggest the next phase: deer surveys. These are trips into the bush to see at first hand the places highlighted by your studies and determine if there are enough animals present to make hunting worthwhile.

The changing of the seasons alters the distribution of deer and so each place probably needs to be seen in each of the four seasons. On these trips plan to cover as much ground as possible; use circular routes so that the same ground is not covered twice. Walk river flats where soft ground will show prints, look at open faces for sign, sidle through heads of creeks and so on. Vary the height of travel and study especially the elevated sunny and sheltered places that were first identified on the map. Don't overlook the country near the road. Often hunters will walk past a side creek near the end of the road thinking that the more remote, the better the hunting. Sometimes this approach means that nobody is hunting these close areas.

Be careful about predicting the number of deer from the amount of footprints and tracks you see, because one deer travelling long daily distances can leave many prints. Sometimes a large group of deer settled in country that does not hold prints well will leave little evidence of their presence. Look for other sign besides footprints to gauge numbers and activity. What you learn about the location of deer will change with the seasons — a good spot now may not be so good in a month's time, but 12 months from now the deer are likely to be back there on schedule. The whole process of studying deer patterns and trying to locate the deer is one of the most challenging and fascinating aspects of deerstalking.

In order to keep up a good stock of venues, a hunter should be looking at new areas almost as often as he hunts known places. Hunting grounds fail from time to time for reasons such as overhunting or disturbance by dogs used to chase deer.

Deer in heavily hunted areas become very sensitive to the signs of man. Continued hunting pressure on deer will often make them leave the area. In practice, this often means that few deer are within the distance of an easy morning or evening shot from a hut. The number of shots fired on the hunting ground should be kept to the bare minimum, as should the lighting of fires. The sound of a helicopter usually produces panic in deer even when they are in heavy bush cover. Where overflying by helicopters is frequent, deer will not venture far from the bush edge, even where no helicopter hunting is actually being done. Helicopter disturbance and hunting is still keeping large areas of open tussock, the hunting grounds of the past, devoid of deer.

A general plan for hunting a new area

There will be occasions when a hunter is in a new area without having been able to carefully evaluate it as we have described. An enthusiastic mate may have invited him to a "great place" where (two years ago in a different season) there were hundreds of animals. So you tramp for hours to get to the place, and there see some excellent examples of well preserved old deer sign, a nice print with a young rimu seedling growing in it and droppings with a centimetre of white fungus growing on them. What to do now? Usually you sit around all weekend while your mate tells of the mighty deer he used to shoot around here, followed by a general paranoid discussion about who shot them all. The trip ends in a depressed return home on a Sunday when even the pubs are shut.

Some hunting strategies and tactics

Let's analyse this scenario. Firstly, the people you blame are highly unlikely to have exterminated all the animals. They are probably still there in the same numbers as your mate saw them, but in a different place.

Finding that place should be the aim on the first day of the hunt. Each member of the party should head in a different direction for the whole day and cover as much territory as possible at a fast walk with little regard for wind direction. Ridge lines should be examined for fresh tracks, stream beds followed looking for crossing points showing fresh sign and river flats similarly examined for well used trails. The emphasis in this search is on looking for well used trails rather than individual tracks. When doing this sort of survey, by travelling ridges, stream beds and river benches, the hunter can cover a lot more ground than bush bashing from one gully to the next. The hunters should spread out as much as possible, each covering a large area to minimise the disturbance to the deer, wherever they are.

That evening in camp, each hunter should give an account of where he has been and what he has seen in an objective and uniform way, so that the party can decide on which area to concentrate the following day. The next day's objective is to find out the level of the deer in the chosen area. The level can change during the day, as animals may bed in one place and ascend or descend to feeding areas, or if they move in response to changes in the weather. Each hunter should be given a particular level to explore. Examples of particular levels are river flat bush edges, river terraces, middle bush level, gully heads and tops.

The hunters should hunt these levels simultaneously, more or less in line heading upwind. In this way as much ground as possible is covered in such a way that if a deer is encountered there is a good chance of bagging it. Detailed attention should be paid now to the individual sign encountered to estimate how fresh it is and in what direction the deer that made it was moving. If a hunter does shoot a deer the others should not change their plans, as to do so would sabotage the information-gathering objective of the day's efforts. The deer shot, for example, may have been in a bedding area in the middle of the day, but what the party still needs to know is where the deer are feeding.

Even if no animals are encountered by the end of the day, the party should have a reasonable estimation of the level at which the animals are feeding, what they are feeding on and where they are bedding during the day, and a more detailed estimate of how many deer are living in the area. With this information the party can now plan to close in on the animals the next day. If, however, results are disappointing, the hunters can revert to the first day's strategy of covering a lot of ground again to find where the deer really are.

Hunting methods

There are a number of different ways to go about hunting a red deer. Often when out for a day's stalking a hunter will use more than one of these methods, perhaps merging one with another.

Hunting river flats

The technique is, essentially, to walk up or down a river valley hunting the grassy river flats. Walk along slowly into the wind, keeping under cover wherever possible, looking for any deer out in the open, eating the less preferred grass or tussock. They do this mostly in spring at night, so the most productive time to hunt is at dusk or in the first light of morning, especially after a moonless night.

On a river flat the wind is likely to be blowing down the valley at daybreak and up the valley at dusk. We find it difficult to know where to make camp so that our scent is not blown all over the hunting ground when the wind changes. An answer can usually be found in the detail of the area. If a camp can be made up a side stream, for example, the problem is to some degree overcome. Certainly do not camp just above or below the best flat in the valley or, worse still, in the middle of it!

River-flat hunting is a good technique for hunters new to the sport. If it is done with care — and sometimes without — a dead deer can be the result. Deer are particularly nervous when out in the open and it is essential to hunt only with the wind in your face. Often during the last moments of light at dusk the wind begins its catabatic shift and starts to blow down-valley at the critical moment of a stalk.

It is particularly important to make an extra effort to identify your target in the poor light in which this type of hunting usually takes place; a telescopic sight on your rifle is precious at these times. Take a torch to find your way home.

Walking a riverbed

This technique is suitable for small to medium rivers running through steep bush country. The idea is simply to walk up or down a riverbed looking for any deer. Where slips have fallen down into the riverbed, grass and shrubs will have grown, providing good feed for deer. The slips also provide places where deer can sun themselves in the winter or after a frost. Deer can also dry off on the slips after a rainstorm, avoiding the heavy drip of the bush. Small open flats in the riverbed may also hold deer.

At river bends stay on the inside to keep out of sight of the next section of river until the last possible moment. Wherever possible, look out from inside the bush, because deer are likely to be fully alert while on these open places. Binoculars can be very helpful for scanning slips and, as always, the wind has to be in your favour.

Hunting the tops along the bushline

Trees are unable to grow at the higher altitudes of big mountains. The transition zone from forest to alpine meadow is typically occupied by small trees, and sometimes shrubs, growing close together. In pure beech forest there is often a clean transition from forest to tussock, and you can remain concealed within the forest edge, yet still obtain good views of the tussock. Unfortunately, the most common transition zone is one of an established scrub belt which is difficult to get through, and visibility is poor when looking out. You are therefore forced outside any cover when looking for deer in the open. The best way to succeed in this situation is to use the folds and valleys of the tops for cover.

When coming on to the top of a ridge or spur to overlook the next basin, you will appear as a visible silhouette on the skyline to any deer below. To avoid this problem lie down and wriggle up the last few metres to the top of the ridge so that only your head and binoculars are visible from below. Another method is to move purposefully at a low crouch over the top to a position below the ridgeline, before stopping to look for deer.

This type of hunting doesn't involve much skill and is a great way to shoot deer on the tops.

Bush stalking

Bush stalking is consistently the most successful and commonly practised hunting method for the wild red deer of New Zealand. But it requires the highest degree of skill, especially in bush with a thick undergrowth. (Fig. 18 depicts the skills and senses required for bush stalking.) The basic questions you need to address about stalking are: where, when, how high, how fast and in what direction?

FIG.18: THE HUNTER'S SKILLS

SIGHT
UP TO 3-4 KM
WITH AIDS (BINOCULARS, TELESCOPIC SIGHT)
COLOUR VISION
FORM AND MOVEMENT
LESS EFFECTIVE
CLOUD FOG RAIN

SMELL RANGE - 10 METRES

INTELLIGENCE
KNOWLEDGE OF DEER LIFE CYCLE + DEFENCES
STEALTH
KNOWLEDGE OF SIGN

HEARING RANGE - ROAR - 1·6 KM
NON-ROAR - 100 METRES

FORMULA FOR SHOOTING
1. POSITIVE VISUAL IDENTIFICATION
   NO OTHER
   SIGHT
   OF LIVING ANIMAL
   NOT A DEAD ANIMAL ON ANOTHER HUNTER'S BACK
2. APPROPRIATE RANGE
3. KILLING SHOT AVAILABLE

Some hunting strategies and tactics

Some of the answers will be found in the knowledge of the spots that deer use year after year for the same purpose. For example, in late spring hinds will be in their traditional nursery areas and in winter they will be in their yarding up areas. Similarly, stags will be in their separate and more widely spread wintering yards. In autumn both the stags and hinds will be on the rutting grounds.

Because walking around the side of a hill is much easier than walking up and down it, it is important to know at what height in the bush to hunt. In spring and summer especially, deer can move over a range of heights. For example, in the early mornings of summer, deer are likely to be feeding heavily in the middle part of the bush between the flats and the tops. As the morning wears on, deer will be returning to their bedding areas above, and in late morning they are likely to be in their beds high up in the bush. You should hunt accordingly. In early morning in spring, start hunting the low bush adjacent to the flats to catch deer returning from the grassy flats towards their beds. Again, as the morning wears on, gain height to stay with them.

The faster a hunter walks through the bush the bigger the area that will be covered, but, unfortunately, more speed means more noise, and a greater likelihood of disturbing deer. A compromise is to walk at an easy pace, which allows you to spend most of your time looking around for deer rather than at your next step on the ground. When you see fresh sign, slow down. We have suggested previously that the style of walking should resemble that of a deer. The best way to get an idea of how they do it is to watch deer on a deer farm walk about over rough ground. All four legs move in a smooth, rhythmic, measured way, which is different to the style of a two-legged human stumbling jerkily along over difficult terrain.

The direction of hunting is limited absolutely by the wind. You must stalk only upwind. If the wind unexpectedly changes you must change the direction of the hunt. When an area of fresh sign is reached try starting a zig-zag pattern into the wind to cover as much as possible of the likely holding area. Sometimes when a strong wind is blowing and the country is steep, gusts of wind come swirling in all directions. In these conditions successful stalking can be difficult. The only consolation is that a deer may not be able to locate you from your smell, which can be to your advantage.

When bush stalking you will use as many of your senses as possible, frequently stopping to look, listen and smell for deer. You should also stop if you inadvertently make a loud noise, such as a cracking branch. You should also stop when a new area becomes suddenly revealed, such as crossing over a spur or looking down into a basin.

If a deer sees or hears you it probably won't depart until it has confirmed its suspicions with another sense, preferably that of smell (see Fig. 9, p. 31). A deer may bark at you in the bush and linger around trying to work out what you are. Sometimes you may be lucky enough to be in country that allows you to silently and rapidly close up on the barking deer, which is usually slowly walking away from you as it barks. In these situations the tactic of barking back will sometimes delay the deer long enough for you to approach it.

A deer that is alarmed and hurriedly rushing off may still sometimes pause at the top of a spur to have a quick look back just before it disappears out of sight. Again, departing deer can sometimes be brought to a halt by a short sharp bark.

Clothing for bush stalking is important for minimising noise and for camouflage in the bush. Because deer are colour blind, contrast is what matters. White legs flashing along among the sombre dark greens of the bush are easily seen, and can be effectively disguised by wearing soft leg coverings that do not make a noise scratching against the bush. Woollen or polypropylene long johns, dyed green or brown using the tie-dye procedure, are an example of a suitable camouflage effect. Jackets should also be of low-contrast colours or camouflage design, and constructed of a material that does not rustle with body movement or make noise when scraped against vegetation.

Footwear is an important, and often personal, consideration for the bush hunter. Some experienced hunters go about in bare feet to achieve the most naturally quiet approach, but for most of us, a good pair of boots are needed. Good boots combine support to the feet with sufficient flexibility to enable them to bend when placed on top of small branches and twigs on the forest floor, and in so doing minimise the number of snapping noises made by the hunter's feet.

While bush stalking you will usually carry an emergency kit, some food, spare clothing and so on, usually in a small backpack or in pouches around the waist. Such packs and pouches need to be of non-rustling material, but the modern materials often used for their construction nearly all rasp badly, generating noise. The rasping can be avoided by wearing a jacket over the top of the pack or waist pouch.

Two hunters bush stalking together

The advantage of hunting in pairs is that a deer disturbed by one hunter often crosses in front of the other, enabling a shot to be made at the deer which would otherwise be lost.

The greatest hazard of hunting, especially in the bush, is getting shot by another hunter who has not clearly identified the target. Accident statistics consistently show that the other hunter is often a hunting companion who was **inadvertently** hunting the same place as the victim. Most hunters prefer to hunt alone, probably for safety reasons. But always hunting alone may encourage a false sense of security: because a single hunter almost never meets other people, he is unprepared for the event when it does occur.

We believe that hunting in pairs in the bush can be both profitable and safe provided two **essential** rules are followed.

The first rule is that both hunters always stay in sight of one another. The second is that the arc of fire of each hunter is restricted to the half circle arc of 180 degrees beginning straight in front of the hunter and extending around the side of the hunter **that faces away** from his companion and ends directly behind him (see Fig. 19).

Lack of visual contact between two hunters can result in one person getting in front of the other — a dangerous situation. When two hunters cannot see one another they should stop moving forward and under no circumstances fire a shot until visual contact is re-established.

A consequence of the first rule is that in denser understoreys the hunters are close together. In such conditions, stalking in pairs can on occasion have little advantage over solo hunting, because the two hunters have to be so close in order to maintain visual contact. In more open bush the hunters can be further apart and a worthwhile amount of ground covered.

When an area of fresh sign is reached, both hunters zig-zagging together can become an extremely complex movement. It is preferable for one hunter, with due regard to the wind and field of fire, to position himself at a vantage point and wait to be picked up by the other stalker at the conclusion of an intensive zig-zag stalk.

When one hunter of a pair sees an animal, a pre-arranged hand signal should be used to indicate to the other that a deer has been seen and a shot is about to be taken. On hearing the shot the other hunter should "freeze", to allow the shooter to listen to the animal's movements and also to avoid the possibility of disturbing a wounded

FIG. 19: THE RULES OF STALKING IN PAIRS

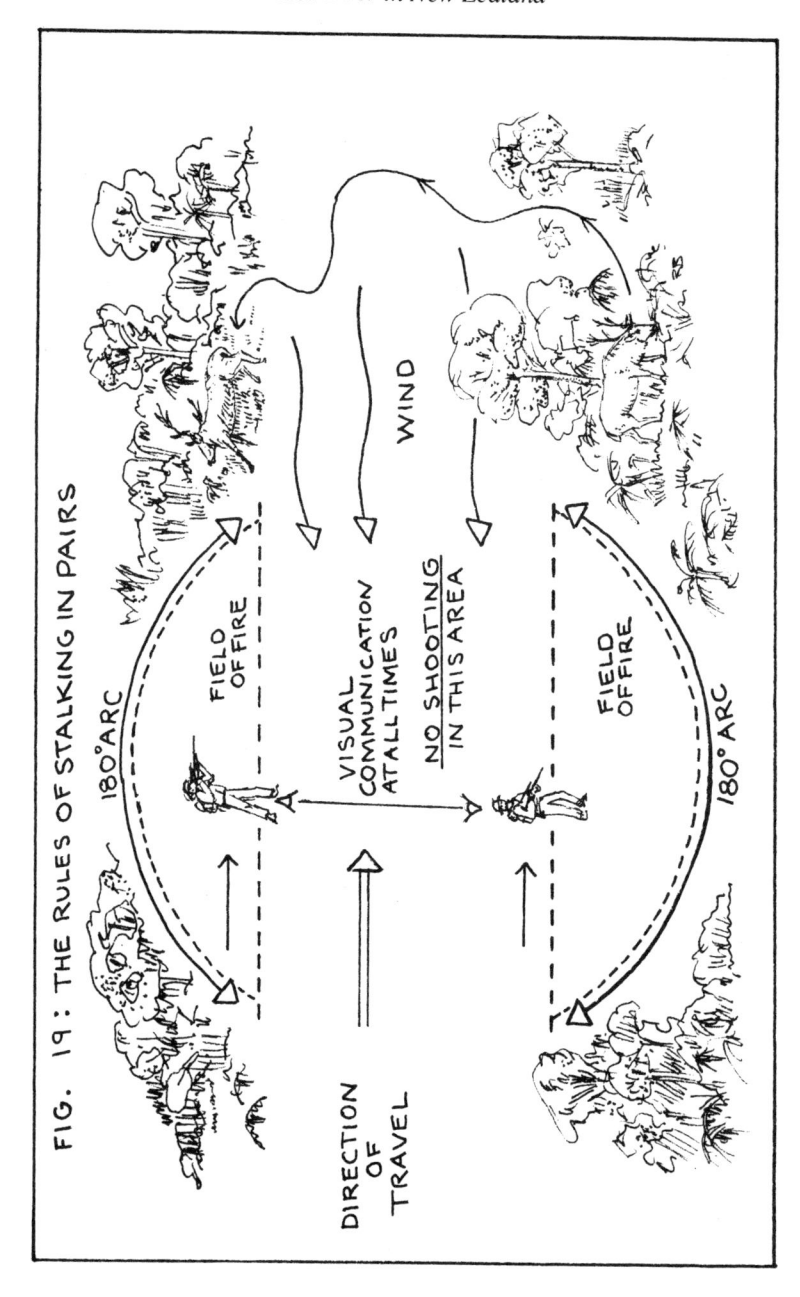

animal which may be in the process of settling down. The second hunter should wait for instructions from the first before moving from his frozen position.

If the deer is between two hunters neither can shoot at it because of the 180 degree rule. One hunter will have to stop and move backwards to allow the other to gain a position from which to take the shot.

Perusal of accident statistics shows that following up a wounded animal is hazardous — many hunters have been shot by their mates when they were mistaken for the wounded deer. If the animal has escaped wounded then one of the pair should stay at the shooting site while the other does the tracking. (See Chapter 8.)

Hunting during the roar

This is the easiest and most thrilling time for hunting. Stags enraged by their passions become incautious and can often be taken with relatively little skill by the novice hunter.

If you have hunted all year in an area you will have built up valuable knowledge of the location of wallows on the rutting grounds. Left undisturbed, stags are creatures of habit. If you see a stag one rutting season at a wallow, you can expect to see it again at the same place the next roar. Stags usually have more than one wallow to enable them to have a choice according to the prevailing weather conditions. The best time to be walking about plotting the layout of the wallows is out of season when the animals are not there. The stags may lose some caution during the rut but the hinds do not, and they will leave the roaring grounds altogether if they are disturbed too much. The stags won't be there without the hinds.

Making a few cautious trips to the wallows just before the rut will give you a feel for the time the deer will start to roar. If, however, you are in an area for the first time during the roar, try to locate the position of the stags by getting on to a high spot and listening for them roaring from their wallows. This is especially effective if you can be on open tops a hundred metres or so above the bushline. As well as hearing stags roaring, you are in a position to occasionally find a solitary stag that has come out of the bush, to listen also, and to roar a challenge to the ones below. Stags seem to be accustomed to being challenged by stags moving down from above, something you can imitate and so perhaps strike success. If practical, you will find that travelling slowly with a small torch at night, into the wind along the tops above the bushline is a great way to plot where the stags are on the roaring grounds below.

You need to be able to imitate the roaring sound of a stag. This comes with practice. Because stags have long necks their roaring reverberates through a long windpipe. Humans need to imitate this reverberation. A simple piece of alkathene pipe about 80 mm in diameter and 250 mm long works as well as any commercially available roaring device. A hole can be drilled in one end to enable it to be slung on a cord around the neck.

Apply the tube to the outside of the mouth and breathe a deep groan down into it — see what happens. Farmed deer usually roar a few weeks before the wild ones. Try visiting a local farm (with the farmer's permission) to listen and give a few roars over the fence — practice improves the performance.

The basic stag roar starts in low volume, rises to a climax, then fades again. Stags will string two or three such roars together on a single expired breath, sometimes ending with a few "coughs", a sharper, shorter sound. Because the roaring rate of a stag (the number of times the animal roars over a given time), signals his size to other stags, always try to deliver a slightly lower roaring rate than the stag who replies to you — he is then more likely to come to you spoiling for a fight. On the other hand, if you roar faster than the answering stag you will probably convince it you are a bigger beast and it will slink away to find a weaker rival, never giving you the chance of a shot.

The biggest and fittest stags roar first and establish the harems. This means that although not many stags will be roaring early in the season, the ones that do are likely to have the biggest antlers. Each stag will start roaring in a set sequence of stages. Initially they will simply grunt at intervals and then begin to roar briefly. Usually, they do not at this stage respond to the roars of other stags or hunters' imitations. As a stag "ripens" into the roar it will respond more readily to other roars. Eventually, in the full heat of the roar, it may even respond to a distant chainsaw! Because a succession of stags is coming into the rut, the shooting of a stag at a wallow does not necessarily mean the end of that spot's hunting potential for the season — the territory may well be claimed by another stag.

The volume of roaring does not indicate stag size, not does the amount of time the stag spends roaring. The older the stag, the wiser it is likely to be. Older stags tend to roar for more limited times during the day, often only late in the evening and early in morning, and in heavily hunted areas may roar only during the hours of darkness. Less experienced animals roar for longer periods as the rut develops. Such animals will initially roar only in early morning and late evening, gradually extending the time in each session until they are roaring intermittently throughout the day. Both young and experienced stags are influenced by the weather: frosty mornings and evenings encourage them to roar for long periods, whereas overcast conditions, rain and high winds will not only delay the onset of the roar, but also inhibit animals that have already begun.

During the season, even if no deer are roaring it is still a good strategy to give a few roars, the idea being to tempt the stags to roar back. This practice works best at the beginning of the rut. At this time the passion of the stags is not at its peak, but they have established each other's whereabouts and are biding their time before contests over status. However, they are sensitive to the intrusion of any new wandering stags, so a hunter walking along and giving a few roars may be greeted by replies from nearby animals challenging the position of this new "contestant" in their midst.

If stags are already roaring, roaring back is worthwhile. Indeed, this can lead to the most exciting, and dangerous, type of hunting — dangerous, because the roaring hunter may be mistaken by another hunter for a stag, and shot.

Do not give any more roars than is necessary, especially if the stag is near, because a deer close by seems to be better able to distinguish between a genuine roar from an imitation. For this reason, hunting in pairs during the roar is preferable. One person can roar at a stag from a distance while the other stalks into the replies. The stag is expecting trouble from the source of the roaring and is often caught unawares when the silent, unseen hunter stalks up. As always, the wind should be blowing in the right direction, because no matter how worked up a rutting stag is, one good whiff of the scent of man and the stag will silently be gone.

When you are close to a stag the thrashing of antlers against shrubs can often be heard. The stag is also likely to walk through the bush in a noisy way, quite unlike the normal stealthy gait. Breathing is often heavy and laboured and can be heard for some distance.

If you are close to a roaring stag, stop roaring and make other rutting noises, which are less likely to be detected by the stag as imitations. For example, shake a shrub lightly or hit two pieces of antler together. Antler striking antler is the noise of two stags fighting and is a powerful stimulus to a rutting stag. You can be prepared for this trick by taking with you on the hunt two sawn-off pieces of antler. Make some noise when travelling through the bush during the roar, as a more noisy progress will often be mistaken for the clumsy approach of a stag.

When a stag is really close its breathing is noisy and its individual footsteps can be heard. If you still cannot see it, stop making noise and concentrate on looking. You must be aware of the wind and the likelihood of the stag moving around downwind of you to find your scent — you must be ready to out-manoeuvre him.

The largest stags will be holding hinds in a harem, and it is the hinds that are usually the biggest problem for the hunter. They will be as alert as ever, and because they are silent you will not know where they are until you see them. The alarm raised by a frightened hind often brings disaster to a careful stalk up to a trophy stag.

Occasionally, you may hear two stags roaring at one another and then silence followed by the clashing of antlers. Stop roaring and stalk the fighting animals from downwind.

Finally, and **most importantly: identify your target absolutely**. It might be us, or your best mate, pretending to be a deer in the roar. We may even be adorned with antlers or a carcass that we are carrying through the bush. Make sure that your target is a live deer and it is the deer you want to shoot before pulling the trigger.

Hunting from a fixed position

In Europe and Britain, hunting red deer from a hide where the hunter sits still and waits for the animals is common practice. Often the hide is up a tree or on top of a specially built stand. The position of the hide requires a detailed knowledge of the deers' routes and feeding areas. This hunting technique is not much used in New Zealand, but in some situations it pays dividends.

Hunting deer coming out on to farmland: If you have permission to hunt farmland, this can be some of the most gentlemanly deerstalking New Zealand has to offer. Simply drive right next to the hunting ground to execute a pre-established plan of waiting for the deer to come out.

Deer will come out on to farmland to graze during the night, particularly in winter and early spring. They have a great love of turnips and will travel miles to reach them (a few turnip crops are quietly grown on farms each year just for this purpose). If you can get permission to hunt on the farm, work out exactly where the deer are coming out of the bush and, with regard to the prevailing wind direction, find a place to hide or make one. A good way to make one in an open paddock is to dig a shallow trench. Be careful to dispose of the dug soil well away from the paddock so as not to alarm the deer with large quantities of freshly turned earth. In changeable wind conditions you may want to dig more than one trench, each one for a different wind direction. Lie down in the trench, or whatever else you have got set up, in the late afternoon and wait for the deer to make their appearance.

If you do not have the permission, all may not be lost. The deer are probably travelling from a nearby public forest for which you can get a permit and access. The animals are likely to be using the same route each night. They will generally use the route of maximum concealment, for example, where a finger of bush or a bushy gully runs out close to the feeding area. If there is a continuous boundary fence they must cross it, so walk the length of the fence on the legal, forest side, looking for their crossing point. Barbed wire is good at catching a few belly hairs from a jumping deer and there should be deeply marked tracks at the points of take off and landing. The route can be followed back into the bush from the crossing point. Follow the trail and look for sites where you can hide in wait. Sometimes, climbing up a tree is appropriate. Choose a number of sites for different wind directions. The deer may be coming out to feed only if the wind is favourable, for example, if it is blowing from the farm to the bush so that they can be warned of danger. If they don't come the night you watch, try again in different weather.

Watching slips: A pleasant way to pass an evening, especially in spring, is to sit across the gully from a grassy slip waiting for deer to come out and feed. The slip should have plenty of fresh sign indicating recent use. In choosing the site of concealment, take into account the prevailing wind and any catabatic changes that may affect it. Before the light fades you should have a clear idea of the distance from your position to the slip, because in poor light, judging the range across a gully can be difficult. Returning to a slip before first light and waiting for daybreak is another variation on the same theme.

Putting out special food to attract deer: Try cutting off some branches of broadleaf or other preferred browse. If you don't want to cut off the branches, you can tie them down with rope so that their leaves come within the browse zone of deer.

Another trick is to broadcast seeds of good food plants over river flats or open slips. A season later you will return to a growing supply of good spring food. Lotus major or clover are the best, especially purple clover. Shake the seeds with red lead before use to prevent birds from eating them. Turnip or swede seed can also be used but it must be dug into the ground. These methods are illegal in public forest and are applicable only on privately owned land.

Some foods can to be carried into the site, for example grain, chestnuts, acorns, karaka berries and commercial deer pellets. A salt lick might work. Food such as turnips or swedes lying loose on the ground don't work, as deer need the anchorage of the tap root to be able to graze them.

Chasing deer with a pack of dogs

This type of hunting is a tragedy. Deer run fast and they will not turn and stand like pigs. Dogs often get lost as they travel long distances behind deer and as the deer being chased crosses the path of another deer the dogs begin chasing a fresh animal. Some deer are savaged by dogs and escape to suffer a lingering death from septic wounds. The whole area becomes thoroughly disturbed and the deer are likely to vacate. This hunting happens with inexperienced pig-hunters using poorly trained dogs. The correct way to use dogs is described in Chapter 7.

Flying into a hunting ground by helicopter

This has become popular in recent years as more hunters have become accustomed to the benefits, and as the hiring of helicopters has become cheaper. The beginning of a one- or two-week hunting trip is an exciting helicopter ride instead of a day or two of exhausting tramping with heavy backpacks. Moreover, you don't have to carry out the meat in a backpack.

Have a clear understanding with the pilot over pick-up procedures. Make sure you both know the day and time of pick-up. Because helicopters cannot fly in all weathers, you may have to wait longer than expected to be picked up. If you are being dropped off on high ground, consider arranging an alternative pick-up point lower down should the tops be clouded in.

Take care of the helicopter. Don't board with a loaded rifle, or allow the rifle barrel to rest on the footrest bar of the front passenger's seat because it can slip down and puncture the plexiglass bubble. Get into and out of the machine only when the pilot tells you to do so, especially when the machine is hovering, because the pilot has to adjust the flying controls for your weight. When pitching camp, keep the landing site clear. The helicopter may have to come back early for you or want to use the site in an emergency. Secure all loose gear on the ground and stack it clear of the landing site before the machine arrives, because a loose ground sheet, for example, can get sucked into, and damage a rotor blade.

Perhaps the biggest danger is your being hit by a rotor blade. The small tail rotor spins around in a vertical plane and when the machine is sitting on the ground it is about the right height to cut the face off any person who walks into it. This rotor is often difficult to see as it rotates around. The golden rule is: always go around the front of the helicopter when going from one side to the other — **never walk around the back where the tail rotor is**. In fact, helicopters **should always be approached from the front** no matter what the circumstances. You should leave the same way.

The main rotor blade on the top is usually above head height when the helicopter is on flat ground but on sloping ground, on the uphill side, the clearance between it and the ground is sometimes less than head height. To avoid being hit by the main rotor blade **always approach the helicopter from the downhill side**. Once inside the machine fasten the seat-belt and give it a good yank to ensure it is solidly in position.

The pilot can sometimes pick up deer carcasses direct from the hunting ground. They need to be clearly marked with dayglow paint for example. A good open area is needed to give generous clearance for the rotor blades. Usually, pilots will operate these potentially dangerous manoeuvres only with experienced assistants who are accustomed to getting in and out of a hovering helicopter and who know how use the cargo load-hook and other gear.

I sat high on the grassy shoulder of one of the many Maungatukutuku foothills behind Paraparaumu feeling guilty. Far below me and a good two miles upwind, I could just make out the roof of my "four by four" parked on the rough gravel track where we had left it. I had climbed to the summit of the ridge almost opposite where it was parked and walked the arduous ridge-top track all the way round and down to where I was sitting, the purpose of the exercise being to reach the top of the side gully into which I was now gazing, without giving my wind to it.

My buddy John Bowman had waited for the full hour it had taken me to accomplish this in the warm confines of the truck with our two dogs, not an enviable task in such a close early-summer evening when the humid warmth gave their doggy smell a special edge. Worse still, following this warming-up session, he had to walk the two miles of river flats that led along the valley floor below me to the base of the densely scrubby gully above which I was now sitting. Then the final coup de grace, a straight-up, zig-zagging course through the very worst of the briar, lawyer, manuka and low ramarama scrub that infested it.

He had just started on this final leg and I could just make out the excited bark of his dog as it careered through the vegetation. Not that this meant anything, John's dog was a well-loved family "bitsa", used to having his head on rabbits and anything that moved during the progress of his evening "walkies". To him this evening's venture was no different to his usual walk and he was letting rip with his usual exuberance. Of my dog Wredd, the Hungarian Vizsla, there was no sound. She knew John well enough to work for him and would be down there somewhere, her usual silent questing self. This was in fact the reason we had brought John's dog. Wredd was more suited to lining up the shooter on a deer and would point silently even with the wind at his back. We were hoping John's dog would upset this routine and bark excitedly when led to deer by Wredd. What with the dogs' double act, the wind up John's back and his deliberately noisy progress we meant to thoroughly disturb the gully and flush any deer within it out at the top, and into my sights. We were in reality hunting "American style", using a flushing technique more familiar to the mule deer and whitetail hunters of the U.S.

In the distance I could easily hear the passing trucks on State Highway One as they toiled towards Wellington, just a mile downwind of me. The evening was one of those still, early summer ones, when sound carries for miles. The slight southerly breeze on my face was barely noticeable as I hunkered down and waited. Below me the sounds of the dog were getting closer and I could just make out John's crashing progress.

Suddenly it was all on. The crashes came faster towards me than John could ever have managed, reaching a climax below me and to my right about 30 metres away. Out of the scrub bounded a moderate stag with a head in branching velvet. He paused for a moment looking suspiciously in my direction, but I knew he could not see or wind me and kept rock still. I was unable to fire as he stood directly above the "V" of the gully through which I knew John was ascending. He cantered to my left, up to the highest point of the ridge where six strands of number nine wire barred his progress. He half turned and started to trot alongside the fence towards me. "Boomwhac." My 308 spoke and I could just make out the sound of the bullet connecting. He turned again and started back toward the gully. "Boomwhac." Another hit and the animal out of my view. I sat quietly in case another animal was below and made the same mistake.

"Halloo . . . did you get him?" my cobber called up from 15 metres below. I kept quiet, not willing to commit myself until I'd seen the carcass. John did not speak again and the sounds of his progress faded off to the right and above me. Finally the noises stopped and I knew he was at the fence and above me. Suddenly, a brown flash and Wredd was with me. She'd picked my wind from higher up and come down the fenceline to me. I pointed downwards. "Go track" I told her, using the word she'd been trained to. There was no need to tell her. Her nose was already well up and she worked past me in the semipoint. She went 15 metres and pointed immobile, then started to furiously wag her tail. It was a clean kill. I followed her down and silently gutted the beast. Then I called her off and she followed me back up the fenceline to where John was sitting.

"Did you get it?" he said.

"No, a clean miss," I replied.

"You lying bastard — I can see the blood on your hands!"

Good old John, always the policeman! — *R.L.*

I was in that difficult position all deerstalkers seem to find themselves in sooner or later, that of being a guide and trying to produce deer "on tap" for a novice hunter.

We had flown in by helicopter the previous day to a favourite spot of mine in the Ruahine Ranges and now, in the early hours of the morning of a new day, we were fighting our way upwards through the sub-alpine scrub to the tussock tops. We made it into the open as the night gave way to the half light of the first morning of our hunt. Graham and I were soon shivering in the hoar frost looking out over the cloudless deep blue of a dawning sky. We were going to hunt the north-facing slopes of a large basin. Radiating out from the centre of the basin like the separated fingers of an outstretched hand were small deep-cut gullies growing stunted and lichen-covered beech trees in among the autumn gold of the tussocks.

When I had been here 6 months before I had seen mobs of hinds and shot two stags in velvet, so I was sure there was a good population of animals — all we needed to do was to find them. Graham was a tramper and 10 years younger than me, so it was no problem for him to head off with me into the wind some 15 metres below and traverse gully after gully looking for the deer. I was having trouble keeping up at times. We heard one faint grunt from a couple of miles around in the basin. But something was wrong. In the places where there had been interlacing ribbons of animal tracks linking all the usual haunts of the deer, there was now nothing except the odd fresh print on the main trails on top of the side ridges that separated the gullies and headed up towards the main ridge some 150 metres above us. The sun was well up when we stopped for a rest after a few hours of hunting. This fine weather was a nuisance because it was early in the roar and a warm day would mean an early finish for the day to the amorous endeavours of the stags.

Although the wind around us in the basin was barely noticeable, a look at the sky revealed a few fast-moving clouds. I thought the weather may close in quickly and, in any case, as there was little sign of deer in the basin, I suggested that we climb up to the ridge top and walk back down the other side to the main valley. We would get there in time for an evening shot.

We stumbled upwards through the tussock to the ridge top. The view was magnificent, but a brisk southerly wind now encouraged us to keep going. As we stalked down the ridge following a well marked deer trail we suddenly heard the electrifying sound of a stag giving a long full-throated roar. The sound was carried up to us by the icy blast of the southerly wind. We quickly slithered down behind the ridge and anxiously glassed the open south-facing slope below, but we couldn't see him. Suddenly he roared again, only to be answered by another stag further down the same cold face. I dragged my plastic roaring horn out from under my "swannie" and groaned down into it with as much volume as I could generate. It was followed by an agonising silence. I didn't think I would be able to compete with that strong wind, which seemed to be strengthening. Abruptly piercing my doubtful thoughts came a long drawn-out sawing reply from the stag below.

We roared back, he replied, and up that ridge he came towards us. We saw him from our hideaway with his neck extended and my brief replies to his questioning roars kept him moving ahead. From time to time he would stop and look upwards, trying to see where we were. Sometimes he would traverse to the left then to the right of the ridge to try to cut our scent, but the wind was true and steady. Steadily on he came, his roars becoming louder and more stirring. When Graham shot, the beast was scarcely 20 metres away. He had his first head. — *R.L.*

7
Dogs for deerstalking

Dogs used for hunting deer in New Zealand fall into three general categories. Firstly, there is the household-pet category. This type of dog normally lives with the family, and because it is of a good "deer breed" its owner believes it will automatically know what to do in the bush. After a few frustrating trips, during which the dog spends its time chasing deer or getting lost or barking all the time, it is left at home in the belief that it is no good as a hunting dog.

The second kind of dog is used in packs by a hunter (usually a novice) attempting to hunt deer in a similar fashion to pig-hunting with dogs. The result is a disaster for the hunting grounds and the reputation of deer dogs. The untrained dogs, usually under poor management, create general panic in the deer population but seldom capture a deer.

The third category of dog, which this chapter is all about, is that used by a competent deerstalker, who often has only a single well trained dog. This dog silently hunts close to its master. The dog uses his powerful sense of smell to locate deer for the hunter to shoot, and also assists in the tracking and restraining of wounded deer.

The well-trained deer dog should hunt silently and remain within sight of the hunter at all times. When a deer is in the locality the dog should signal this fact to its master by its bearing or attitude. If the deer is close, but has not been seen, the dog must not chase off but should track it slowly, so that the hunter can quietly follow behind. When the dog sees the deer it should freeze and "point". When the hunter has taken his shot the dog should remain motionless until signalled to move on by its master. The dog should continue to remain in sight of the hunter and silently follow the trail of the wounded deer, signalling to the hunter when it is found. The dog may also be able to restrain the wounded deer and kill it by strangulation, achieved by gripping the throat firmly enough to close off the windpipe.

All this is a lot for a dog to learn. However, with the right dog and a great deal of commitment, time and patience from its owner, it can be achieved.

Choosing a dog

A lot of time and money will go into training and keeping a hunting dog, so take great care over selection to increase the chance of getting the best dog available.

When dogs are used for hunting game birds, rabbits and hares, their task is essentially to bring the game to the hunter. With deer hunting their task is to bring the hunter to the game — a fundamental difference. We have found that a dog trained in one type of hunting may become confused when introduced to the other. For this reason, we believe that a deer dog should be used only for deer hunting; the choosing of an older dog for deer, already trained for other types of hunting, is likely to be a frustrating experience.

When choosing a dog, a number of desirable qualities should be looked for. The dog must have a good scenting ability and the inborn quality of "pointing". This is a visible state of arousal that the animal has scented deer. "Full pointing", which usually occurs when the dog can see the deer, is characterised by the dog becoming immobile with its head held in a peculiar posture, often with one paw raised and gazing with an almost unblinking stare in a fixed direction. "Semi-pointing", which occurs when the dog has scented game but cannot see it, is characterised by a sudden slowing of gait and the erection of the hairs along the spinal strip. The dog should also be co-operative. In the big-bodied breeds of dogs, co-operation is more likely to be found in females than males. The dog should also be brave, brave enough to restrain a wounded stag, for example. Finally, the dog should be intelligent; brighter dogs are easier to train.

Almost any breed that is big enough to restrain a wounded deer could be trained as a deer dog. But the best breed to choose is a question that is debated endlessly among hunting-dog owners. All have advantages and disadvantages.

A number of breeds used in Europe for deer hunting are unavailable in New Zealand or, if available, come only from show stock. We will discuss only three of the more commonly available breeds of large dogs with which we have had experience: the Hungarian Vizsla, the Weimaraner and the German Short-haired Pointer. We have also seen other breeds successfully trained for deer, including the Labrador, the Large Musterlander and the German Wire-haired Pointer. Unfortunately, we have not had enough personal experience of them to form detailed opinions of their advantages and disadvantages of hunting in New Zealand conditions.

Hungarian Vizsla

We must admit some bias here. The best dog I (R.L.) have ever had is a Hungarian Vizsla. However, we will attempt to remain objective.

The advantages of the Hungarian Vizsla are its intelligence, complete silence in the bush, and a good sense of smell. It also has a good full point and a good semipoint. Hungarian Vizslas generally have a good character and are biddable.

The disadvantages of the breed are its lack of an instinctive throat-hold and its short hair, which leaves the animal cold in winter. They are a sensitive dog and can be damaged easily by heavy punishment. Their high intelligence can at times get them into trouble; they will sometimes think they know where the deer has gone when following a scent line, cut corners, and thereby lose the trail.

German Short-haired Pointer

The advantages of the German Short-haired Pointer are its intelligence and good natural point.

The disadvantages include the fact they are noisy animals when walking in the bush. They also have a strong tendency to give a "yip" (a small bark), when they are excited or distressed. This habit may belong only to strains of which we have had experience, and perhaps can be avoided by buying from a better working strain. They have a thin coat, which leaves them cold in winter, and the bitches are a bit on the small side for deer. Generally speaking they are not particularly brave.

Weimaraner

The advantages of the Weimaraner are its good sense of smell, good full point and semipoint, and instinctive throat-hold. It is large enough to pull down a fully grown stag.

The disadvantages are their lack of high intelligence, which makes them difficult to train, and their tendency towards disobedience.

General advice for buying a pup

Pups for sale can be tracked down by looking in kennel club "litters due" notices as well as in shooting magazines, daily papers and by word of mouth.

Having located a litter in which you are interested, ask to see the written pedigree of the pups because a pedigree will ensure there is no cross-breeding and will identify the real father. It is important to choose a dog bred from working stock rather than from show stock, as dogs with a long pedigree of being bred only for show sometimes lose their hunting qualities. Pups should have spent at least the first 6, preferably 12, weeks of their life with their mothers before being taken away.

When choosing from a litter watch the litter being fed. If they are still suckling, the bitch will have to be removed from the litter for a time and then brought back to feed the pups. When food is introduced see which pup arrives at the food first and is the bravest in its fights with brothers and sisters. Look for the largest and best-fed pup and one that uses its nose the most.

Ask for the names and addresses of buyers of pups from previous litters and ring them up to hear how they are getting on. Ask about the qualities of scenting ability, pointing, co-operation, bravery and instinctive throat-hold. If possible, watch the pups' parents working on deer and observe them for these qualities.

Training a dog to work on deer

Do not start training until the pup is at least 6 months old — we recommend that it be at least 12 months old. To make the description of the training easier we have split the explanation into four stages. At the completion of the last stage the dog will be able to work on wild deer.

Stage one
This stage embraces the basic training common to all well-behaved dogs. The dog needs to be taught to sit and stay, to come when summoned and to walk steadily at the heel of its owner. There are a lot of good books about how to do this basic training and dog obedience classes can be very helpful to a novice owner. If you do go to a dog obedience class remember the final purpose of the training, and be wary of any training that may be counter productive to this end. One local dog obedience instructor, for example, has the view that well trained dogs should not sniff around! Because of the availability of books and clubs we don't go into the details of basic training here. Getting basic training right is important, to enable you to control your dog well before you go on to the next stage.

Stage two
The objective here is to train a dog to follow a blood trail from the hunter to a deer. The dog must be at least 6 months old before starting this second stage of training.

The substitute we use for a freshly killed carcass is a deer skin that has been simply dried in the air without applying any chemicals. It will retain the deer scent for the dog to become familiar with.

The other ingredient needed is liquid deer blood. This cannot be bought readily in a shop, but can be obtained fresh from a deer abattoir. It needs to be prevented from clotting, which can be done by adding sodium citrate, a safe, non-poisonous chemical available in a powdered form from dispensing chemists. It should be added to the fresh, warm blood at the rate of 0.6 g per 100 ml, or 6 g per litre. To preserve the blood until needed, keep the bottles in a deep freeze. For a complete training programme about three 2-litre bottles will be needed.

Start the training as simply as possible. Find a flat, open paddock and keep the dog out of sight while you prepare the following exercise.

First, the dried skin should be laid out on the ground with the hair side uppermost. The skin should be anchored to a neighbouring tree, or a peg in the ground, by a length of rope so that the dog cannot take off with it. To encourage the dog to take an interest in the skin, or to increase the interest he may already have, a small piece of raw venison thawed out from the freezer can be placed on top of the skin for the dog to find and eat.

Next, with the dog out of sight, lay a blood trail of about 25 metres to the skin from a peg in the ground. Put a holed cap on a bottle of liquid deer's blood and drop blood on to the ground as you walk, holding the bottle well away from your body. However, in laying trails this way, you will also be leaving a trail of human scent. To make sure the dog is learning to follow the blood and not the human scent, the two trails should be kept well separate. A better way to maintain this separation is to use a slightly more sophisticated set up. Attach a plastic tube to the bottle top, and tape the tube along a pole. Hold the pole out at right angles and squeeze the blood through the tubing. By occasionally changing the pole from one side to the other, the blood trail can be made more independent of the human scent line. Finally, a small adjustable tube clamp can be attached to the tubing to enable you to vary the rate of blood drips.

Now collect your dog and attach a long lead (about 3 metres) to a loosely fitting collar. Take the dog to the peg and encourage it to sniff around by indicating the ground and showing interest. You may even need to get down to the ground and sniff around yourself to get the message across — an amusing thing to see a trainer doing! As soon as the dog does some rapid sniffing, which indicates he has found the scent, encourage him further. Do this again when he begins to find and follow the trail. If he strays from the trail do not pull him back, but allow him time to re-establish contact with it.

Once the dog reaches the skin, allow him to find the small piece of venison and eat it. Sit down on the ground with the dog at the skin and feed it another small piece of venison. After about 10 minutes, return the dog to its place of concealment and lay out the skin at the end of another straight trail, but in a different area on fresh ground, and again run the dog. Repeat the whole exercise three or four times more then finish for the day. Never train for more than half an hour, and less if the dog loses interest. Never pull on the lead if the dog goes wrong and don't punish the dog if he makes a mistake. Encourage the dog to feel that training is fun, so that it will look forward to the next training session. You should have no more than two training sessions a week.

Gradually increase the length of the trail up to about 50 metres and then introduce curves and finally sharp bends. When the dog is proficient at these tasks, start the training again, this time in dense cover.

This routine will train a dog to track animals while keeping close to its master at all times. When the dog is comfortable tracking the blood trail on the long lead without tending to run ahead pulling on the lead, the lead can be dispensed with. If at any time the dog starts to range away from you, the long lead can be brought back into use again. Always sit down next to the skin when the dog has brought you to it, and give him rewards of small pieces of venison to eat. Some dogs will bristle up and semipoint when they first reach the skin, and they should be encouraged with praise if they do.

Stage three

The dog can now track a line of deer's blood, a very useful skill when tracking wounded deer. This next stage is to train it to trail other deer scents, to enable it to become an indicator dog useful to a hunter looking for undisturbed deer in the wild.

The scent trails deer leave as they travel in the bush are a cocktail of body smells, the strongest of which come from the special scent glands which they use for marking territory. Perhaps the easiest to use are the tail or anal glands, a pair of dark oily structures situated underneath the tail, one on each side of the tail bone, below the skin. Tails from dead deer can be collected easily and kept in a freezer until they are needed.

Some care is needed to prepare the tails for use. Thaw them out, remove their skin and carefully cut out the dark-coloured glands. Make up a simple salt solution of 1 per cent salt and 99 per cent water by weight. Put one pair of tail glands into a kitchen blender (perhaps when your wife is out!) and add 150 ml of the salt solution. Churn it up until smooth. The resultant brew we will call the "scent solution".

Add some of this scent solution to the blood before making the next trail. Start by adding 150 ml of scent solution to 500 ml of blood and at successive training sessions add more scent until the dog is able to track pure scent solution. Any tendency for the dog to semi-point when first encountering the trail or reaching the skin should be reinforced with praise.

Stage four

This final phase trains the dog to get used to work with live deer. The essential ingredient is to have the cooperation of an understanding deer farmer.

First, make some detailed arrangements with your friendly deer farmer. You will need a paddock which deer have just vacated, but one of the adjacent paddocks should still contain deer. Walk the dog slowly from the gate into the empty paddock, allowing the dog plenty of time to pick up the many ground scents there. After a time allow the dog to quietly approach the fence between it and the deer. Any tendency of the dog to run on should be firmly resisted. When the dog sees a deer he will probably point. The dog should be allowed to remain on point for a few seconds and then be rewarded with meat and walked gently away from the paddock. This lesson should be repeated until the dog consistently follows the scent trails and comes on to point, or semipoint, whenever it sees a deer through the fence.

For the final stage you will need a bottle of whisky (for the farmer), an iron nerve — and a firm grip on a reliable long leash just in case things go wrong.

Most deer farmers have at least one reasonably tame deer. Get the farmer to put one of these quiet deer into a fresh paddock by itself and then introduce the dog into this paddock in the same way as in the previous section. The result should be the same as in the previous exercise: the dog follows the scent line until it sees the deer and then points or semipoints. If the paddock has bush or scrub, so much the better. With luck the deer will be bedded in the cover and not be seen by the dog until the two animals are close to each other.

By now the dog is ready to graduate from its training programme — ready to be taken on a hunt to develop in the real world of hard knocks and rough country. To keep in form, the dog should be taken on a hunt at least once a month. If this doesn't happen or if it is not performing particularly well in the bush, give a refresher course of these training lessons.

Some comments on European training methods

Not much has been written in New Zealand about training deer dogs, and what has been written often relies heavily on European experience. We believe that some of what has been suggested is not the most suitable for New Zealand conditions.

In Europe the essential purpose for training dogs for deer hunting is to have them track and find a deer that has been shot. In New Zealand, the primary purpose is to have the dog indicate live deer to the hunter. We have found it difficult to train a dog to behave one way towards a dead deer and another way towards a live one, which is why we have developed our training programme to produce a dog that hunts silently while always remaining close to the hunter. The dog is then useful for work on both live and dead deer.

In Europe, the dog ranges away from its master as it follows the trail of a wounded deer. Because these dogs often travel considerable distances away from the hunter, they must be taught how to signal to their distant master when they have found the kill. Three signal methods are used, and each dog is taught only one. One method is by the dog repeatedly travelling from the kill to the hunter and back again without barking; another is by the dog barking at the kill until the hunter arrives; and the third is by the dog returning to the hunter with a special wooden marker in his mouth. The marker is called a "bringsel", which the dog normally carries slung from its collar until he finds a deer, whereupon it is transferred to the mouth.

If your dog is to be allowed to hunt away from you, we believe that the first of the three methods is the most suitable. The barking method is not good, as the dog is likely also to bark at live deer. Training to the bringsel method is time-consuming and probably unjustified on New Zealand dogs, whose main role is to indicate live deer.

Thank goodness for local knowledge, I thought to myself, as I sat and shivered in a cold southerly breeze at the top of a side ridge just under the main spine of the Southern Haurangi Ranges. From where I sat I could see right down the 6-kilometre length of steep-sided river valley, up which my buddy Tom Drew and I had struggled the night before by torch and battery headlight. Our progress had been slow and tedious and we arrived late at the stream-side campsite. A quick appraisal of the state of the frost on the little riverside flat decided us to sleep up on one of the spurs. Ten metres made a fair difference to the air temperature, but even then I was glad of the warmth of the two dogs we had brought, as they lay jammed between the two sleeping bags. It was just as cold when we got up two hours before first light and headed for the tops.

Our route was straight up the side of the valley wall and then along the thickly bushed ridge-top track in a broad sweep around the top of the river's terminal basin. Deer sign had been virtually non-existent — an occasional fresh print in the well-worn track, to which the dogs paid scant attention. Droppings were nowhere to be found. Having reached the mid point of the terminal basin ridge, my mate told me to hunker down while he headed down to get his bearings. Here I waited for him. Things did not look promising. What little I could see of the understorey in the half light of dawn looked to be all twig and no tucker for deer.

After a few minutes Tom returned as silently as he had left. "Yes, this is it," he announced. "They are usually in the side gully directly below us at this time of year. I'll drop down this side spur, you carry on round to the next side spur and then drop down. Then we'll have the gully covered from both sides. Be careful not to drop into the guts of the creek, as you'll find it benches out lower down and in this cold weather they'll be high on the benches."

As I dropped down I wasn't so sure. The understorey was so eaten out you could see 50 metres in any direction. I angled out over the side ridge to sneak down on the opposite side to the favoured gully, at intervals sneaking up and carefully looking into the still dark recesses down towards the little stream that could be heard faintly meandering through. I was moving quite slowly but descending quite rapidly using this technique. As my pace was a studied similarity to Tom's, I didn't get too far above or below where he would be on the opposite side of the little gut. I'd been stalking with him a good few times and was well able to judge his pace.

I'd gone down about 15 metres when I realised that the ridge I was following was starting to broaden out into a well flattened shoulder. As I descended into this area, I started to notice well cropped broadleaf shrubs ahead. They had been so well browsed that they had that characteristic absence of lower branches, reminiscent of the trees in well-grazed farm paddocks. Things started happening quite quickly after that. I slowed down and the dog went forward. I could see her sniffing at some tracks a little to the right about 10 metres ahead, so I started to really stalk. The dog walked slowly on, knowing her job, her eyes everywhere. Ten minutes and 25 metres later, I could see we were getting into a "hot" area. The print sign was getting very heavy, so much so that the area in places looked like a cattle yard. The prints were fresh in a wet clay, not dried at the edges, and showing prominent balling. This was undoubtedly a winter yarding area for stags. Good old Tom, he'd spent half his life in the Pirinoa district and certainly knew his ground! You could spend months wandering this country and easily walk past such a small area, so similar to all the surrounding hills, yet this one spot favoured. As the sun came slowly up I could see why. The ridge on the opposite side of the gut was high enough to keep out the cold southerly but not too high to keep out the warmth of the sun.

Suddenly I noticed that my dog had gone. I looked silently backwards and forwards, not daring to step. Then I saw her. She was on the top of a small ridge about 10 metres to my left, completely "frozen". I could see she was looking off the top of this ridge and down the other side in the manner that I had done further up when the ridge was steeper. However, from where I was I could not see what she was looking at. I inched slowly towards her, studying her. She was well locked on, her gaze fixed on a patch of coprosma scrub about 30 metres below. I had not walked over the small ridge, knowing that such an action must reveal me to whatever was on the other side. Instead, I had half crouched and walked up it until I was at the same level as a small pepperwood seedling stand just on the ridge top, and poked my head quietly over this. You can imagine what I saw in the clump of coprosma — nothing, absolutely nothing. Yet the dog continued to indicate it, every hair on her spine standing, her nose raised to that well-loved smell.

I stood in that uncomfortable half-crouched position, rifle at the ready, for fully ten minutes. I'm sure my eyes were each on half-inch stalks, I was straining that hard to see what the dog was indicating with every fibre of her being. She never faltered, yet I, for all the experience I professed to have, was letting her down. I couldn't see a damned thing. Slowly, ever so slowly, I straightened up from the half-crouched position. Still nothing. At any minute I expected action. Surely any deer would be alarmed by the sight of a progressively evolving disembodied head suddenly materialising from the middle of a pepperwood stand. The dog moved forward half a step, then locked up again. It, whatever it was, was still there. Carefully, so carefully, I took a step forward through the pepperwoods.

"Harrumph," the desperately close bark of a full-bodied stag. "Crash," a pause, "Harrumph". Then I saw him, a fast-moving blur further down the ridge. He had been doing the same thing as me, not in the coprosma patch, but on the other side of it where he'd been looking over the top, right at me! The dog, from its lower position, had seen its feet. I had only just seen him when he had started to run and was clear of the coprosma. Just great bounds and he was gone, a mighty beast, just his strong smell carrying to me. "Oh blast, I've stuffed it up yet again."

Then, from the other side of the gully, came the echoing blast of a .308 and the "whack" of a bullet connecting.

Good old Tom! — *R.L.*

8
Shooting and tracking wounded deer

Much has been written about the technique of shooting deer. Nearly every book published on deerstalking contains diagrams showing numerous "vital points" on the animal at which the hunter can aim. The practical fact of hunting is that most experienced hunters use only two shots: the lung shot and the neck shot. Matt and Bruce Grant's book *The Sharp Shooter* contains an excellent section on how bullets kill and the preferred aiming points, principally the "hilar" kill zone.

The hilar kill zone (see Fig. 20) is the area of the chest containing the large blood vessels that feed blood from the heart to the lungs and vice versa. The area also contains the so-called great blood vessels which feed oxygenated blood from the heart to the rest of the body, but it does not include the heart itself or the edges of the lungs. A bullet entering and expanding in the hilar area ruptures large blood vessels and causes a sudden massive blood loss. The animal is unable to travel more than a few metres before it falls and death is almost immediate. In contrast, a bullet striking the heart directly will stop the heart, but relatively little blood is lost, sufficient remaining in the blood vessels for the animal to run surprising distances, often a hundred metres or more.

The hilar kill zone can be clearly viewed when the animal is standing side on, but when the animal is at an angle to the shooter different portions of the zone can be shielded from the bullet (see Fig. 21). Thus in a quartering-towards-the-hunter shot, a shoulder will partially screen this area. More importantly, in the quartering-away-to-the-left shot, all the hilar kill area is screened from the hunter by the left hindquarter. The region of the chest visible below the curve of the left hindquarter contains the heart, which screens off the rest of the hilar area. This means an attempted hilar shot in this position will result in a heart shot at best. The only other shot in this position is the difficult head shot which often results in a wounded animal (frequently jawless) that dies a painful and lingering death.

The neck shot (Fig. 20) drops an animal almost instantaneously from a combination of blood loss and spinal shock, but the kill area can be seen to be much smaller and more difficult to hit in all except close-up shots.

FIG. 20

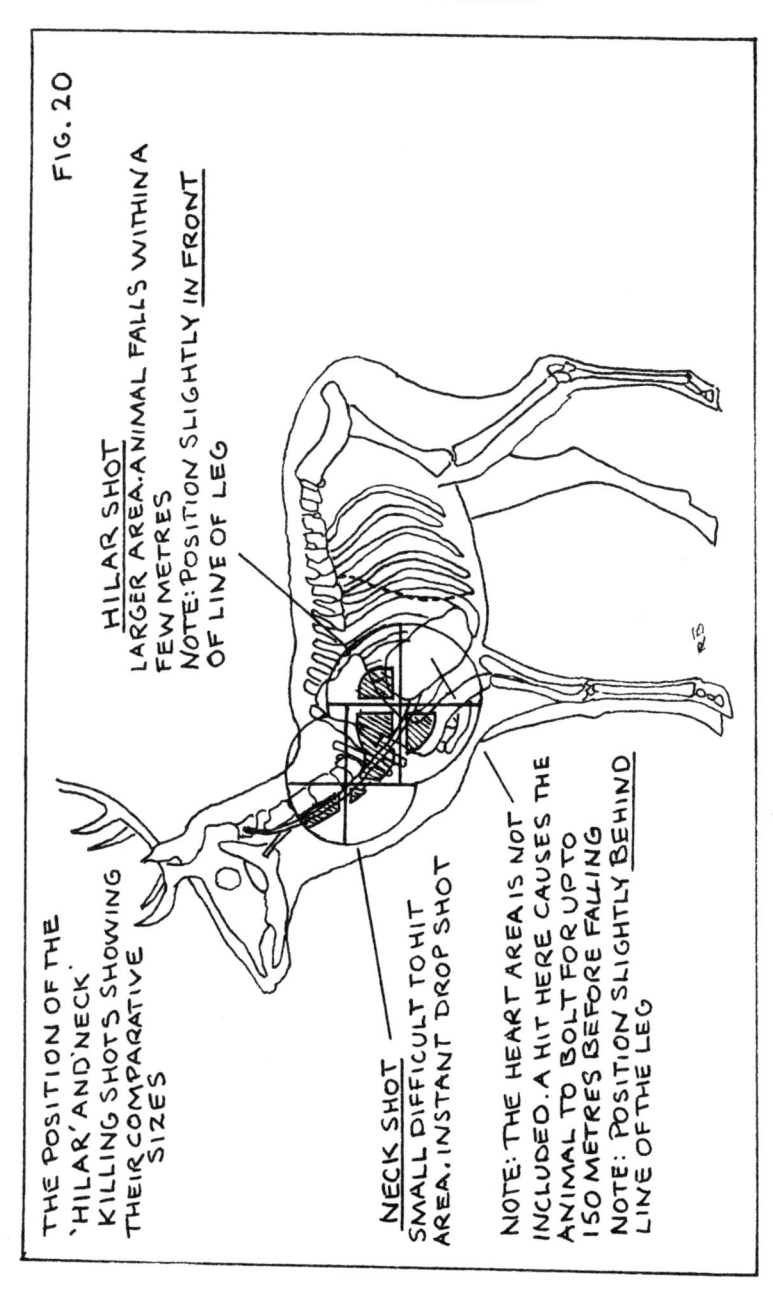

THE POSITION OF THE 'HILAR' AND 'NECK' KILLING SHOTS SHOWING THEIR COMPARATIVE SIZES

HILAR SHOT
LARGER AREA. ANIMAL FALLS WITHIN A FEW METRES
NOTE: POSITION SLIGHTLY IN FRONT OF LINE OF LEG

NECK SHOT
SMALL DIFFICULT TO HIT AREA. INSTANT DROP SHOT

NOTE: THE HEART AREA IS NOT INCLUDED. A HIT HERE CAUSES THE ANIMAL TO BOLT FOR UP TO 150 METRES BEFORE FALLING
NOTE: POSITION SLIGHTLY BEHIND LINE OF THE LEG

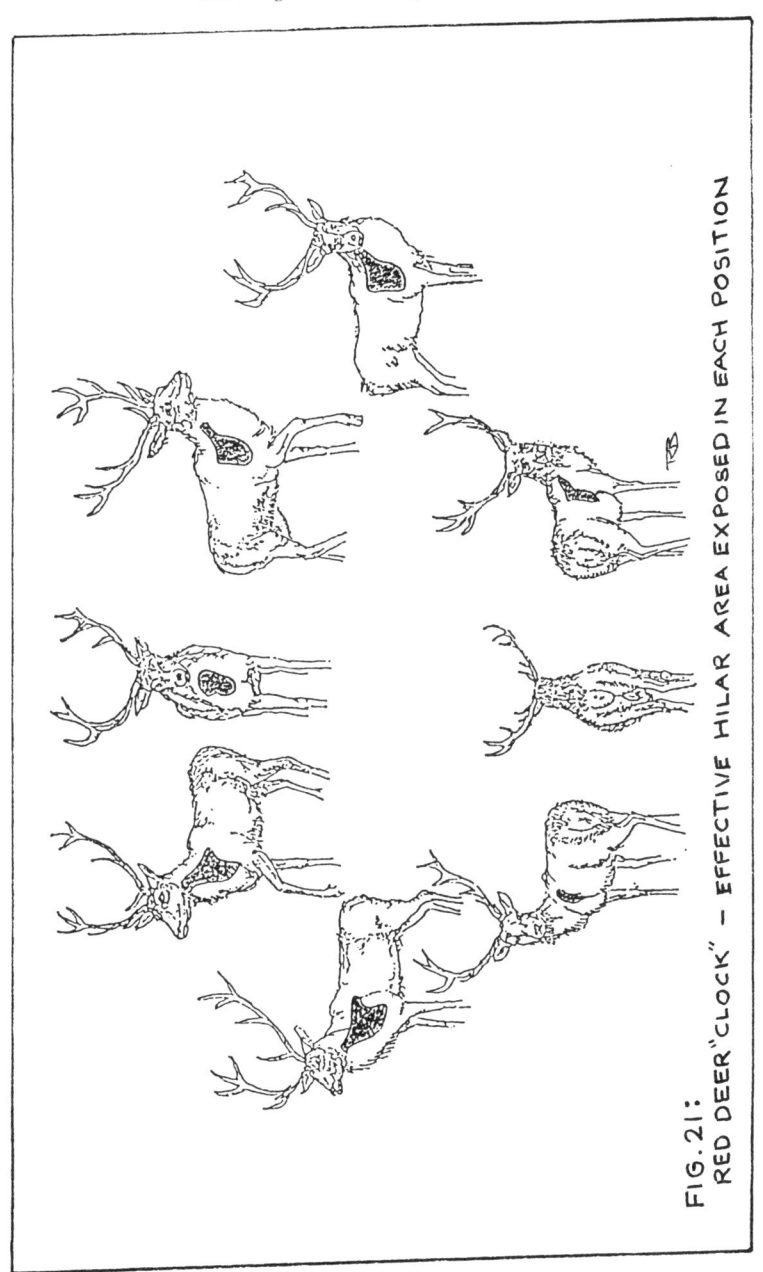

FIG. 21:
RED DEER "CLOCK" – EFFECTIVE HILAR AREA EXPOSED IN EACH POSITION

At all times try to avoid wounding animals. Making a clean quick kill gives a feeling of satisfaction, whereas having an animal escape badly wounded gives disgust. We believe that many deerstalkers give up the sport because of the horror of seeing a mortally wounded animal in agony, but still mobile, escape from some bad shooting.

When taking a shot at an animal, try to rest the hand that holds the fore-end of the rifle on something, but never rest the fore-end of a rifle directly on a hard surface, as this will throw the shot high. Better still, lie down and place the rifle on a steady, rested hand to line up an accurate shot. In practice, you rarely have the chance to do either of these, and free-standing shots without the aid of a rest are the norm, particularly when bush hunting.

Try to practise shooting every day to become competent at shooting from the standing position. Add weights to the fore-end of an air rifle to make it handle like a hunting rifle and then have daily target practice in the controlled environment of a basement or a shed.

When shooting at a target at any distance other than the zero point, the point of impact of the bullet will be above or below the point of aim. Beginners should consistently zero their rifle to the same distance, so that they can get used to estimating the variations of the impact point at shorter and longer ranges than the zero point. The zero point of a hunting rifle should be a relatively short distance — 100 metres is probably the most useful range to which to zero, and for bush stalking the range should never be greater than this distance.

As well as being precisely shot-in on a rifle range, your rifle should be of a good fit. Try it for fit wearing bush clothing and not shirt sleeves. A good fit means that you can quickly bring it up to the shoulder and find the sights clearly aligned on the target. A good fit enables accurate "snap" shooting at an alert animal when there is little time to spend taking the shot. Snap shooting does *not* mean the criminal behaviour of taking a quick blind shot at something moving in the bushes.

Rifle wobble, difficulty of judging bullet variations from zero point and the need for speed when taking shots, all mean that shots at deer in the bush will be less accurate than shots on the rifle range. For this reason, the larger killing zones, the hilar and neck shots, are to be preferred.

The major advantage of the two killing zones we recommend is that a variation from these ideal points of aim is still likely to result in a traumatic injury for the deer and a quick death.

Hilar shot

A bullet directly striking the lungs will make a loud, solid "whack". The deer is likely to jump and run forward a few paces if hit in the hilar zone but up to 100 metres if hit elsewhere in the chest. It runs with its neck outstretched before falling over with all four legs threshing. Death is from massive internal bleeding, but if the bullet is not exactly on the point of aim there is still a good chance of a dead deer, as described below.

1. If the bullet is at the correct elevation but too far back:
   (a) about 150 mm too far back and slightly low — a heart shot. The animal visibly jumps and immediately runs off at speed, collapsing dead up to 100 metres away.
   (b) about 300 mm too far back — a hollow sound when the bullet strikes, indicating a gut shot. The animal jumps on being hit and sometimes kicks out with its hind legs before running off with a hunched up appearance. Depending on where hit in the stomach, it may be difficult to track down.

2. If the bullet is of correct elevation but too far forward, it is a neck shot (see below).

3. If the bullet is simply too high:
   (a) up to 150 mm high — still a lung shot although not a hilar shot. The animal will not bleed profusely but will usually fall within 100 metres.
   (b) over 300 mm high — a spine shot. The hit makes a good solid sound and the animal drops instantly. If the animal stays down the spine has been destroyed, but the animal has not been killed and will need a finishing shot. If the spine has suffered only concussion the deer will get up after a few moments and run off and may be difficult to track down. If the deer falls down instantly, always stand ready to administer a killing shot should it get up again.

4. If the bullet is simply too low:
   (a) up to 150 mm too low — still a hilar shot.
   (b) over 300 mm low — a foreleg shot. There is a solid "bony" sound of the bullet hitting, and the animal falls over more slowly than after a spine shot. It threshes around before getting up and running off slowly and noisily. The animal can usually be tracked down with skill.

Neck shot

The neck shot is in effect a spine shot.(See Fig. 20, p.124.) When correctly delivered there is usually a solid sound of the bullet hitting bone and the deer drops instantly.

1. If the bullet is at the correct height but too far forward:
   (a) up to 75 mm too far forward — still a good spine shot.
   (b) more than 75 mm too far forward — the jaw may be hit. There is a "bony" sound as the bullet hits, the deer drops immediately but gets up and runs off normally with little noise.

2. If the bullet is the correct height but too far back, it is still effectively a good hilar shot.

3. If the bullet is simply too high:
   (a) up to 75 mm too high — poor placement, causing spinal concussion. The animal is likely to fall down but then get up and run off.
   (b) more than 75 mm too high — bullet strikes without sound, causing a slight neck wound, sometimes cutting the long dark nape hairs (see below). The animal flinches and runs off virtually uninjured.

4. If the bullet is simply too low the animal usually drops immediately from spinal concussion, then gets up and runs a few metres before falling over once more, threshing its legs around, before dying as a result of the destruction of all the big blood vessels going to the brain.

The important difference between the neck and the hilar shots is that the neck shot instantly grounds a deer but needs to be more accurate than the hilar shot. After a hilar shot the deer is likely to run off some distance before falling dead. In heavy undergrowth, without the aid of a dog, tracking down the fallen deer may need some skill.

Tracking wounded game

When a deer runs away after being shot at, you will need to know whether it was completely missed. Clues can be gained from how quickly the deer runs off.

A deer peacefully grazing will be greatly alarmed by an explosion but it will not know from which direction the sound came. The

Shooting and tracking wounded deer

animal hesitates. Often at this stage the novice hunter, using a bolt-action rifle, reloads and the deer hears the unnatural metallic sound, locates the hunter and is gone. If, however, the bullet **hits** the deer, the sudden physical shock of the impact causes **immediate flight**. An alerted deer one that, for example, has heard the hunter's approach and is looking at him when the shot is fired and misses, will also run once the shot is fired. An experienced hunter, therefore, can often tell that a deer has not been hit by watching carefully for a momentary pause between the shot and the animal's reaction.

A bullet striking an animal makes a different sound according to where it hits. The noise made by the departing deer can also indicate a hit: an uneven run, a noisy crashing departure, for example. A glimpse of the animal running unevenly can also suggest a wounding. Even if none of the above are seen or heard and a miss seems certain, a search should still be undertaken, as impressions are often misleading.

After you have fired a shot, stand still, listen to the noise of the animal's departure and the direction in which it heads. Staying absolutely still for some time after the shot is to be recommended. In areas where deer are relatively undisturbed, a deer shot at but missed may come back, curious about the big noise. Other deer in the same group may be concealed in a positions nearby and only after some time may decide to come out of hiding. If the deer shot at was a hind with a fawn concealed nearby, she may come back for her fawn. A single shot, because of its suddenness, will not unduly alarm deer.

A wounded deer will endeavour to reach a place of safety and concealment where it lies down. After 10 minutes or so its wounds begin to stiffen up and the animal has difficulty in getting up and running off again. If, however, a freshly wounded deer is immediately followed, the animal will keep moving in order to escape, and by maintaining mobility may be able to keep going for a long time. The prudent hunter, therefore, should wait if possible before tracking a wounded deer. Some authorities recommend a wait of 2 to 4 hours when a gut shot is suspected. Unfortunately, such long waits are not always possible: for example, it may be late in the evening, or a long way from camp. In persistent rain an immediate search is called for, before the signs of blood and prints are washed out. Always remember that even lightly wounded animals are liable to lie up, and cautious tracking after a long wait can lead to a second shot at the deer as it gets up from its bed.

Before you decide to move from your firing position, mark the location so that you can find it again if necessary. Quietly move over to the spot where the deer was and mark this also. Search the place where the animal was standing and all the ground within 3 metres. Look carefully for tufts of hair that might have been cut from the deer by the bullet — small bunches of hair as opposed to individual hairs that might have fallen out naturally and be lying there. The part of the animal hit can be identified from the appearance of the tufts, but remember that the deer's coat changes colour through the seasons (see p. 80).

1. Long and thin with black stripes: high neck or back wound.

2. Thin grey hair, medium length: body wound anywhere in the middle section of the deer's body.

3. Thin short grey hairs: a leg wound.

4. Thicker, grey/white hairs: a lower gut wound.

You will probably find other signs of a hit at the site where the deer was standing, for example, fragments of bone, indicating a leg wound, or blood, the most commonly looked-for clue.

Even in mortally wounded animals, often little or no blood is found at the exact location where the animal was shot, and the blood trail may not begin for up to 10 to 40 metres away. The appearance of blood from a wounded deer can give information about the part of the body struck by the bullet:

1. Bright red frothy blood: a lung shot.

2. Dark red blood occurring in large drops: a gut shot in the liver.

3. Watery, light, sometimes greenish/yellow-coloured blood, smelling strongly of deer: a gut shot in the intestines.

4. Many small medium-red colour droplets in spray lines on the ground: a shot in a leg or the jaw.

After searching the site where the deer was hit, try to follow the deer's escape route. The highest points of any blood smears on the shrubbery along the way give a fair indication of the height of the wound. If prints are visible, look for irregularities caused by a leg wound, for example drag marks from a foot. Look also for blood sign on the rim of one hoof print, resulting from blood running down the side of a wounded leg, and for poor registration caused by a wounded leg. If you follow the trail a long way, make marks as you go so that you can find it again if you should lose it.

Seriously wounded deer can be just as cautious and silent as healthy ones. When following a wounded deer, places where it has stopped and even laid down to rest will usually be found. Such places can give another indication of the type and severity of the wound by the amount and type of blood and other tissue fragments present there. The gradual lessening of blood in a trail over a long distance indicates that the wound is not severe and the animal's recovery mechanisms are coming into play. Your sense of smell is often helpful when searching for wounded and dead deer. The final location of a carcass, particularly that of a stag, is often revealed by its smell.

If you cannot find any trail of the wounded animal, go off in the general direction taken by the deer and have a good look for sign. If this doesn't work, return to the marked point where the animal was shot and start a circular search pattern, walking in gradually increasing circles around the site until sign is cut. If this time-consuming search still doesn't produce results, again take the general direction of the departing deer and explore the next steep scrubby gully or basin you come across. Badly wounded animals rarely travel uphill, but generally sidle or travel downhill and do not travel as far as one might expect. In these situations a good tracking dog will easily follow lightly wounded animals for hours.

When approaching deer that is wounded, or appears dead, do so cautiously and with a loaded rifle. The "dead" deer may leap up and rapidly depart. Hunters have been seriously wounded by the threshing antlers of a dying stag. When finishing off a wounded animal an extra bullet is never wasted.

The Waitahu in the Buller is a surprisingly difficult place to shoot. Although it is straightforward beech forest and low in elevation compared with the mountainous ranges that start on the other side of Reefton, it has a distinctive "U" shaped cross-section to its main flow and tributaries that makes stalking on anything but the river flats hazardous and arduous. The lower reaches of the valley on the southern shoulder are occupied by an open-cast coal mine, and the lower flats are a popular picnic spot for the locals of the nearby town: in all, a recipe for a bunch of very skittish deer. They come out on the river flats only briefly in the spring, and then only in the few minutes of first and last light. Further up the valley, beyond the mouth of the first main tributary, the Montgomery, the river is less disturbed by the sound of picnickers and dynamite. However, to reach this area a four-wheel-drive vehicle is needed to traverse the tortuous bog-hole-ridden Forest Service track that winds 5 kilometres to the hut. Also, at least three days are required without any rain, as even the more modest of the spring deluges of the West Coast rapidly swell the river, making it unfordable above the hut, especially when carrying a carcass.

A weekend off duty, with the prospect of more fine weather following two fine days, had me finishing work in record time, driving the partially dried track's length, and fording with relative ease the first part of the Montgomery to gain its recently constructed walking track.

There were still a good two hours before sunset but in these high-sided valleys the light was already beginning to fade. The wind was pleasantly light and blowing downriver into my face as I hurried along the track until it petered out, whereupon I crossed the river into the first small flat. In the winter these flats are desolate places for all the little river's charm: only blue-green scabweed and a few mosses held on to the stony surface of them. Now, however, in the early spring a thin green beard of fresh grass was sprouting in a few more fertile places. I noted this with anticipation as I rapidly traversed small flat after small flat, scouring them for sign.

The stony subsoil made poorly yielding ground that would not accept the signature of a print easily. On the third small flat I slowed down. The print sign was still scant. A few rims of partially slipped moss made for sign of very indeterminate age, but up ahead, about 40 metres away, I could see some large wet splashes on the stones well clear of the margin of the little river. As I sneaked up towards them I used as cover the stands of manuka that bordered the adjacent beech forest, looking always outwards on to the open flats. I was glad I was wearing my traditional garb, the swannie and long-johns making no harsh rasping noises against the reluctantly yielding scrub. As I ghosted along I saw places under the little manuka stands where the earth had been held by them against the winter ravages of the swollen river. In these places a heavy green sward had developed, greener than the best of the exposed flats.

I drew slowly nearer the wet stones. Yes, the wet marks were clearly linked with faint deer tracks on either side of the boulders, and there was the good old smell of wet deer! I soon lost the limited trail in the manuka scrub. Slowly I zig-zagged the flat, going into the wind. Then out of the corner of my eye, just under a particularly lusty manuka, I saw a white fluttering. At first I thought it was a fantail, but then the manuka bush quite definitely shook. I froze. After about a minute the bush moved again and out from the side stepped the foreleg of a deer. I traced its outline upwards to see the blackish silhouette of a deer's head and neck. Even as I looked, the head came down and cropped at the grass just in front of the foreleg. I could see it clearly now but could not get a killing shot. I waited, rifle half raised, a good 5 minutes. The rifle was starting to weigh heavily in my hands when the animal slowly stepped into full view. He was a spiker, his thin reddish spires not yet loosened by the approaching spring. I centred the cross-hairs on the base of his neck and squeezed off the shot.

At the moment of the explosion the animal vanished from view, the sure sign of a hit. Had I hit him true? I held my ground, listening intently for the tell-tale sound of a deer crashing away up into the safety of the beeches. Nothing. I fought the urge to rush out to where he had been, knowing that if I had wounded him he would have been panicked into running. I waited just a few minutes, time for him to lie down quietly and the wound to stiffen. Had I allowed sufficient depression? When I aimed, the deer had been only 15 metres away but the rifle was zeroed for 100 metres. I mentally relived the shot. No, I could definitely remember dropping those cross-hairs about 5 centimetres. Did I hear the bullet strike? No, it had been so close that the explosion of the round would have covered the noise of the strike. After 5 minutes I slowly stalked to the spot. No carcass to be seen but a clear well splayed track running directly along the edge of the manuka belt. Slowly, listening all the time, I followed it. After 10 metres a bright splash of blood, and my spirits lifted. Another 10 metres and the splashes were all around. Then, in the last metres of the flat, just inside the manuka belt, I saw the white curve of an upturned belly.

The evening was suddenly extra marvellous. I examined the carcass, resisting the temptation to gut it. A good neck shot but the animal went 30 metres! The exit hole was almost as small as the entry wound. I use silvertip ammunition and experience has shown me that the bullet will not expand well in close shots unless it hits the bone. The bullet had severed the carotid artery, missing the narrow spinal area. The animal had bled to death as it ran. "Should have taken a hilar shot even at that short range," I murmured to myself as I dragged the un-gutted beast towards the river. It was starting to bloat quite nicely. Out with the 10-metre length of nylon cord I always carry, a quick cut in the space behind the tendon in one hind leg, a good non-slip knot and into the river went the carcass. Off I went running along the river bank, cord in hand, steadying the carcass on its free float down to the hut.

The Waitahu might be difficult to hunt but it's damn good to get the carcasses out of! — *R.L.*

9
From forest floor to kitchen table

There is much pleasure in giving well-presented cuts of venison to family and friends after a successful hunt. In this chapter we will demonstrate methods of keeping your hard-won venison clean and uncontaminated. During butchering more can be learned about your deer — information such as the animal's age, general condition and diet which can be useful in hunting the same area on another occasion. Diseases such as tuberculosis and hydatids can be detected. Detection is important, because not only will it enable you to avoid contracting these diseases from contaminated meat, but also the hunting fraternity as a whole will be able to build up hard evidence of the incidence of disease in wild deer populations.

The first observation
When you have just shot a red deer, a creature of the wild lies before you on the forest floor, ready to reveal its quiet secrets. When you have confirmed the sex and general size, take a little more time for thought and run through questions like these:
1. Is the animal in good body condition? Perhaps the bones project somewhat more than they should, indicating hard times; on the other hand, it may be a fat, well-upholstered animal.
2. If it is a hind, is it in milk? You can test for this easily by stripping one of the teats as you might a cow.
3. What is the animal's age? Indications are given by the body conformation, the state of wear of the cleaves, and the configuration of the antlers. The best indicator of age is the teeth. If you intend to cut off the head and discard it, this will be the only time to examine them. If you are going to keep the head as a trophy and want to have an accurate age assessment, take the lower jaw too (Chapter 10 gives details on tooth ageing using the lower jaw bone).

Hanging a deer
The best way to gut a deer is with the animal hanging by its head from the branch of a tree. By hanging up the animal it can be kept

free from contamination by soil, dead leaves and other ground debris, but how do you hang up a heavy animal such as a mature red deer? Two hunters can often lift a lighter animal, but on your own you will find it difficult. One way around this difficulty is to carry a miniature pulley system, which can be purchased from a hardware shop. This consists of two double blocks threaded with a light woven nylon cord, and although only weighing a few hundred grams, it can easily lift the heaviest stag. Tie it to a sturdy branch as high up as you can reach. Insert the lifting hook into a rope loop tied around the animal's neck or antlers. In this way the animal is lifted by its head up to a convenient height. One or both forelegs are then lashed sideways to a handy branch, so the carcass doesn't spin around.

We have three reasons for suggesting you hang the carcass by its head rather than from its heavier and stronger back legs. Firstly, when the animal is hanging in this position the gut falls deeper into the animal and so tends to put less pressure against the upper belly wall, making it easier to cut the belly skin without cutting the underlying gut. Secondly, the oesophagus (the tube that leads from the mouth to the stomach) is easier to deal with because the gut is falling away from it. Finally, the post-mortem examination, particularly of the lungs, is more readily undertaken in this position.

If the animal cannot be lifted up it can be gutted while lying on the ground. The animal should be lying on its back, preferably on a slight slope with the head higher than the hindquarters. Problems come, however, when halfway through the procedure the carcass begins to slide further down the hill. With stags this can be prevented by pushing the animal's chin upwards so that the antlers dig their tines into the ground. The tines can then be driven into the ground by standing astride the head with one foot on the main beam of each antler and alternately shifting weight between the two.

The value of hygiene

When gutting and butchering a deer, cleanliness is important. Contamination of the meat with hair, gut contents, droppings or urine should be avoided, as they sometimes harbour bacteria harmful to man. Puncturing the bladder or intestines is likely to result in large areas of meat surface being contaminated. All deer should be assumed to be infected and stringent precautions should be taken to avoid contamination. In England, for example, the risk of contamination is taken so seriously that any deer gut-shot is automatically condemned as unfit for human consumption.

New Zealand deer herds carry at least two bacteria that are spread by contamination of meat with gut contents or urine, and are known to be harmful to man. The frequency of their occurrence in wild herds is unknown, but the likelihood of a hunter becoming infected from a poorly butchered carcass is probably low. However, illnesses caused by these bacteria are sufficiently nasty to make special care with butchering worthwhile.

Probably the rarer of the two bacteria, *Yersinea enterocolitica*, causes a disease known as yersiniasis. Its effects on humans can vary considerably: it can cause a short-lived episode of diarrhoea and vomiting (similar to a bout of food poisoning), or a more severe long-lasting diarrhoea leading to septicaemia, which in weaker individuals can cause death. Probably the more common bug is leptospirosis, which is one well known to farmers. It infects a variety of New Zealand wild and farmed animals and there is no reason to suppose it does not also infect deer. There are a number of substrains, each one having a slightly different effect on humans. Illnesses vary from the "flu-like" one (known as "lepto" in farming circles) to the more severe "hepatitis-like" one, complete with mild jaundice.

Gutting a deer

The most important point in cutting the belly open is to avoid also cutting the underlying stomach and intestines, allowing gut contents to contaminate the meat. The first cut in the skin should be in the middle of the belly (see Fig. 22), about 10 centimetres long. Draw the knife down slowly in a single cut through only the thickness of the skin. More light strokes of the knife are applied to this cut until the belly cavity is only just penetrated. You can then insert your fingers into this hole to make it a little bigger. With two fingers inside the belly cavity make a V-shape and introduce your knife, cutting edge uppermost, between them. By running the ends of the fingers ahead of the knife you are able keep the intestines away from the gut wall ahead of the point where the knife is cutting. As the cut gets longer you can put your whole hand inside to perform this function.

The next objective is to sever the oesophagus and windpipe at the neck. If you are headskinning the animal, you will have to cut and "punch" a lot of the skin away from the neck to get up underneath the skin to the point where the oesophagus should be cut through

Fig. 22 — Skinning Out

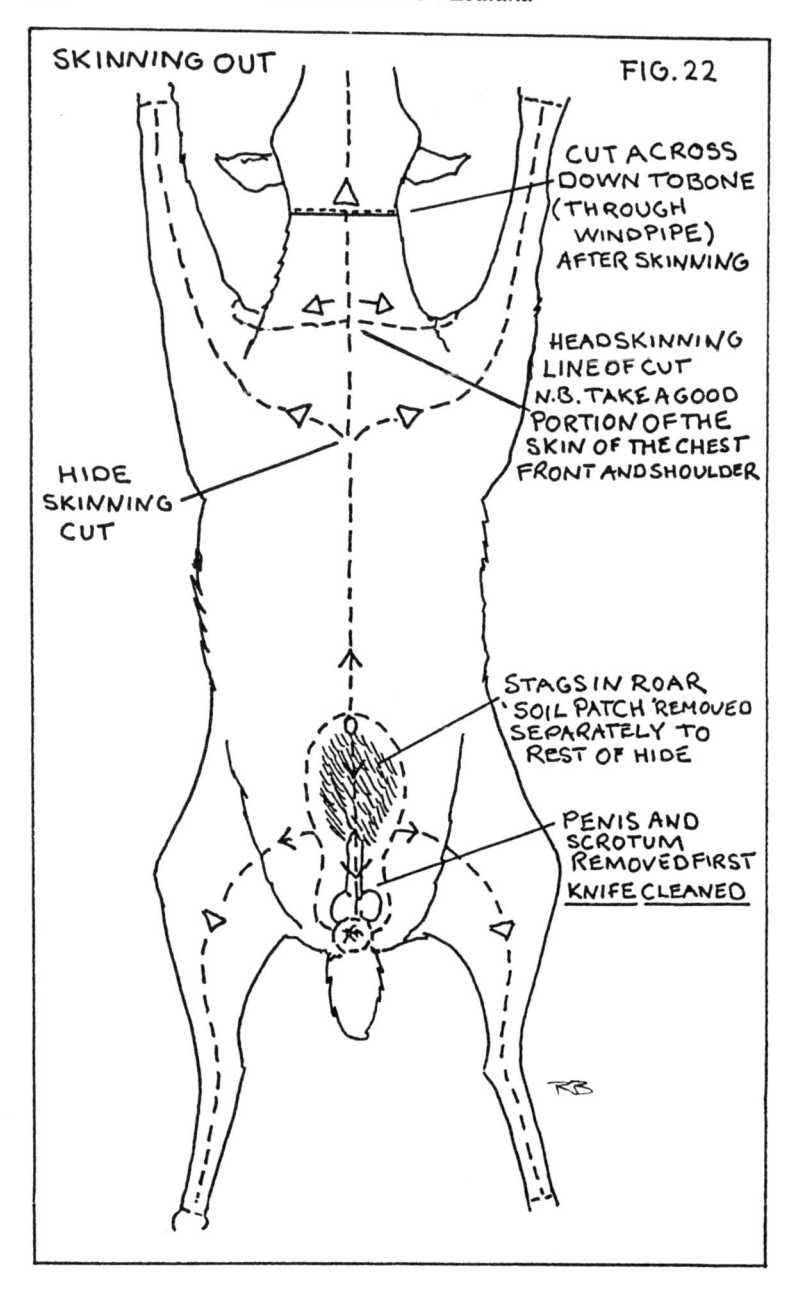

From forest floor to kitchen table

(see Fig. 23). If the animal is not being headskinned, this site is reached by simply continuing the belly cut line up over the chest and on to the neck. To cut the oesophagus, make a deep cut at right angles to the line of the neck from the front back towards the neck bones. In making this cut you will feel the knife cut through the windpipe. After cutting through the windpipe continue the cut until you reach the neck bones. In this way you are sure of cutting through the oesophagus.

Now put your hand into the gut cavity and by feeling around near the diaphragm (the muscular wall that separates the lungs from the guts) find the lower end of the oesophagus. Cut the diaphragm in a semicircle around the oesophagus so that it is free and can now be pulled down from the neck. Once pulled free, the oesophagus should be tied in a simple knot to prevent the stomach contents coming out.

Now that the belly is cut open and the oesophagus free, the stomach can be gently lifted out of the belly cavity; the other intestines will follow until the point where only the lower gut, still attached to the anus, is left inside.

Pull the animal's tail away from the body, and make a circular cut in the hairless skin around the anus (and vaginal opening in the female). Once the skin is cut, insert the knife deeper all the way round. In this manner the bowel tube is cut free from all its attachments at the point where it passes through the pelvis. This frees the lower bowel, allowing the whole intestinal tract to be removed and placed in a safe position for later examination. Next, the bladder and, in hinds, the uterus (see Fig. 23), should be gripped firmly from inside the belly cavity and pulled upwards and outwards. They should come out quite easily as their outside openings will have been freed by the anal and vaginal cuts.

The liver and kidneys are still in the abdominal cavity. Remove them, unless you intend to sell the carcass, in which case they should be left attached (their positions are shown in Fig. 23). Removal is simple. To remove the liver cut through its attachment to the diaphragm and it should come free, often bringing with it the right kidney. To remove the kidneys, grip them and firmly pull them away from their position on the back wall of the belly cavity. Cutting through the small tubes that lead down to the bladder should free them. The liver and kidneys should be placed in a shaded position ready for the post mortem. They also make first-rate eating.

The next task is to open the chest cavity. Cut through the soft part

Figure 23. The Gross Anatomy of the Red Deer.

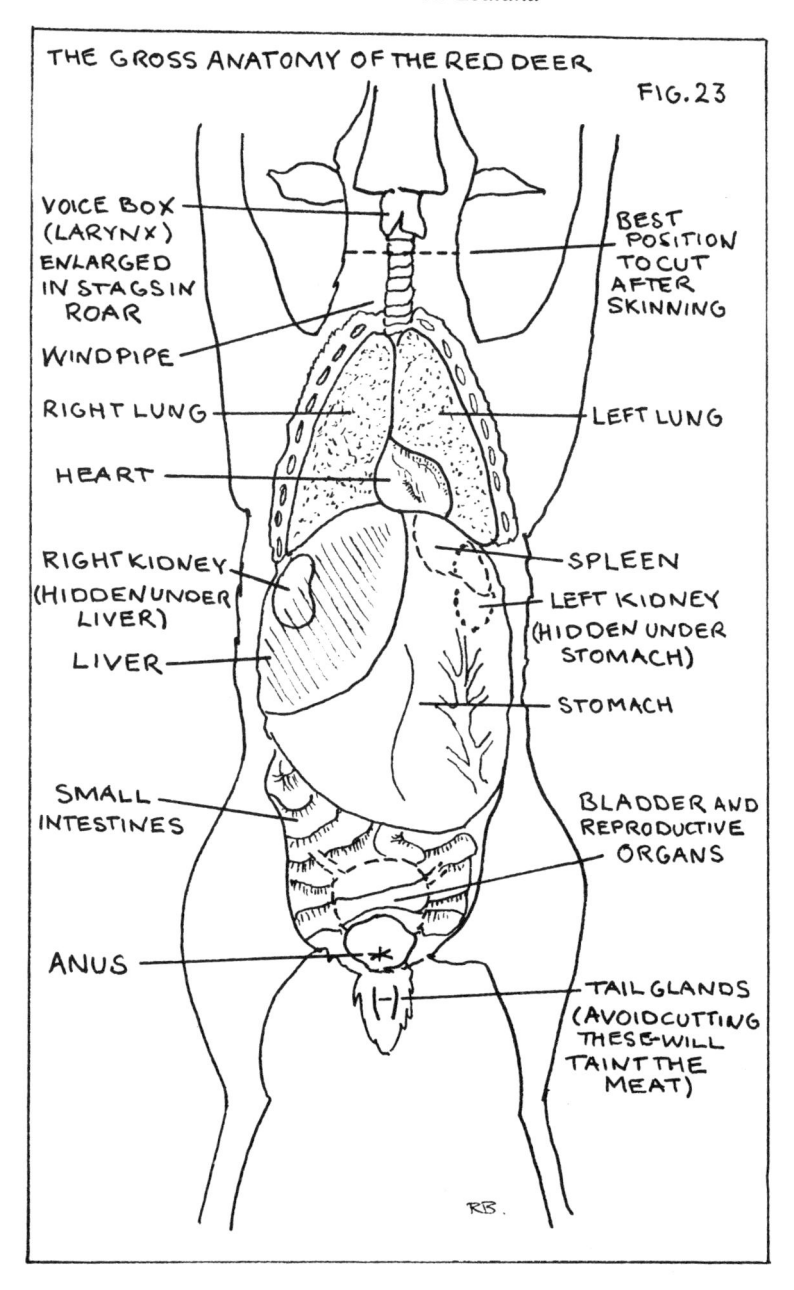

of the ribs where they are attached to the breastbone at the front. Cut upwards in and out of the rib cage with a sharp knife in a sawing motion, and keep going right to the top of the chest so that all the ribs are severed. The chest cavity can now be pulled open and the diaphragm cut free right around in a big circle where it joins the rib cage. Now grab the windpipe at the top of the chest just before it goes into the neck and pull firmly outwards and downwards. The windpipe, attached lungs and heart should now all come out leaving an empty chest cavity. They should be placed with the liver and kidneys ready for the post mortem. *Note*: if you intend to sell the carcass, you must leave the lungs, heart and windpipe in the chest.

The post mortem

Every joint of meat you buy at the butcher has come from an animal killed at a licensed abattoir, a legal requirement in New Zealand and in most western countries for the protection of the consumer. The protection is two-fold. Firstly, the animals are killed and dressed in a hygienic way to prevent the carcass from becoming contaminated with urine, faeces or hair from the slaughtered beast. Secondly, the carcass and its offals are examined by a qualified meat inspector who is trained to identify the presence of diseases communicable to man. Our new deer-farming industry has set up licensed abattoirs all over the country to perform these functions for their high-quality farmed venison product. Wild deer sold to an abattoir must have their heart, lungs, liver and kidneys still attached to enable a post mortem.

In the same way that abattoirs protect the general public, the deerstalker has a duty to do his utmost to avoid giving contaminated or diseased meat to his family or anyone else.

If you have followed the correct procedures for gutting and organ removal, you will have achieved the first function of the abattoir — that of preventing contamination of the meat. The second and more difficult function is the detection of significant diseases in the carcass and offals. Some diseases of deer can be communicated to humans eating an infected animal.

The most important disease, easily identified by post mortem, is tuberculosis. This disease, in man and animal alike, causes a "wasting away", often to the point of death. The treatment in humans requires a long course of drugs with unpleasant side effects. A number of cases of tuberculosis have been confirmed in both wild and farmed

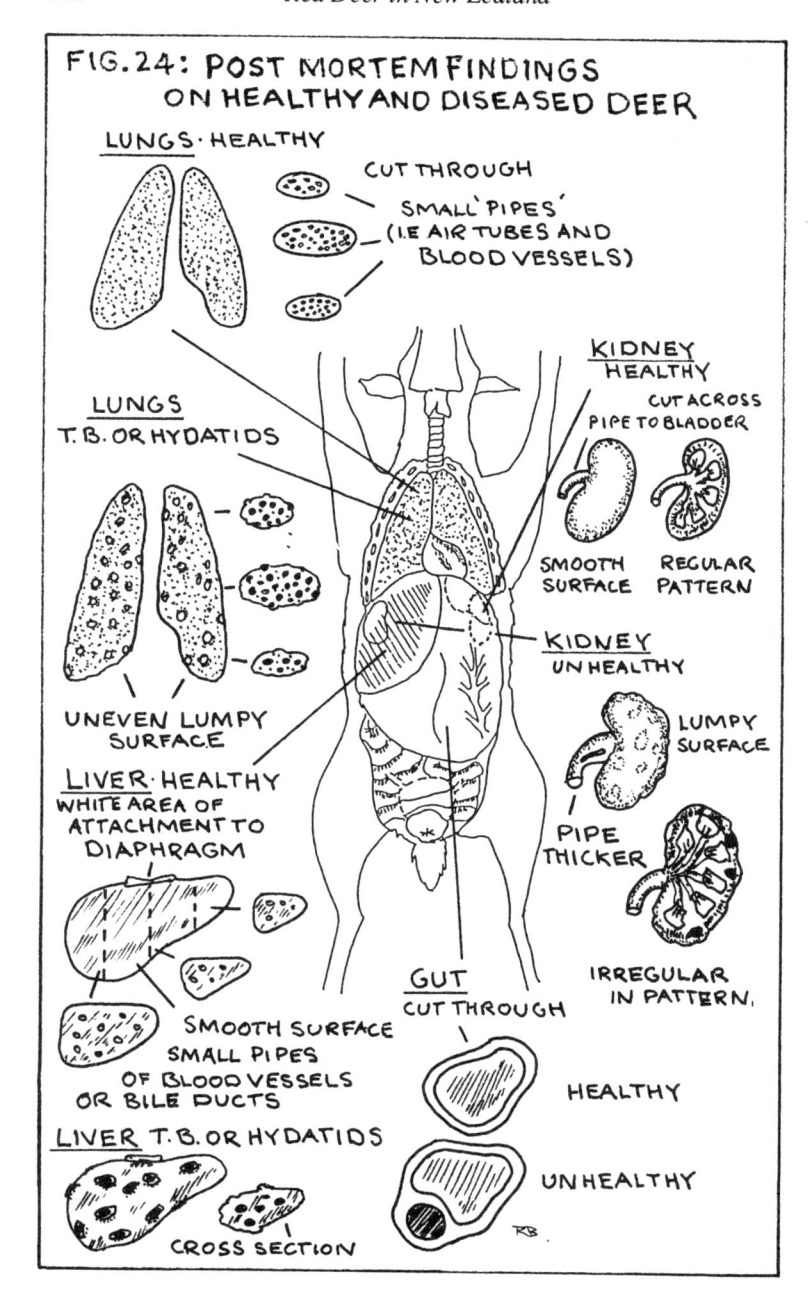

Fig. 24: Post mortem findings on healthy and diseased deer

New Zealand deer. Conveniently, the disease usually leaves a "signature" visible to the naked eye, on the parts of the animal it infects. This signature (or signatures, as there can be many of them) consists of a small, round, white lump either in the middle of or alongside the organ of the body in which the tubercular bacterium is living. Each lump is made up of an inner ball of soft, cheesy material (dead infected cells) and an outer thin layer, like orange peel, of tough, white, fibrous material (a layer of scar tissue the body has laid down against the infection). Generally speaking, the longer the animal has had the infection, the bigger the white lumps, because of the gradual increase in size of the ball of dead cells in the centre of each lump.

The other disease to look for in the post mortem is hydatids. In the same way that sheep are infected from eating grass contaminated with eggs from the droppings of infected dogs, deer can also contract the same disease. This disease also leaves a signature on the infected parts of the body — a lump, or cyst. Hydatid cysts consist of an outer peel of white tissue and an inner cavity filled with a clear, colourless fluid.

Tuberculosis can infect a bone or muscle, but it is more likely to be found in the major organs of the body removed during gutting. By far the most common sites of infection with hydatids are in the liver or lungs — rarely are they found in muscle.

In looking for signs of infection, first examine the carcass that is now open and empty of internal organs. Looking inside the chest cavity you should see a smooth curved inner surface to the ribs on which alternate layers of rib and muscle will be visible. Any lumps on this inner surface should be viewed with suspicion, particularly if the lung had stuck to the rib-cage and had to be prised off. Any such lump should be carefully cut into to see whether it has a cheesy or fluid centre. Next, look into the belly cavity and again look for lumps and places where the guts have become stuck to the inside of the belly wall.

Now examine the carefully placed pile of organs:

Lungs

Each lung should be still attached to the windpipe. Look at each lung carefully. A healthy lung should be a uniform light pink colour throughout, light in weight, dent readily when lightly pressed with the fingertips, and have a texture and feel similar to candy floss. Look carefully for any projecting lumps or white areas just under the surface of the lung, particularly if the smooth outer lung covering is rough or puckered at this point. Now feel for lumps. At any point where you can feel a lump, cut down through the lung towards it and then look at the cut surface. Sometimes you will find you have cut down to a lung tube, which is quite normal. If you are not sure if it is a tube or a hollow hydatid lump, try threading a piece of grass into it. If it is a lung tube the grass will slide in easily and go in a long way; if it is a hydatid cyst the grass will come to a stop after a short distance. Look and feel each lung in turn. If you find nothing, cut each lung into slices 2 centimetres thick with a sharp knife. Look carefully at both surfaces of each slice for evidence of lumps that have been cut through.

Liver

This is the dark purplish-black organ found just under the right side of the diaphragm. Don't confuse it with the spleen, a flatter, more disc-shaped structure found under the left side of the diaphragm.

Look carefully at the surface of the liver. It will have two whitish areas on it: one in the centre of the rounded surface where it was cut from the diaphragm, and another underneath on the opposite side. Any other white areas or areas of roughness or puckering should be cut down into and through in the same way as for the lungs. Look for the same white lumps. If no abnormality of the surface is found, cut the liver into slices 1 to 2 centimetres thick and inspect each slice for lumps. The many small hollow tubes that have been cut through are quite normal, but look for any larger ones. If you are suspicious, cut slowly, peeling the fresh slice apart from the remainder of the liver as you cut, looking for the telltale spurt of fluid of a cyst being cut.

Kidneys

These are the plum-coloured, bean-shaped structures removed from the back wall of the belly cavity. Again, examine each carefully, looking for irregularities on the surface. Each kidney should have only whitish marks at the middle of the inside curve, rather like the white marks on broad bean seeds. Feel the kidney carefully for hard lumps within. There should be none. Now slice each kidney lengthwise and parallel to the flatter front and rear surfaces (see Fig. 24), cutting each kidney in half to expose a delicate symmetrical design within each. Look for any white lumps or cysts that distort this regular pattern.

The intestines
This is the most difficult part for the novice. Begin by finding the stomach. Now grasp between your thumb and forefinger the intestine tube leading from the stomach. With your free hand pull the tube of the intestine progressively through the grip made by your thumb and forefinger until you have pulled its entire length through. As you pull, feel the thickness running between your thumb and forefinger. Any part that suddenly increases in thickness should be carefully cut into. Normally the wall of the intestine is thin, about 5 millimetres thick at most, and any large lumps in the wall, especially if containing a cheesy centre, should be viewed with suspicion. As you near the end of the intestine during this procedure, you will often find droppings still within the tube of the gut. With experience you will be able to identify them as such by moving them within the tube. If they do not move cut down into them and look directly. If in doubt you can cut down the whole length of the intestine and thus lay bare the whole delicate structure of the lining of the gut. Look for any irregularity of pattern caused by a projecting lump or cyst, and if in doubt cut through it.

After following this procedure with a couple of carcasses, you will be reasonably adept. Any suspicious areas should be carefully preserved in a polythene bag and taken to your local MAF officer. You will find him keen to help. If you think you have killed an infected animal, wash your knife and hands carefully and discard all meat, hide and trophies. If you do not discard these things, at least do not eat any meat until it has been cleared by the MAF.

Carrying the carcass
A whole carcass can usually be carried. You may want to carry it back to the hut to have more time to butcher it, or, if near the road, carry out the whole lot. Fig. 25 shows how to prepare a carcass to carry it like a backpack. For your own safety, tie some colourful material over the carcass to avoid being mistaken for a live deer and shot at by a trigger-happy hunter. If you don't have any special material, a colourful nylon raincoat will do.

If the hut or vehicle is some distance away, the hindquarters and back steaks only can be removed and carried out. They contain 70 per cent of the meat (see Fig. 26). Rather than waste the meat of the front legs they can be boned out and the meat carried with the back steaks in a daypack or inside a shirt or jacket above a tight belt.

Fig. 25: "Haversacking" a deer

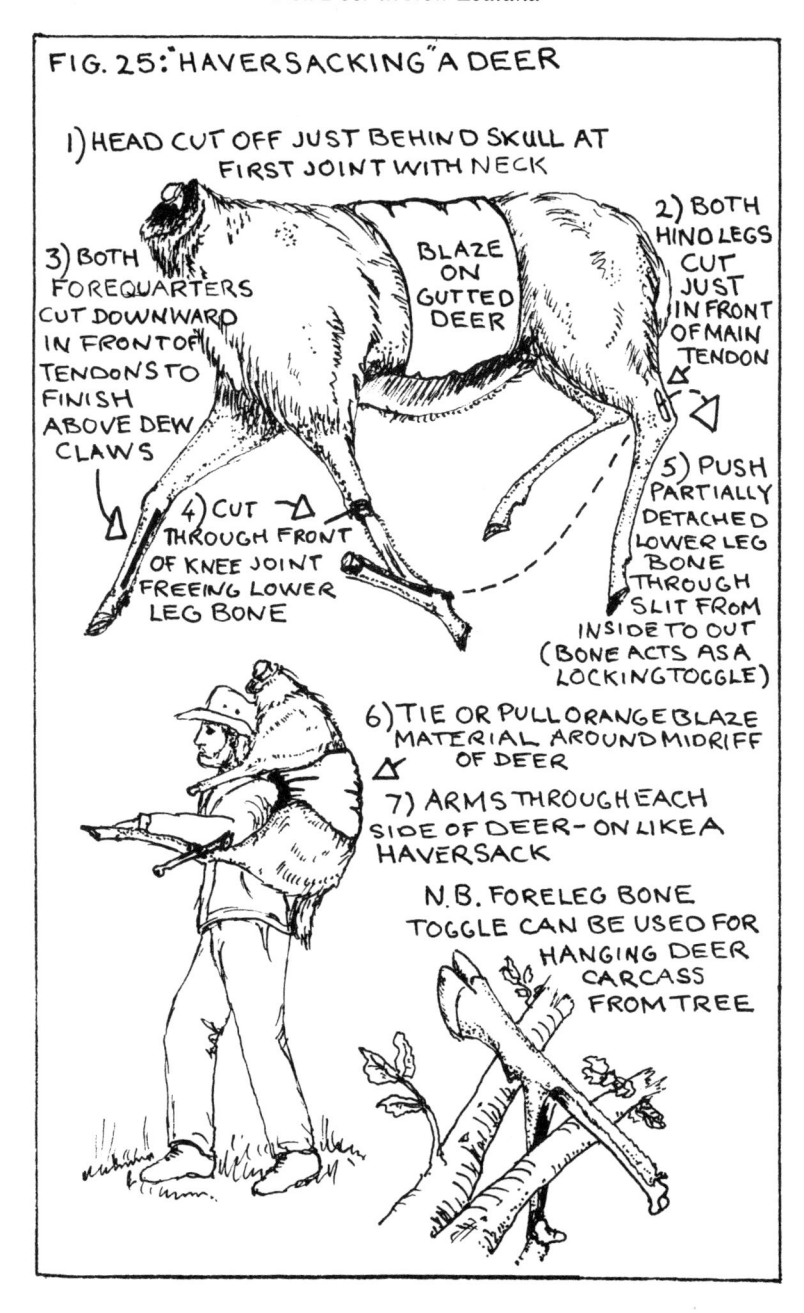

1) Head cut off just behind skull at first joint with neck
2) Both hind legs cut just in front of main tendon
3) Both forequarters cut downward in front of tendons to finish above dew claws
4) Cut through front of knee joint freeing lower leg bone
5) Push partially detached lower leg bone through slit from inside to out (bone acts as a locking toggle)
6) Tie or pull orange blaze material around midriff of deer
7) Arms through each side of deer – on like a haversack

N.B. Foreleg bone toggle can be used for hanging deer carcass from tree

From forest floor to kitchen table 147

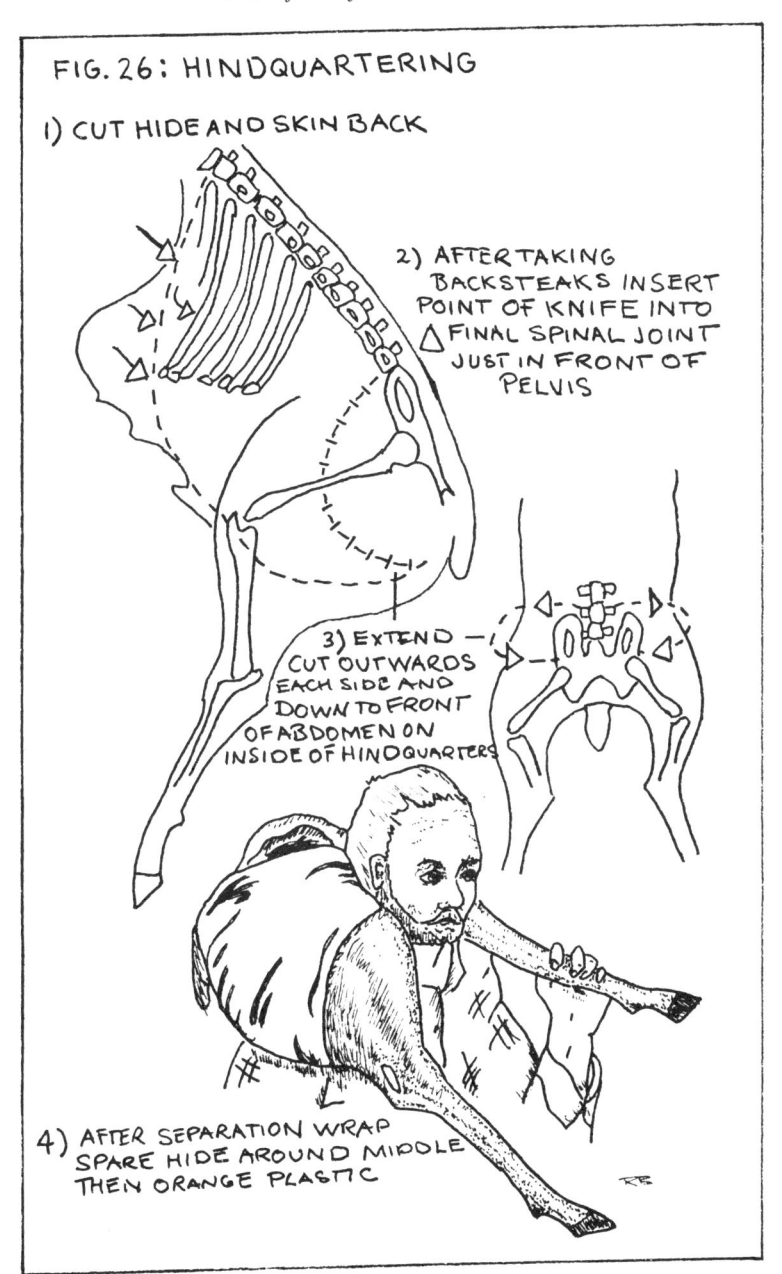

FIG. 26: HINDQUARTERING

1) CUT HIDE AND SKIN BACK

2) AFTER TAKING BACKSTEAKS INSERT POINT OF KNIFE INTO FINAL SPINAL JOINT JUST IN FRONT OF PELVIS

3) EXTEND CUT OUTWARDS EACH SIDE AND DOWN TO FRONT OF ABDOMEN ON INSIDE OF HINDQUARTERS

4) AFTER SEPARATION WRAP SPARE HIDE AROUND MIDDLE THEN ORANGE PLASTIC

Removing the skin

The skin must be removed cleanly before quartering and boning-out, so that hairs do not contaminate the meat. Fig. 22 (p. 138) shows where the knife cuts should be made in the skin. One line of cuts is made around the brisket for the purposes of headskinning a trophy, but a different line is made if you want to remove the entire hide and not keep the headskin. Once the belly cut has been made the other skin cuts are easily made with a sharp knife by running it, blade upwards, up under the skin so as to cut the skin from the inside out.

At the edges of the skin cuts, some knife work is used to separate the skin from the underlying fat and muscle until enough is freed to grasp and begin "punching". In this technique a fist is used to push and punch the skin at the line of separation, to further separate the skin from the body. Often the skin will come away with a firm pulling. The less the knife is used, once the initial cuts are made, the cleaner the skin will come off, and the freer it will be of attached pieces of muscle and fat. Avoid punching near bullet entry and exit wounds, as bullet and bone fragments lying just under the skin can cause nasty cuts to knuckles. A hanging carcass is easier and cleaner to skin than one on the ground. Once the legs, neck and the sides of the belly have been freed, a final big pull downwards along the back to the tail completely removes it except for its attachment to the tail. Cut off the tail close to the hindquarters, by cutting through the muscle and soft gristle piece in its centre, so that it is left attached to the skin. Fold the edges of the skin inwards and then fold the whole skin lengthways, roll it up and tie it with string.

Figs. 27 to 31 illustrate how to remove and care for the headskin of a stag if you wish to keep it as a trophy.

Quartering

The carcass is now hanging in a tree ready to be butchered. Before you take the meat from the bones each limb needs to be removed from the carcass so that it can be handled separately. There are four limbs, hence the name quartering. Figs. 32 and 33 show how to cut a carcass into quarters. After removal of the limbs the eye steaks are removed from the inside of the backbone. Quartering also includes removal of the back steaks.

From forest floor to kitchen table   149

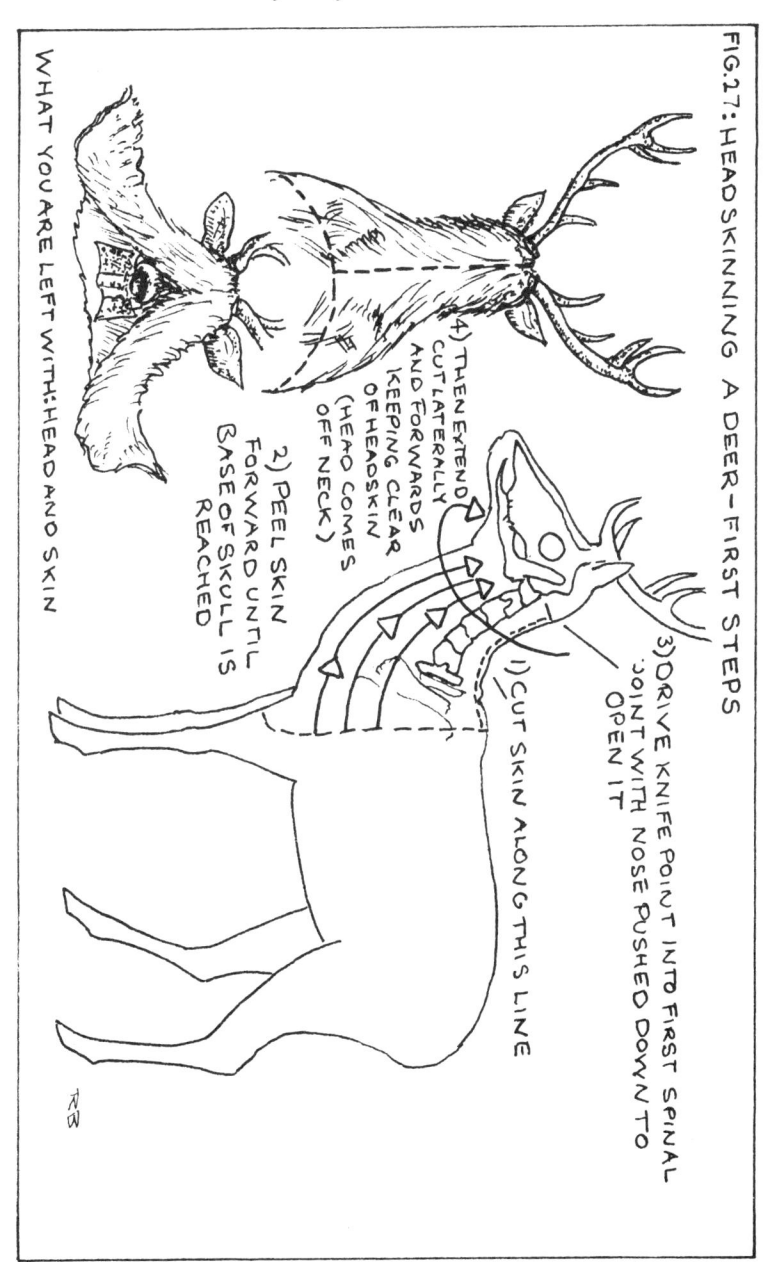

FIG.27: HEAD SKINNING A DEER - FIRST STEPS

1) CUT SKIN ALONG THIS LINE

2) PEEL SKIN FORWARD UNTIL BASE OF SKULL IS REACHED

3) DRIVE KNIFE POINT INTO FIRST SPINAL JOINT WITH NOSE PUSHED DOWN TO OPEN IT

4) THEN EXTEND CUT LATERALLY AND FORWARDS KEEPING CLEAR OF HEADSKIN (HEAD COMES OFF NECK)

WHAT YOU ARE LEFT WITH: HEAD AND SKIN

FIG. 28: HEAD SKINNING (CONTINUED)

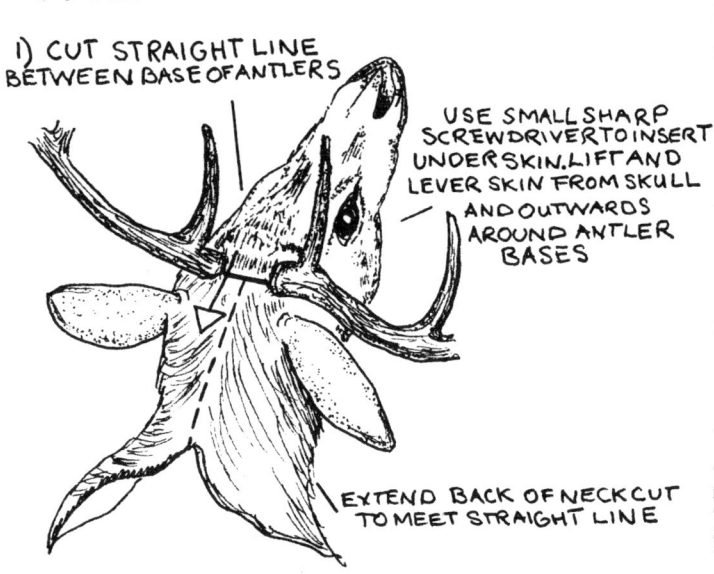

1) CUT STRAIGHT LINE BETWEEN BASE OF ANTLERS

USE SMALL SHARP SCREWDRIVER TO INSERT UNDER SKIN. LIFT AND LEVER SKIN FROM SKULL AND OUTWARDS AROUND ANTLER BASES

EXTEND BACK OF NECK CUT TO MEET STRAIGHT LINE

2) A PEEL BACK FREED SKIN FROM ANTLER BASES, SKULL AND SPINE IN MID LINE DOWN BACK

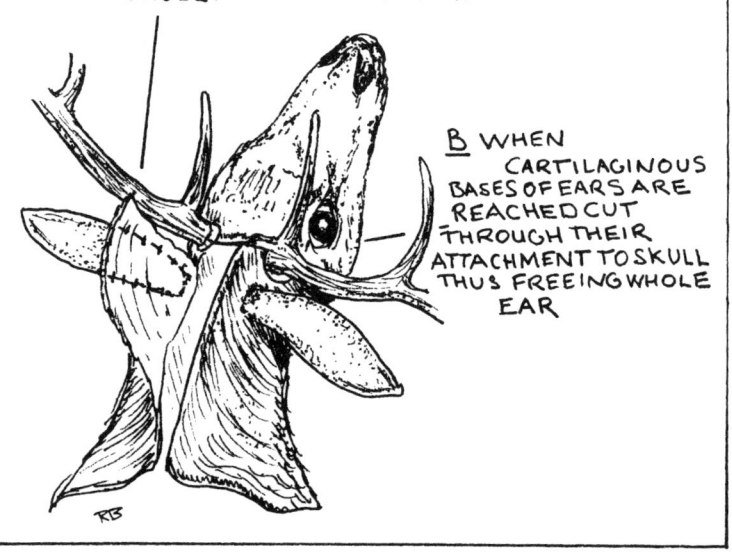

B WHEN CARTILAGINOUS BASES OF EARS ARE REACHED CUT THROUGH THEIR ATTACHMENT TO SKULL THUS FREEING WHOLE EAR

From forest floor to kitchen table 151

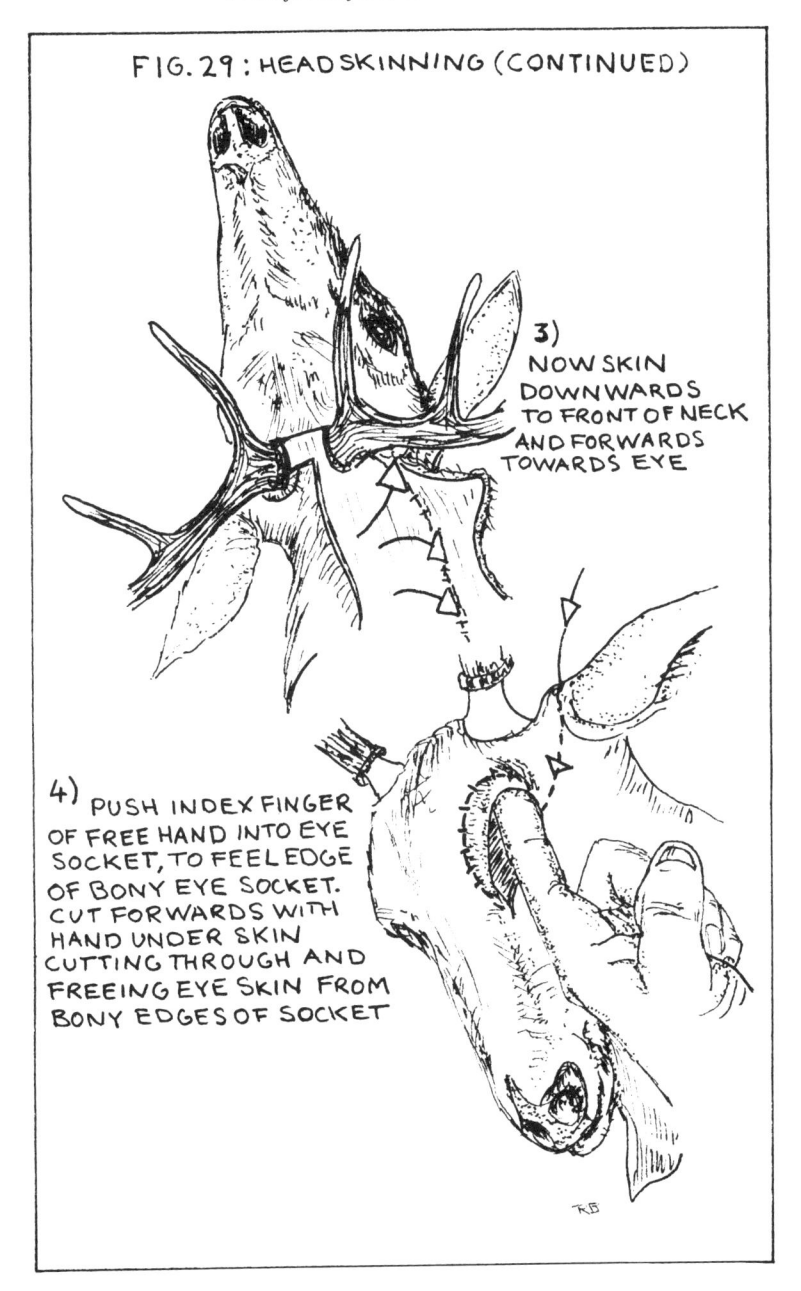

FIG. 29: HEAD SKINNING (CONTINUED)

3) NOW SKIN DOWNWARDS TO FRONT OF NECK AND FORWARDS TOWARDS EYE

4) PUSH INDEX FINGER OF FREE HAND INTO EYE SOCKET, TO FEEL EDGE OF BONY EYE SOCKET. CUT FORWARDS WITH HAND UNDER SKIN CUTTING THROUGH AND FREEING EYE SKIN FROM BONY EDGES OF SOCKET

FIG. 30: HEADSKINNING (CONTINUED)

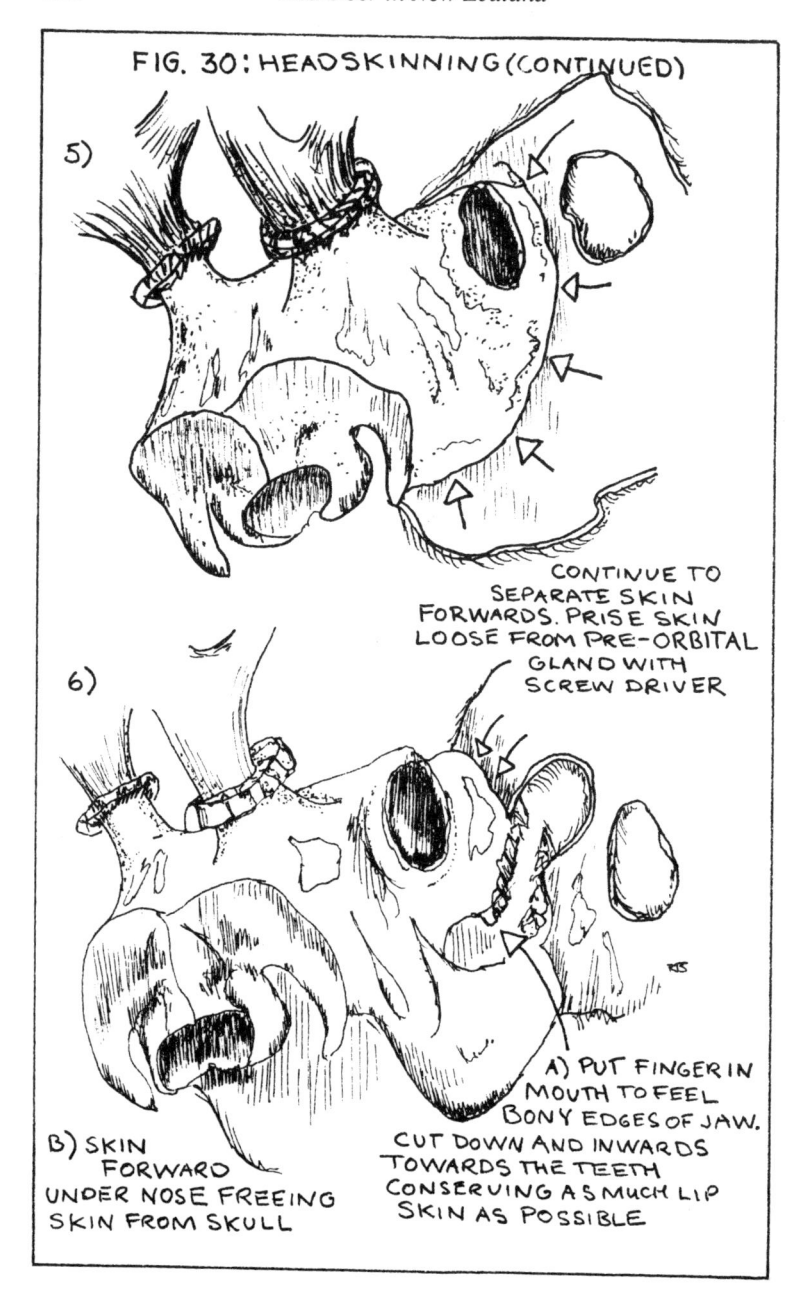

5)

CONTINUE TO SEPARATE SKIN FORWARDS. PRISE SKIN LOOSE FROM PRE-ORBITAL GLAND WITH SCREW DRIVER

6)

A) PUT FINGER IN MOUTH TO FEEL BONY EDGES OF JAW. CUT DOWN AND INWARDS TOWARDS THE TEETH CONSERVING AS MUCH LIP SKIN AS POSSIBLE

B) SKIN FORWARD UNDER NOSE FREEING SKIN FROM SKULL

FIG. 31: FLENGEING OUT HEADSKIN

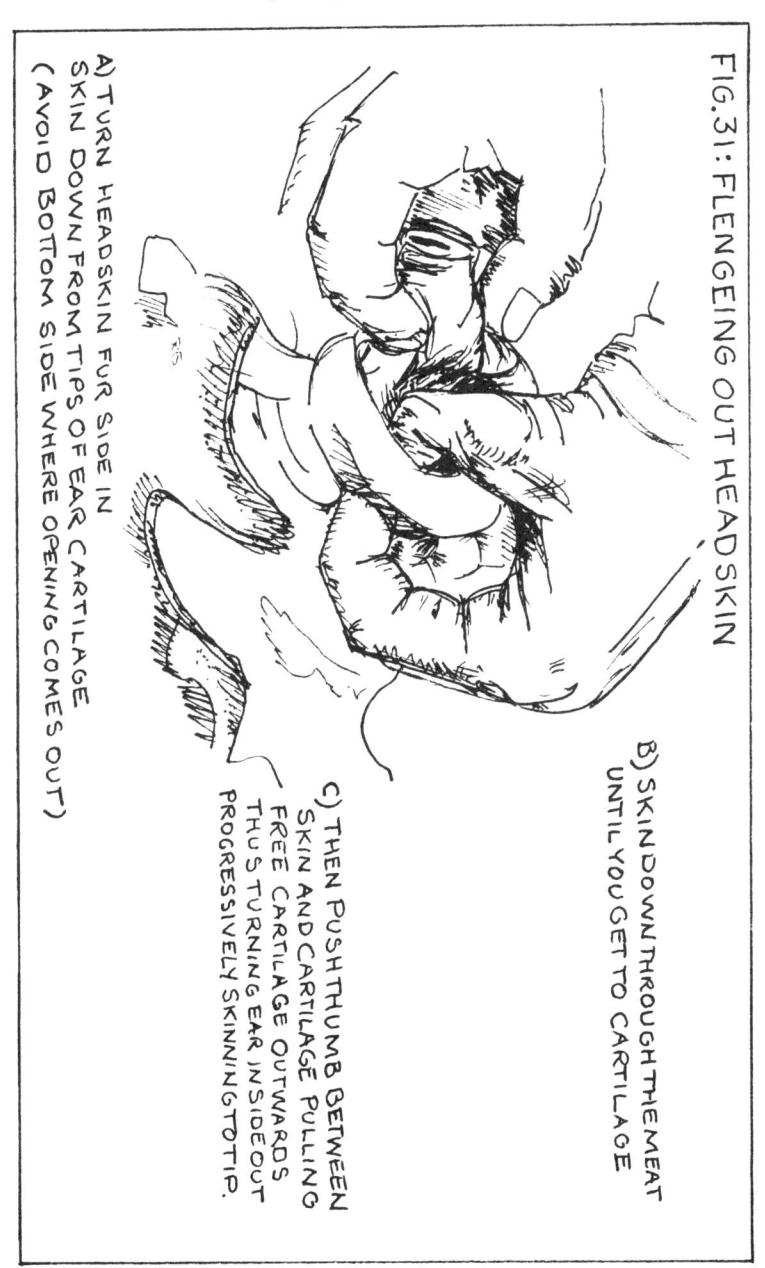

A) TURN HEADSKIN FUR SIDE IN. SKIN DOWN FROM TIPS OF EAR CARTILAGE (AVOID BOTTOM SIDE WHERE OPENING COMES OUT)

B) SKIN DOWN THROUGH THE MEAT UNTIL YOU GET TO CARTILAGE

C) THEN PUSH THUMB BETWEEN SKIN AND CARTILAGE PULLING FREE CARTILAGE OUTWARDS THUS TURNING EAR INSIDE OUT PROGRESSIVELY SKINNING TO TIP.

FIG. 32: QUARTERING (SEE ALSO FIG. 33)

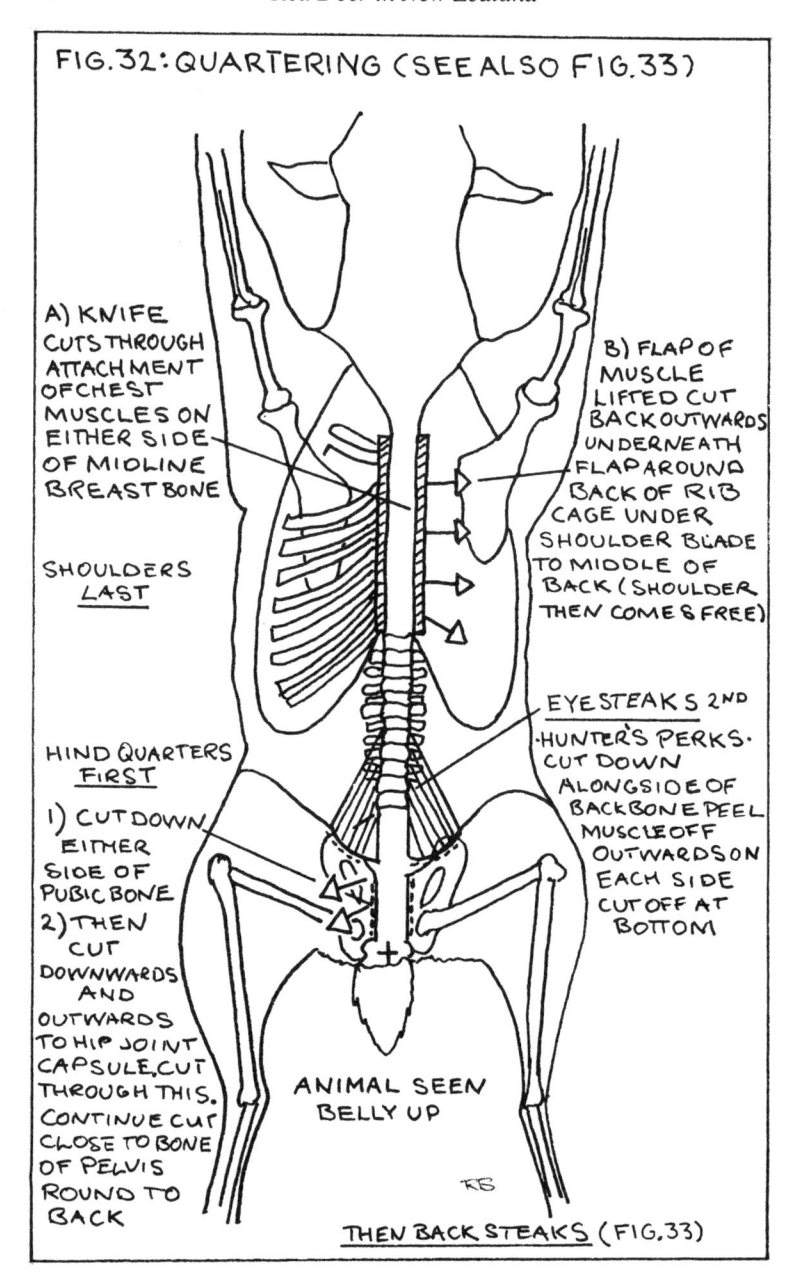

A) KNIFE CUTS THROUGH ATTACHMENT OF CHEST MUSCLES ON EITHER SIDE OF MIDLINE BREAST BONE

SHOULDERS LAST

B) FLAP OF MUSCLE LIFTED CUT BACK OUTWARDS UNDERNEATH FLAP AROUND BACK OF RIB CAGE UNDER SHOULDER BLADE TO MIDDLE OF BACK (SHOULDER THEN COMES FREE)

HIND QUARTERS FIRST

1) CUT DOWN EITHER SIDE OF PUBIC BONE
2) THEN CUT DOWNWARDS AND OUTWARDS TO HIP JOINT CAPSULE, CUT THROUGH THIS. CONTINUE CUT CLOSE TO BONE OF PELVIS ROUND TO BACK

EYE STEAKS 2ND
·HUNTER'S PERKS·
CUT DOWN ALONGSIDE OF BACKBONE PEEL MUSCLE OFF OUTWARDS ON EACH SIDE CUT OFF AT BOTTOM

ANIMAL SEEN BELLY UP

THEN BACK STEAKS (FIG. 33)

FIG. 33: QUARTERING (CONTINUED)

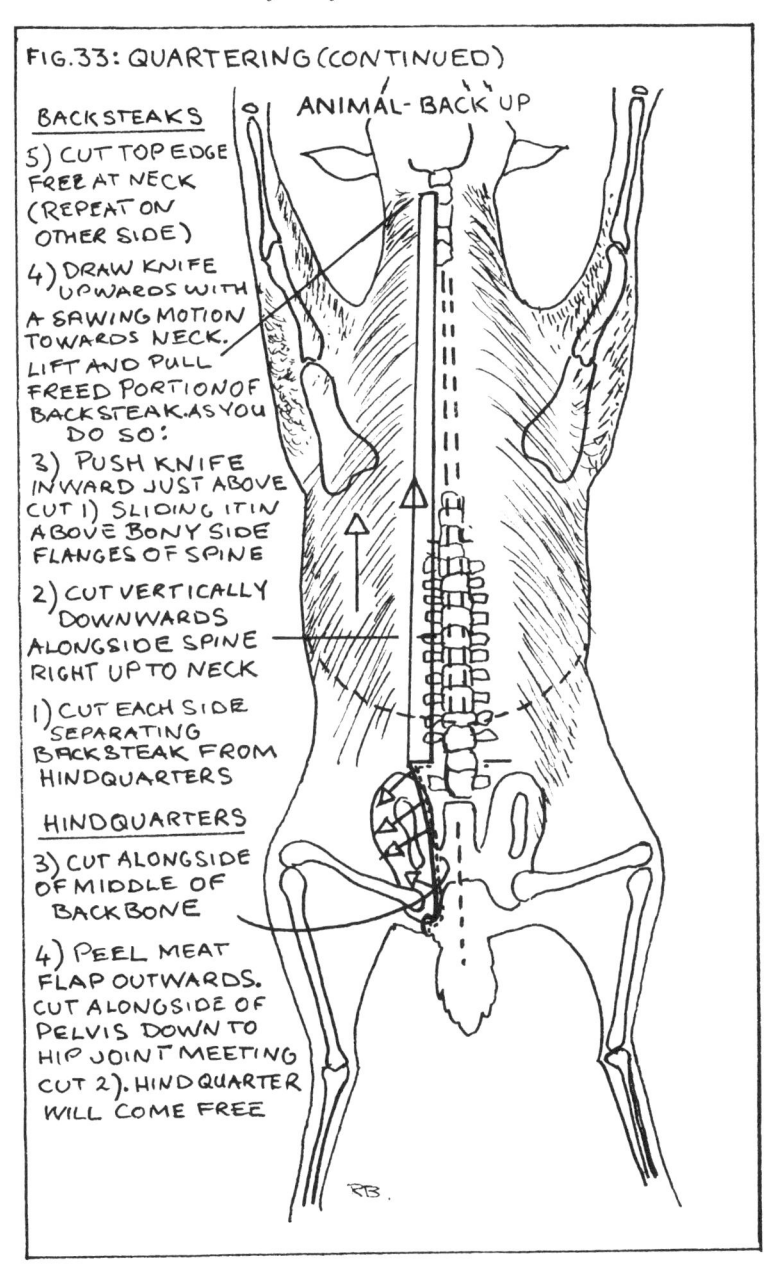

ANIMAL - BACK UP

BACKSTEAKS

5) CUT TOP EDGE FREE AT NECK (REPEAT ON OTHER SIDE)

4) DRAW KNIFE UPWARDS WITH A SAWING MOTION TOWARDS NECK. LIFT AND PULL FREED PORTION OF BACKSTEAK AS YOU DO SO.

3) PUSH KNIFE INWARD JUST ABOVE CUT 1) SLIDING IT IN ABOVE BONY SIDE FLANGES OF SPINE

2) CUT VERTICALLY DOWNWARDS ALONGSIDE SPINE RIGHT UP TO NECK

1) CUT EACH SIDE SEPARATING BACKSTEAK FROM HINDQUARTERS

HINDQUARTERS

3) CUT ALONGSIDE OF MIDDLE OF BACKBONE

4) PEEL MEAT FLAP OUTWARDS. CUT ALONGSIDE OF PELVIS DOWN TO HIP JOINT MEETING CUT 2). HINDQUARTER WILL COME FREE

Boning-out and preserving

Boning-out a leg of venison means removing the meat from the bone. The bone can be discarded to reduce the weight. Fig. 34 shows how to bone-out both front and back legs.

One advantage of boning-out meat is that it can be more readily preserved under the cool waters of a mountain stream away from blowflies and wasps. Fig. 35 shows how to do this with two good quality plastic bags. If the liver, kidneys or heart are being kept this way, store them in a separate bag or they may taint the other meat.

A whole carcass can be conserved by opening it up to the air and hanging it high in a tree where a breeze is more likely (see Fig. 35). A breeze will help to keep the flies away and also dry the exposed meat more quickly to give it a tough surface skin which is more resistant to fly blow.

I'd been in the hunting block, in one of my favourite spots in the Ruahine Ranges, for four days and had little to show for it except lack of sleep! First I had eliminated the river flats as a source of venison. The flats were so free of sign you wouldn't think there were any deer for miles. The spring flush was long gone even for the silly spikers. Next I'd tried the high tops at dawn and dusk, hunting into the wind along the bushline. On the morning of the second day I'd had a bit of luck. As I made my way down a ridge that bore only a thin strip of tussock along the top of its otherwise bush-clad spine, at a range of 75 metres I spied a spiker which was grazing a small swampy basin. The stalk had been simple and the shot true. As I was skinning out the beast, I had said to myself that this was where they were and a good few more would follow. Three stalks later I was less confident. Most of the high country around my campsite had been covered. I had spied no further animals, not even any loners, like the spiker, outside the protection of a hind group or stag company.

The next morning I had tried stalking the bush, varying my height from midway up the steep slopes to just under the bushline. It had been a waste of time for two reasons. Firstly, the undergrowth was tinder-dry and impossible to stalk quietly — true "cornflakes" conditions. Secondly, again there was no decent

From forest floor to kitchen table 157

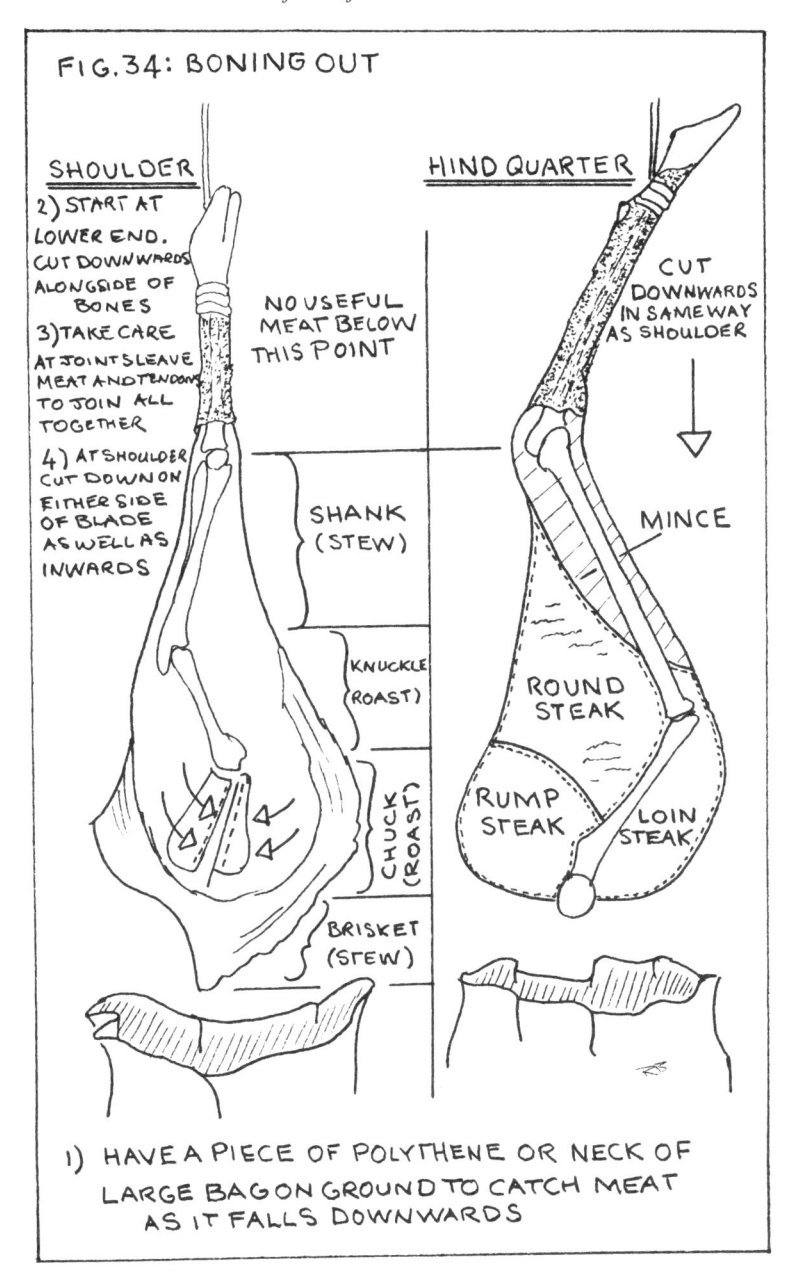

FIG. 34: BONING OUT

SHOULDER

2) START AT LOWER END. CUT DOWNWARDS ALONGSIDE OF BONES
3) TAKE CARE AT JOINTS LEAVE MEAT AND TENDONS TO JOIN ALL TOGETHER
4) AT SHOULDER CUT DOWN ON EITHER SIDE OF BLADE AS WELL AS INWARDS

NO USEFUL MEAT BELOW THIS POINT

SHANK (STEW)

KNUCKLE (ROAST)

CHUCK (ROAST)

BRISKET (STEW)

HIND QUARTER

CUT DOWNWARDS IN SAME WAY AS SHOULDER

MINCE

ROUND STEAK

RUMP STEAK

LOIN STEAK

1) HAVE A PIECE OF POLYTHENE OR NECK OF LARGE BAG ON GROUND TO CATCH MEAT AS IT FALLS DOWNWARDS

FIG. 35: PRESERVING THE MEAT

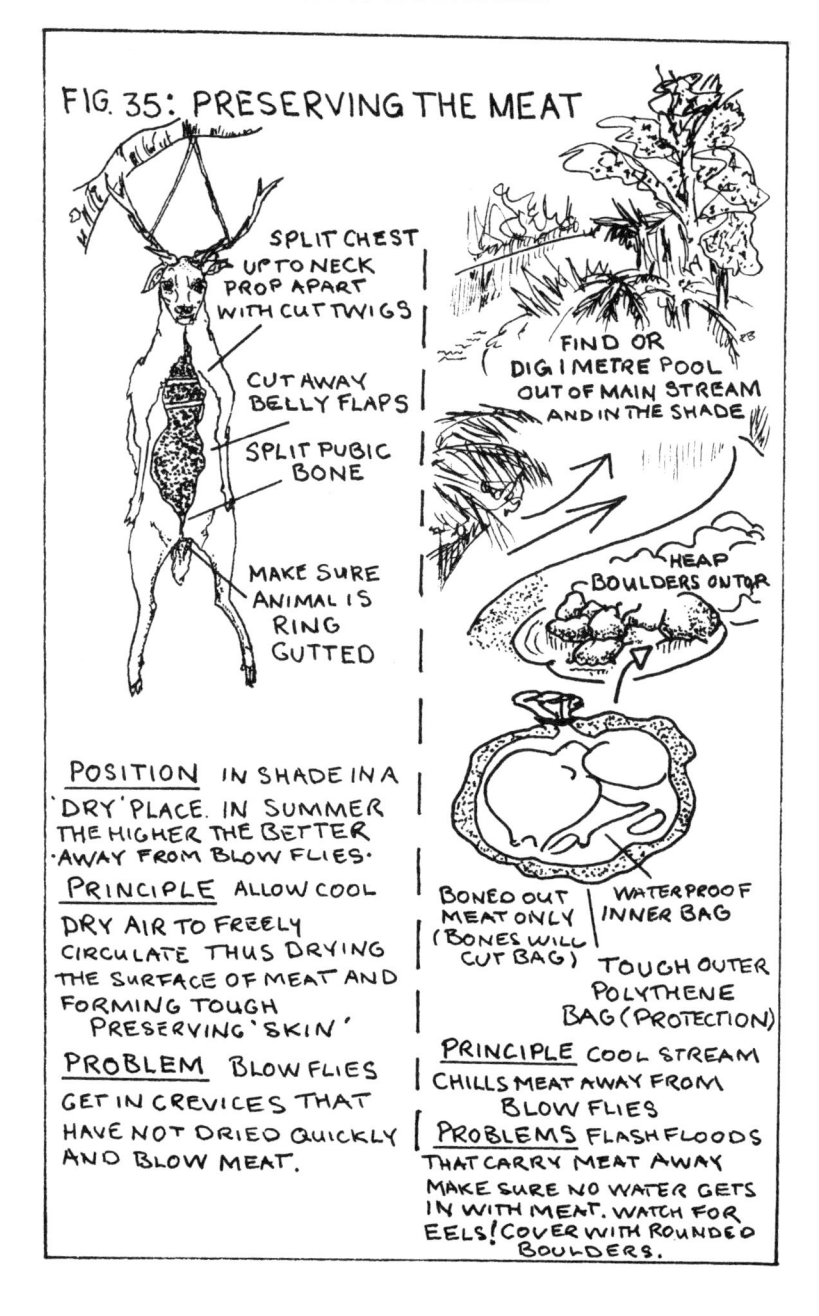

SPLIT CHEST UP TO NECK PROP APART WITH CUT TWIGS

CUT AWAY BELLY FLAPS

SPLIT PUBIC BONE

MAKE SURE ANIMAL IS RING GUTTED

FIND OR DIG 1 METRE POOL OUT OF MAIN STREAM AND IN THE SHADE

HEAP BOULDERS ON TOP

POSITION IN SHADE IN A 'DRY' PLACE. IN SUMMER THE HIGHER THE BETTER AWAY FROM BLOW FLIES.

PRINCIPLE ALLOW COOL DRY AIR TO FREELY CIRCULATE THUS DRYING THE SURFACE OF MEAT AND FORMING TOUGH PRESERVING 'SKIN'

PROBLEM BLOW FLIES GET IN CREVICES THAT HAVE NOT DRIED QUICKLY AND BLOW MEAT.

BONED OUT MEAT ONLY (BONES WILL CUT BAG)

WATERPROOF INNER BAG

TOUGH OUTER POLYTHENE BAG (PROTECTION)

PRINCIPLE COOL STREAM CHILLS MEAT AWAY FROM BLOW FLIES

PROBLEMS FLASH FLOODS THAT CARRY MEAT AWAY MAKE SURE NO WATER GETS IN WITH MEAT. WATCH FOR EELS! COVER WITH ROUNDED BOULDERS.

amount of fresh sign. I lay in my fly camp at midday, dozing and wondering where the hell the deer could be. My helicopter pilot friend who had flown me in talked about a little side creek not far upstream from my campsite, saying that he had seen a bit of deer sign while flying over it the previous week. I wasn't too hopeful of the prospects in that little gully. Having shot this area a good few times, I had tentatively explored most side creeks, including the one he had mentioned. As far as I could remember this particular creek had not seemed very promising, as it led into a steep-sided gorge after the first 50 metres of its boulder-strewn run. Nevertheless, I decided to give it a go. There seemed to be nowhere else worthy of exploration and I also remembered how cool it had been in the deep cleft when I last explored it. The weather was at present particularly hot and had been so for a good few days. Perhaps the deer were making use of the little valley's coolness.

That evening I ascended the staircase of wet boulders that led from the main river into the side creek's deepening shade. As I climbed I was feeling less and less hopeful. The gorge loomed ahead just as bad as I remembered it and to make matters worse there was a gentle breeze at my back. I quickened my pace, knowing that under these conditions I was in no position to surprise any animals in the valley that lay ahead. At least I had enough time to explore the enclave thoroughly before darkness fell. After half an hour the gorge quite suddenly fell away and I found myself gazing on to a well-marked small flat about 15 metres wide, through the middle of which coursed the now less swiftly flowing stream. This was a definite improvement! The valley walls on either side were, however, as steep as before, just a little more widely separated. I followed the broadening strip of mini "river flat" onwards a further kilometre. Fresh sign was abundant, but it was obvious that any animals coming down to graze would have to do so from above, there being no access down the steep-sided valley walls. This direction was of course the very one up which my scent was busily blowing. There was only one possibility — a bit of a gamble.

I carried on along the flat a little further until I reached a slightly less steep-sided portion. Slinging my rifle, I climbed upwards, feet skidding on the muddy shale of the steep-sided slope. After 15 metres of this shaky going I came up under an eroded bush edge, roots hanging in the wind. Thankfully, I pulled myself up over the rim and sat down, secure in a thicket of young beech. The objective had been achieved. I could see at least a hundred metres ahead, having a bird's-eye view of a generous strip of "river flat". I looked down, just once. It was quite a steep scramble all right. I didn't fancy going down in the dark by torchlight.

Settling down, I prepared for a long wait. It was two hours before the light went completely, one and a half to sunset. I knew I would have to wait at least the latter to find out whether my plan had worked. Looking up I could see the clear blue sky of a calm summer's evening. I sent up a silent supplication that it would last.

All of a sudden, I didn't know where I was any more. I was cold and stiff. Then it all clicked into place, I'd been asleep. Four days of violently disturbed sleep pattern had caught up with me. Gazing around, I could see the light had almost gone; the western sky was a deep maroon. But my plan had worked — the catabatic wind had shifted and blew down the valley into my face. Screwing up my eyes, I peered ahead at the dimly lit flat. I could barely make out anything. Raising my rifle I screwed the vary-power scope's magnification down to zero. Fortunately, it had a good luminosity factor and I intended to make the best use of it. As I raised my rifle to gaze at the farthest point of the flat, my eye caught the smallest movement down on the green expanse immediately below me. Quick as a flash I had those cross-hairs pointed down, and there, looking up at the barrel of my rifle, were two hinds. My four hungry children turn up their noses at venison steaks, but once the meat is converted into sausages, hamburger paste and pies it does not take them long to chew through a beast. Luckily, I was carrying my favourite rifle, a .308 semi-automatic Heckler and Koch. I spent the rest of the hours of darkness gutting, carrying the carcasses back to camp, boning them out, bagging the meat and putting it into the deepest, coolest river pool I could find before the heat of the coming day. The next day? I slept through the whole damned day! — R.L.

10
Ageing: conformation, antlers and teeth

All hunters at some time are surprised at the difference between the carcass of an animal lying on the ground and their impression of what they shot at. Distance and size are hard to estimate, and although telescopic sights provide a clear identification of shape and colour, they distort size.

Age and size are not simply related. The relationship between size and age varies with the quality and quantity of food available. The wild deer of Scotland, for example, seldom grow to be big animals, and yet when some of them were shipped out to Otago in 1871 and liberated they produced a herd of large deer in the ungrazed lands of the South. The age and type of animal can be studied before and after it is shot, as we now describe.

Conformation

Conformation is the way an animal is constructed: the proportions of the various parts. A knowledge of conformation will help you to judge the age and sex of a deer.

The conformation of fawns and young deer changes rapidly as they grow. Their heads change shape. Observe the distance between the front edge of the ear and the front edge of the eye of a fawn, and that between the front edge of the eye and the tip of the nose. In young fawns these two lengths are almost equal — the eye to nose distance is usually only slightly greater than the eye to ear distance. As the animal matures the nasal bones grow relatively faster and change this ratio. By the time the animal is 3 years old the eye to nose distance is one and a half times the eye to ear distance (see Fig. 36).

A young fawn has a round bulbous forehead with a straight nose. As it grows older, the forehead becomes flat and the nose slightly concave.

Fawns have straight backs, but as they grow muscle development in the forequarters changes the contour of the back. The developing forequarter muscles push upwards to make a bulge in the outline of the back, which becomes noticeable in both sexes at 3 to 4 years of age and continues to grow to 6 or 7 years of age. This bulge is most

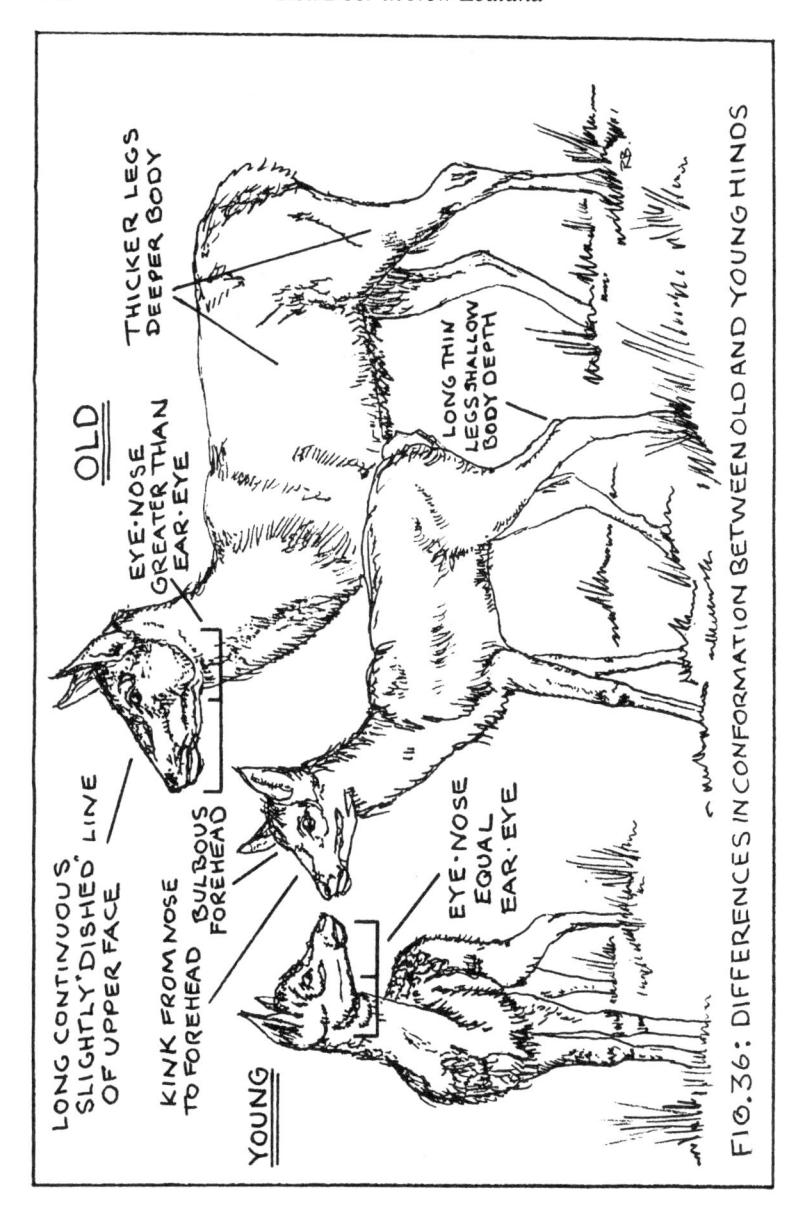

Fig. 36: Differences in conformation between old and young hinds

developed in stags because they develop a greater muscle bulk for fighting.

In early spring, when stags have shed their antlers, you need something other than the presence or absence of antlers to establish the sex of a deer. The shape of the neck is a useful substitute. The neck's contour changes with age and differs between the sexes. Fawns of both sexes begin life with short straight necks, which are only about the same length as the distance from the tip of their nose to their ear. As the animal grows the neck grows relatively faster, to become a long elegant feature of the female. Hinds develop a thin neck, the topside of which shows a continuous curve, which is greatest where the neck joins the shoulder. The underneath of the neck is curved most at its mid-point. Mature hinds have a thin sinuous grace which is especially noticeable when they have their summer coats. Because stags use their necks for carrying antlers and fighting, they develop a thicker, straighter neck. The upper border of their necks, viewed from the side, forms a line which drops to a point below the top of the front shoulders, giving a definite kink in the outline of a stag's back. The underside of a stag's neck is deeper than a hind's and has a bulged, pouched appearance. As a stag grows older its neck becomes progressively thicker, especially near the base. During the rut the stag's neck swells.

A stag goes through a number of other changes as it matures, and the ability to estimate a stag's maturity from a distance is a useful skill. The older a stag, the lower the head is carried when walking or standing. Fig. 37 shows how the angle between the top of the muzzle and the ground progressively changes from about 30 degrees to about 60 degrees as the stag ages.

The stag's body conformation also changes with age. Initially, as we have seen, shoulder muscle development is poor but hindquarters are large and powerful. Young stags are therefore "back heavy". With age, as the shoulder muscles develop and the hindquarter muscles shrink, the animal becomes "front heavy".

Estimating a stag's age from the headskin

To estimate the age of a recently shot stag, or a mounted trophy that has its original headskin, the colour and form of the hair of the forehead between the front of the antlers and the bridge of the nose can be used. (See Fig. 38.):

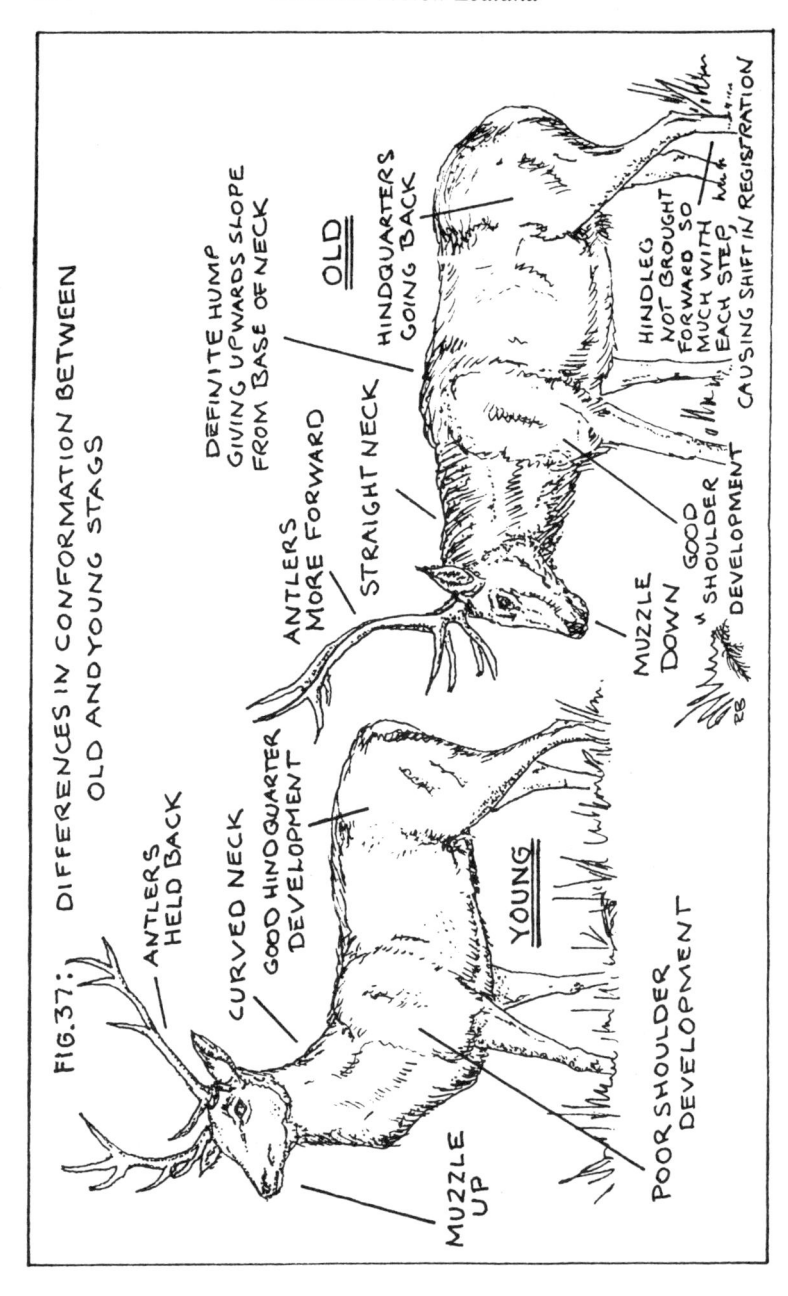

FIG. 37: DIFFERENCES IN CONFORMATION BETWEEN OLD AND YOUNG STAGS

FIG. 38: ESTIMATING A STAG'S AGE FROM THE HEADSKIN

10 YEARS PLUS
ALL HAIR OF FOREHEAD STRAIGHT AND GREY

8-10 YEARS:
POORLY DEFINED CURLY PATCH NOW GREYING

3 TO 4 YEARS:
WEDGE-SHAPED AREA OF CURLY ERECT HAIRS

5 TO 7 YEARS:
POINT OF WEDGE BLUNTS AND RECEDES

1 TO 2 YEARS:
FLAT HAIRED AREA EXTENDS FROM BASE OF ANTLERS TOWARDS NOSE

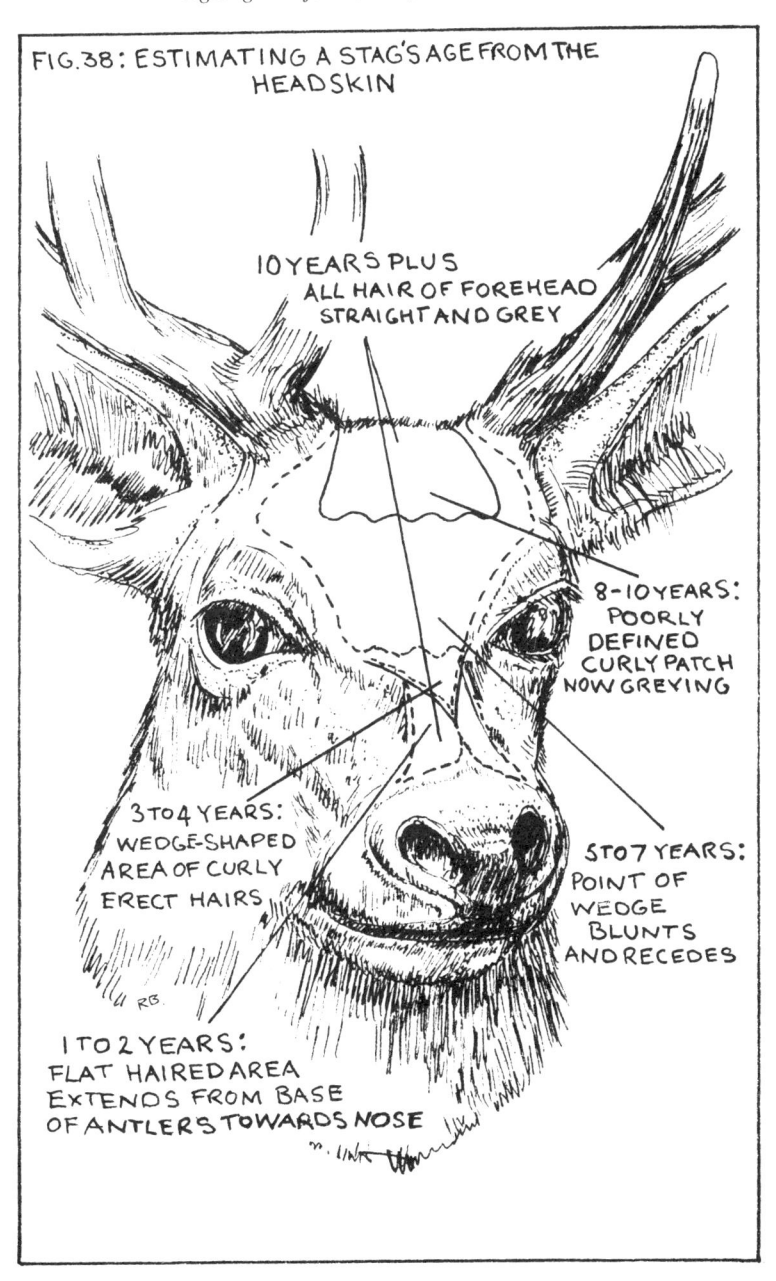

- 1 to 2 years old: dark, even-coloured hair lying flat from the base of the antlers towards the nose.
- 3 to 4 years old: a wedge-shaped region of curly and upstanding hair.
- 5 to 7 years old: the point of the wedge begins to lose its sharpness and becomes a transition zone as the area of long curly hair recedes upwards.
- 8 to 10 years old: the patch of curly hair now has poor definition and hair begins to turn grey.
- 10 years plus: the hair is now straight and grey, and a few grey hairs grow on the muzzle.

Antlers

The way deer grow and then shed large external bones every year is an extraordinary natural phenomenon which has prompted a lot of scientific interest.

The points on the top of the skull from which the antlers grow are called the "pedicles". Newly born male and female fawns show no difference in the shape or feel of their skulls. At 6 months of age two definite bumps can be felt on the top of a male fawn's skull, which indicates the start of the growth of the pedicles. If a female fawn is given injections of the male hormone testosterone, she will develop pedicles and subsequent antlers; if a male fawn is castrated at birth, thus stopping testosterone production, he will not develop pedicles. Although the antlers are shed each year, the pedicles remain unchanged. Damage to a pedicle will result either in the development of a deformed antler every year, or the total loss of the ability to produce an antler.

The flat top of the pedicle is called the "table". The table has the blueprint for the design of the antler, and it is from here the antler grows. Occasionally something is wrong with the blueprint and no antler develops. Such antler-less stags, known as "hummels", are sexually developed in all other respects.

After an old antler falls off, a ring of dark hairy skin containing a lot of blood vessels grows over the site of the old antler. This "velvet" deposits a rubbery cartilaginous substance underneath its surface, which gradually accumulates to produce progressively enlarging antlers. The diameter of the velvet never increases after it is first laid down; the antlers grow only at the growing tips. Thus, on stags with

Ageing: conformation, antlers and teeth

even short growths of velvet, the thickness of the base of the finished antlers can be seen. The rubbery cartilaginous structures are transformed into strong bone by the deposit of large quantities of calcium salts, which also progressively block up the blood vessels and so restrict the flow of blood through the velvet. The last thing to form, the coronet at the base of each antler, is a final ring of calcium in the style of a tourniquet, which totally blocks all blood flow to the velvet. When this happens what is left of the velvet dies and is shed, to reveal the dead bone underneath, which of course is the new antler ready to be polished up by its proud owner. The structure and nomenclature of a fully grown antler is show in Fig. 39.

The time at which stags shed their antlers and start to grow new ones is governed by day length. The antlers are used in the autumn rut and are kept during the winter before being shed in spring. They must be shed for the continued health of the animal. As they are made of bone that lacks blood vessels to keep it alive, the antlers begin to rot almost from the day they are completed. This rot will

FIG. 39: ANTLER NOMENCLATURE

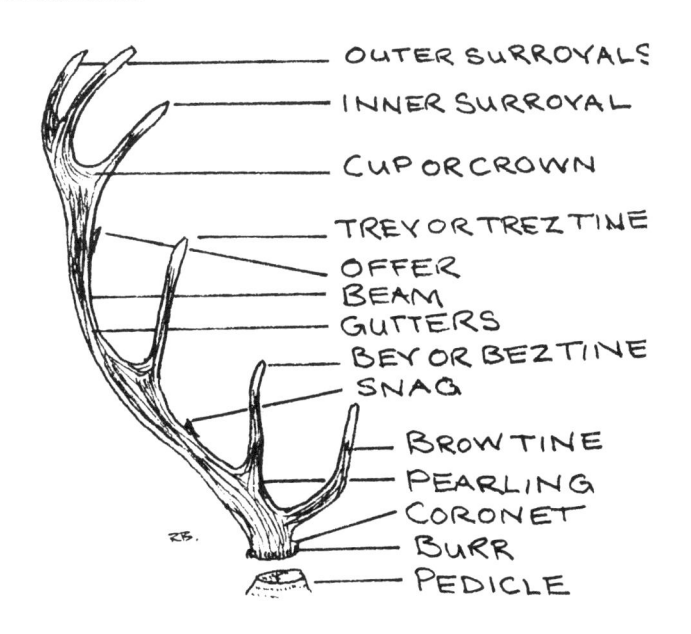

- OUTER SURROYALS
- INNER SURROYAL
- CUP OR CROWN
- TREY OR TREZ TINE
- OFFER
- BEAM
- GUTTERS
- BEY OR BEZ TINE
- SNAG
- BROW TINE
- PEARLING
- CORONET
- BURR
- PEDICLE

spread into the bones of the stag's skull if the antlers are retained.

Shedding is quick. When the blood level of testosterone declines below a certain level, special bone-dissolving cells are triggered. These cut inwards, forming a clean disc shape at the base of each antler just above the pedicle.

As the stag matures the antlers are shed earlier each year until adulthood, when they are shed in early September. Therefore the date of shedding of antlers can be used to judge an animal's age.

Estimating the age of a stag from the size and shape of antlers is difficult in practice. The variability of quantity and quality of food, together with the inherent characteristics of the particular animal, create a complex of interacting effects. If feed is adequate, a stag will increase the size of its antlers each year until old age when they will "go back", that is, they become smaller and misshapen. In Scotland, feed conditions, though generally poorer, are perhaps more uniform than in New Zealand, where variable springs produce wide variation in available feed in different years. As a result Scottish stags appear to display a more reliable relationship between age and size of antlers.

Scottish hunters have categorised antlers according to the age of stags. They have also named each stage of the beast's growth, which we don't do in New Zealand. The Scottish names for female deer 1, 2, 3 and 4 years old respectively are: calf, hearst, young hind and hind. Below we give the Scottish categories for antlers and age. New Zealand names for deer are given, with the Scottish stag names included in parentheses.

1st year: fawn (calf) — pedicles after 6 months.
2nd year: spiker (brocket) — two upright straight horns.
3rd year: young stag (pricket) — uprights, brow tines.
4th year: stag (staggart) — uprights, brow tines, bez tines.
5th year: 8-pointer (stag) — uprights, brow tines, bez tines, trez tines.
6th year: 10-pointer (warrantable stag) — uprights, brow tines, bez tines, two trez tines.

Antlers have a very complex structure. At a microscopic level a series of elastic fibres are surrounded by carefully placed crystals of calcium bone. The fibres provide strength along the lines of stress and the crystals provide hardness, a structure similar to that of carbon-fibre, reinforced, glass ply fishing rod. The result is a light structure with great strength and flexibility under load.

The essence of a stag fight in the rut is a pushing match between the two animals. The antlers ensure that the two contestants are efficiently locked together so that the contest is more a trial of sustained strength than one of skill or chance advantage. The brow tines function as eye guards to prevent the opponent's bez tines slipping down and causing eye damage. The bez, and all other forward-facing tines branching from the main beam, act as engaging and interlocking points with the opponent's antlers. This interlocking mechanism is efficient and largely trouble free. Two rutting stags can engage and disengage swiftly and only rarely do stags become permanently locked together.

Antlers travel well in the bush because when the stag throws his head back the tips of the tines all point backwards, so that passing vines and branches slide over without becoming entangled. Stags can travel rapidly along densely overgrown trails with their heads thrown back.

The average weight of a mature set of antlers is about 2.5 kilograms in New Zealand, which means that a lot of calcium-rich vegetation must be consumed. The various liberations of deer in this country have given us a number of genetic lineages from which our present-day deer are derived. Some herds have the potential to grow better antlers than others because of their breeding, but they must always have good food to realise this potential.

Ageing

The most accurate way to age deer is by examining their teeth. Deer have two sets of teeth in their life, just as we do. As deer get older their milk teeth fall out, their main (permanent) teeth appear and then these begin to wear down in a predictable pattern.

The outside of a tooth is made of white enamel, underneath which is a soft layer of yellow dentine and then a subsidiary layer of browner dentine. The enamel is hard and wears slowly to show first the yellow dentine and then the brown.

A tooth is higher on its sides that at the centre. The crowning enamel wears quickly away to expose a strip of dentine along each side of the top of the tooth. As the wearing continues the layers of dentine are exposed with a corrugated appearance, rather like corrugated iron, the corrugations running at right angles to the jaw bone.

The dentition of the upper and lower jaws of deer and the names of the teeth are shown in Fig. 40. The front teeth (incisors) are used for biting off vegetation and the molars and premolars for cudding.

FIG. 40: SKULL OF RED DEER SHOWING DENTITION

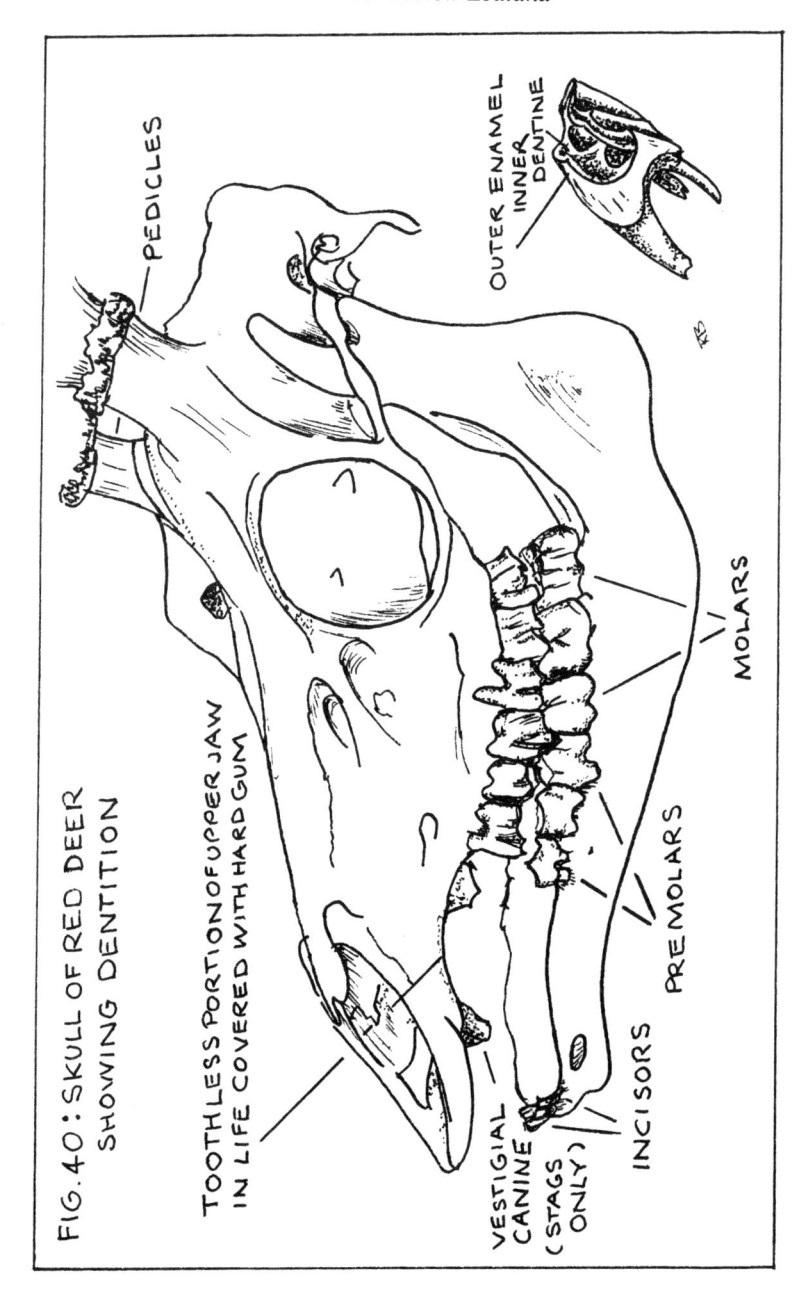

Ageing: conformation, antlers and teeth

Deer wear their three premolars down first in the order 1st, 2nd, 3rd followed by the 1st, 2nd, 3rd molars, because as each chewing tooth wears down it allows more wear on the tooth behind.

The dental formula gives the number of teeth in each half of both jaws in the pattern upper jaw/lower jaw. So "incisors 0/3" means no incisor teeth in each half of the upper jaw and three in each half of the lower jaw. Red deer have the dental formula: incisors 0/3; canines 0/1 (female) or 1/1 (male); premolars 3/3; molars 3/3.

The formula shows that stags have an extra canine tooth in their upper jaw.

The table below shows dental wear with age in the lower jaw of deer. You can use this table to work out accurately the age of the animal.

Age	1st PM	2nd PM	3rd PM	1st molar	2nd molar	3rd molar
4 months	+(double)	+(double)	+(treble)			
8 months	+	+	+	X(double)		
10 months	+	+	+	X	X(double)	
2 years	X	X	+	X	X	X(treble)
2yr 6mth	X y/d	X y/d	X y/d	X y/d	X y/d	X y/d 1/6" Chewing edges
3 years	x b/d	X y/d	X y/d	X y/d	X y/d	X y/d 1/8" Chewing edges
4 years	X b/d	X y/d	X y/d	X y/d	X y/d	X y/d PMs not sharp
6 years	Teeth an even broken platform and showing brown dentine, worn cheekside					
8 years	surfaces of all PM smooth flat 1st molar uniform b/d (ub/d) Edge 2+3 molar blunt					
10 years	Xub/d	Xub/d	Xub/d	Xub/d worn	Xb/d all surfaces smooth	Xb/d
14 years	Xub/d	Xub/d	Xub/d	Xub/d worn	Xb/d worn all teeth dentine decay	Xb/d

Key

+	Milk tooth
X	Permanent tooth
y/d	Yellow-brown dentine, visible in longitudinal strips on each tooth.
b/d	Yellow dentine worn to predominantly brown colour.
ub/d	Dentine now worn to uniform plug to tooth edges (not in strips)
Worn	Tooth worn down to just above the gum.

I used to shoot in the Westport area on the West Coast of the South Island. On one side of the Buller River is the road and on the other side the railway line. I used to cross over that formidable river in a rather fragile rubber boat and hunt the dense podocarp forest on the railway line side.

For the first few trips I cheerlessly fought through dense kiekie stands, almost continuously disengaging my woollen balaclava from bush lawyer entanglements and pulling out scratchy flakes of manuka bark that could find their way to the most personal of places. It was a hell of a place to look for deer but I kept looking because they were there in reasonable numbers: I found every sort of fresh sign and could almost hear them laughing at me. One morning I spent 40 minutes quietly sneaking upwind to a spot 50 metres the other side of the railway line where I knew there were deer beds. I found them still warm, but that was all — I just couldn't get there quietly enough to catch the deer before they vanished and I never even heard them steal away.

One crisp Sunday morning I was sitting among the sandflies on the railway line, munching on scroggin after two hours of close encounters of the most frustrating kind, when a red-brown head cautiously surfaced above the green entanglement not 20 metres from me. I sat stock still with my jaw in mid chew as the deer peered intently up then down the track with its radar-like ears scanning for fully two minutes before deciding all was well. It walked purposefully out across the railway sleepers . . . then I moved, face full of scroggin, frantically forcing an unloaded rifle into active service. The bulging-eyed deer stood there for a few crucial moments of indecision before beginning to bound away, taking a few short desperate strides, vainly trying to reach its green sanctuary. But the deer didn't make it, I got my cross-hairs on to that young spiker's back and up to its neck, squeezing the trigger just as the first green tendrils of security began to envelop it. For the first time of hunting that place I had some venison for my pains.

The next weekend I was back, encouraged by my success, to explore more carefully the strip between the railway line and the river. Here I realised the bush was more open and there were belts of catchment board-planted willow, lots of entangled briars but also patches of rank grass. Plenty of deer sign but as usual no deer.

Ageing: conformation, antlers and teeth

Three days later I talked to a railway worker who rode the slow-moving Buller coal trains and who often saw deer on the track in early morning and late evening near the place where I had shot the spiker. I began to put the jigsaw puzzle together. Two more trips and I had it worked out.

The unmodified bush of the area had little of the deers' preferred browsing plants growing but the dense strip above the railway line was a secure place to hide up in during the day and was only a stone's throw away from the best local feed available, which was the rank grass and willows below the line. It was a simple matter to walk the railway line to find their favourite crossing places, hide up just off the track at the times when they made their way from bed to feed or vice versa, and then simply show them the way to my deep freeze! — *R.L.*

11
Red deer evolution: grass or tree eaters?

All life on earth depends ultimately upon the ability of plants to trap energy from the sun. Animals eat plants and other animals survive by eating these animals, an example of a food chain. Deer are herbivores and they in turn provide food for carnivores.

The theory of evolution is an explanation of the process of species changing over time. By undergoing change, species are able to occupy "vacant" biological niches. Fossil records show that the adaptation of species to their new niches has resulted in ever-larger numbers of species, each new one tending to be more specialised.

Deer and cattle have a common primitive ancestor. These ancestors were wide-ranging feeders: they were able to survive equally well on a diet of trees, herbs or grasses.

An expanding population of this primitive herbivore species would have created intense competition among the individual animals for the available food. Some individuals might, for example, have been born taller than normal, enabling them to survive better in the forest as they could reach up higher than others. In times of scarcity these animals could survive while the others might starve. The ones that survived were able to breed and so pass on their genes and rear taller offspring. These forest-adapted herbivores were the ancestors of modern deer, the Cervidae.

Other individuals might have had larger flatter teeth more suited to grazing the short grasses of the open grasslands, giving them a survival advantage outside the forest. These animals were the ancestors of the modern cattle and antelopes, the Bovidae.

Fig. 41 shows the evolutionary tree of deer. Fossil records show that the earliest primitive deer were a lot like the rare and endangered musk deer of Asia. Musk deer, shy, solitary animals, live deep in the forest, have no antlers and weigh only 10 to 15 kg. They are known as "concentrate" feeders because they eat only carefully selected fruits and the growing shoots of plants, both of which are rich in nourishment, in contrast to grass which is low in energy and needs to be eaten in bulk. During evolution, some deer developed larger

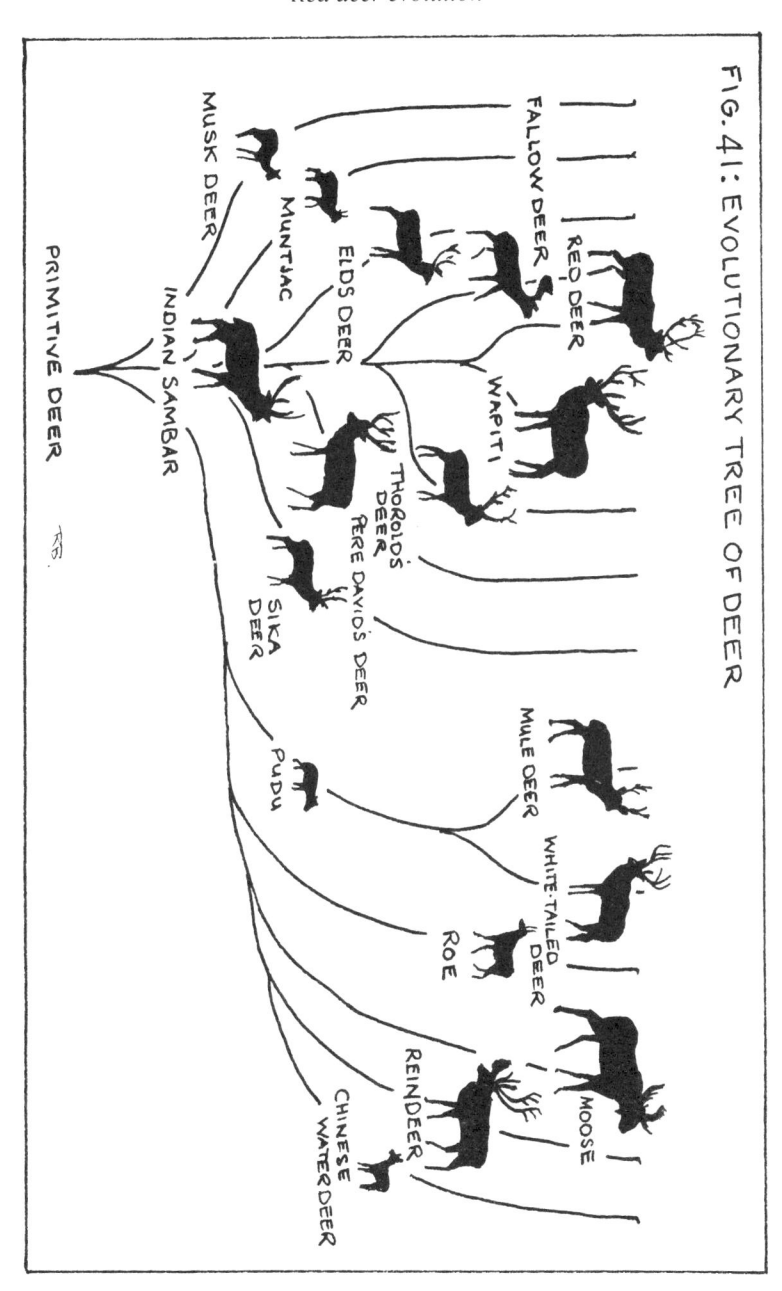

FIG. 41: EVOLUTIONARY TREE OF DEER

stomachs than the norm, and with the aid of specialised bacteria and other micro-organisms living in their stomachs, were able to eat and digest the less nutritious leaves and coarse grasses of the forest floor. In times of food shortage in the forest, these animals were able to venture out on to the grasslands and behave as grass eaters in competition with the Bovidae.

A study of the stomachs of the various deer species of the world reveals how far down this particular evolutionary path each species has come. Some species, like the white-tailed deer, have not evolved much further than their musk deer-like ancestor: they are concentrate feeders and have a relatively small, simple stomach. Other deer, like the fallow and sambar, have larger stomachs that are more able to handle roughage. Fig. 42 categorises deer species according to their feeding habits, and shows red deer to be about midway between the two extremes.

The red deer's stomach can digest fresh young grass but cannot cope with mature dry summer grass. This enables the animal to come out on to grasslands in times of food shortage in the forest, and is probably why this species is so successful.

The stomachs of stags are better able to handle a diet of greater bulk and poorer quality than hinds, which means the stags can live on poorer areas and leave the most nutritious areas to the females. And when a herd of red deer expand into new territory, the hinds stay on the areas of good concentrated nourishment while the bulk-feeding, wider-ranging stags take the risks of exploring new country first. Stags can take such risks because if a few of them die it does not unduly affect the breeding potential of the herd.

Stomachs, of course, are only one feature of the evolution of deer. Forest-living deer have tended to increase in height and develop long necks to browse higher, features which can be seen in the red deer.

A peculiarity in the evolution of deer has been the development of antlers. Primitive deer did not have them and a few species still lack them: the musk deer and water deer. At the other extreme, the extinct Irish elk had the largest antlers of any deer.

Why did antlers develop? The most popular scientific opinion is that they developed as weapons to improve the competition among males for a harem of females. "Primitive" species of deer that don't have antlers don't hold harems, but instead seek out a single female on heat and guard her secretively in the forest. They live dispersed throughout the forest. In contrast, the more "advanced", harem-holding species live

Red deer evolution 177

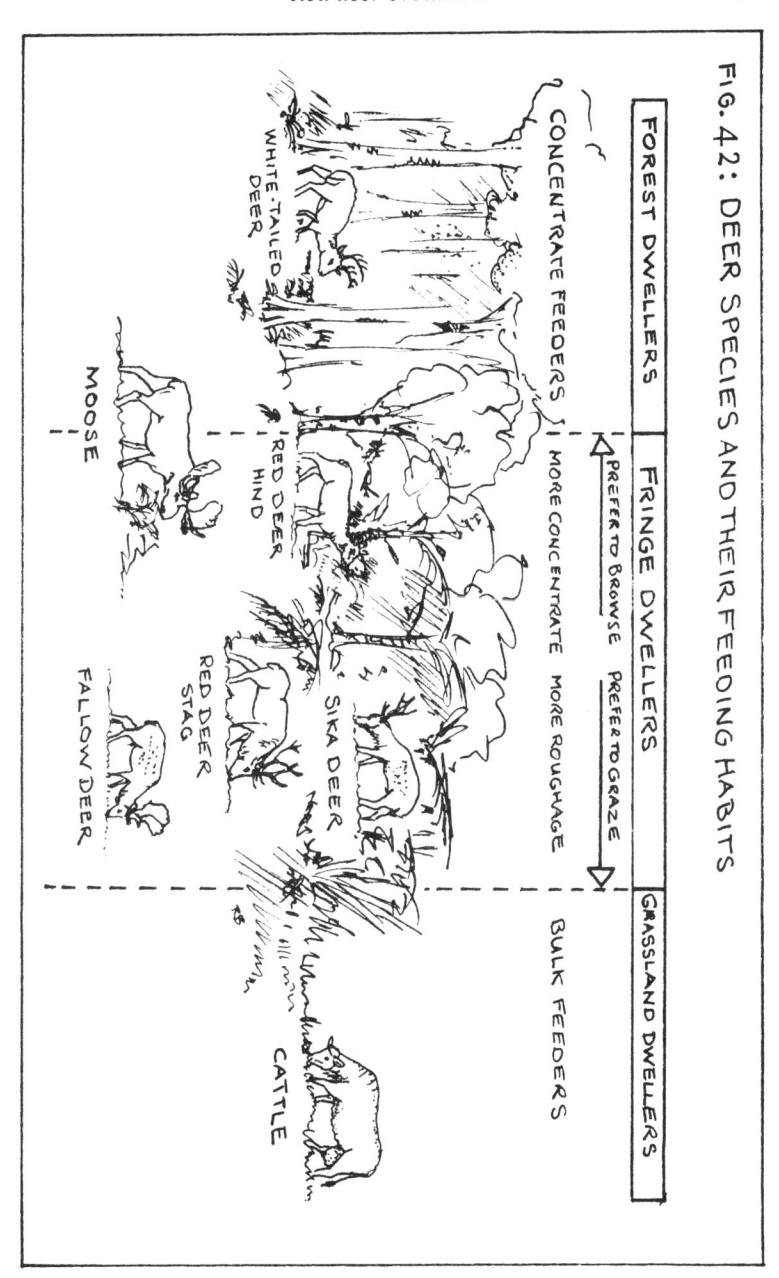

FIG. 42: DEER SPECIES AND THEIR FEEDING HABITS

in groups that concentrate together during the rut. The strongest and fittest stags hold the largest harems and can therefore quickly spread their genes throughout the population. In this way, the best genes are selected and spread throughout the herd. Unfortunately, there is an anomaly in this otherwise neat explanation: for some unknown reason reindeer females also have antlers.

Of all the deer species the red deer, or *Cervus elaphus* in scientific terminology, is perhaps the most versatile. Many species previously classified as separate are now thought to be local variations of *Cervus elaphus*. The Scottish deer (*Cervus elaphus scoticus*) and the Scandinavian deer (*Cervus elaphus elaphus*) are essentially the same, the Scottish deer being a smaller version of the Scandinavian ones. The situation is, however, even more complex. The inability of a species to crossbreed with another is sometimes used by biologists as an indicator of the "separateness" of species. Yet the North American wapiti (*Cervus elaphus canadensis*) has rather disastrously crossbred with the red deer in New Zealand, and wapiti have effectively died out as a separate species in this country. Similarly, red deer and sika deer look to be quite different species, yet they have crossbred in the wild in New Zealand. This does not occur commonly, but over a period of time, as hybrid animals mix in with both populations, a new population of mixed-race animals may arise in the central North Island. Again, experimentally, sambar and sika deer have also been crossbred. It is probably only the difference in height between the two species that prevents this occurring in the wild.

Cervus elaphus has demonstrated a phenomenal ability to adapt and colonise new territory in New Zealand. It now has a new diet of Australasian greenery. Helicopter hunting has made it wary of the tops. All-year-round foot shooting has emphasised its strong nocturnal traits. It grows to a large size because of its freedom from parasites and the abundant feed. Perhaps we should give it the new name of "Cervus elaphus neozelandicus"!

Whatever the name, the modern hunter must be sufficiently versatile and adaptable to match the ever-changing habits of this exceptional species.

I had first discovered it in the spring, and wondered at it. As I was wading through the deep blue-green pools of an unusually low Maropea River, I noticed on the edges of an earthy side bank, the thin, paired, vertical grooves of a deer's toe scrape. They had been made some time ago, covered as they were by spider webs. Nevertheless, I peered over their mute signature to discover a well-marked deer trail leading to a small bush-encrusted flat. I followed the trail away from the water and into the sombre peace of the understorey. I had gone barely 50 metres when I found it, an unusually large wallow, its steep, well-polished clay sides fully 5 metres apart, separated by a stretch of brackish water that still bore a faint taint of its autumn occupants. It might have been well used in the fever of the roar, but I could see by the thin film of algae blooming in its depths that it had not been disturbed since. What caught my imagination, apart from the sheer size of the excavation, was a single well defined set of tracks embossed on the dried mud surrounds.

Even though the animal making them had walked at a leisurely pace showing good front foot on rear registration, the cleave marks of both front and rear prints were well separated, a sign of great weight forcing them apart. Not only were the cleaves well separated, but the rear and front prints showed well the outward and inward rotation that comes only from good body size and condition. Finally, the prints were just plain "big", an article of faith for believers in Donne's rules! I vowed there and then that with the coming of the roar I would return.

It was late March and the rotary wing of Brian Goodwin's Taihape-based "boot-leather saver" had barely set me down before I was off up the river, itching for a look. Yes, he'd been there, and recently too: the water of the wallow now a uniformly opaque chocolate brown, the single trail replaced by a labyrinth of interlacing pathways, all fresh and gleaming wetly. I quietly retraced my steps until a few metres upriver, downwind from the spot, I sat and watched the sun go down, listening all the while for the faintest roar. As I sat, I looked above the little flat at the great scar of a giant shingle fan that started just downstream of the wallow site and wound upwards above it for almost 300 metres. Above it there was barely another 30 metres of beech forest before the summit. Why would a stag come all the way down here to wallow, I asked myself. Then I remembered the hard granite of the upper slopes — not much nice gooey mud up there. The sun was almost down and with the coming of darkness I made my faltering way through wet stones up the river to the hut. As I walked I could feel the first good frost of the season nipping the nape of my neck. Perhaps tomorrow morning?

Getting out of the bag at 4 a.m. was bad enough, but it was doubly difficult that morning with a frost to greet me and the billy water frozen solid. I resolutely gulped my tea and porridge and prised on my socks and boots to hurry down the river well before first light. I sat for a while in my position of the previous evening, waiting until the light came up enough to stalk the bush and see 10 metres ahead. I carefully checked my scope for fogging, all the while listening. Not a sound. As silently as I was able on the frozen stones, I back-tracked up the river until I was 50 metres upstream of the wallow and the slip. The light was improving all the time as I slowly ascended the bush-clad slopes.

By the time I had reached the ridge top the first thin rind of the sun's rising disc was visible over the Sparrowhawk bivouac away to my right. I checked the wind — good, still upstream. Slowly I stalked the ridge top as it ascended to the peak above the slip. I had calculated that on such a morning as this, no well bred stag would be down the valley where the mud was frozen solid, but high, where the frost-cleansed air would carry his lovesick moaning for miles, perhaps from just above the shingle slide, where its natural amphitheatre would best amplify the sound. As I approached the thin fringe of bush above the slip I slowed, especially cautious. A few metres into it I stopped astride the ridge and listened — still nothing. Carefully I unzipped my waist pack and removed the roarer. Perhaps at this early date encouragement was needed. I gave a single quite short but loud moan. Almost immediately from below me, right from where I judged the rim of the slip to be, came a deep guttural reply, then a long silence. I was tempted to descend towards the source of the sound, but knew that trick. Some 5 years previously I had been in just such a position as this in the Paringa. I had spent a good hour roaring a stag to the ridge top only to have him sucker me into descending a scant 10 metres to meet him. That had been enough for him to sneak around above me and cut my wind. The last I had heard of him had been a sharp alarm bark. The silence continued. I was beginning to question whether I had heard the answering call at all. I cautiously let out another moan. Again, and closer this time, a single answer. I judged him to be about 50 metres away at least, for I could hear no sound of his approach. Another long long wait. Ten minutes went by. All the while the sun was coming up. Finally in desperation I gave just one more roar. Even as the first sound was groaning out, I knew I'd blown it! Almost simultaneous with its start, gazing over the top of my roarer, I glimpsed a heavily antlered head emerge from behind the bulk of a stunted beech not 10 metres distant. I valiantly completed my rendition half knowing that at that distance he couldn't fail to pick me as a fake. As I dropped the tube the head disappeared and with an accompanying "Baugh" he was gone. I walked to the spot where he had stood and examined the print. Yes he was almost certainly the same stag that had occupied the wallow. His defences, honed by thousands of years' evolution, held a good few tricks I had yet to learn. — R.L.

Glossary

abomasum compartment of a ruminant's stomach which receives the cudded food from the omasium and in which digestion begins.

anal glands pair of dark oily structures inside the tail on either side of the gristle. They are the source of a powerful scent used in sexual advertising and boundary marking during the rut. Also called tail glands.

antlers bony outgrowths produced by the pedicles on the skull in male deer (and female reindeer). Renewed annually, these structures are used in combat during the rut.

ball prominent rounded area of projecting spongy material in the heel portion of each cleave. More prominent in stags.

bark short resonant noise made by deer when alarmed.

beam main antler upright which bears the tines.

bez tine second forward-facing tine at the base of each antler. Used for interlocking with an opponent's antlers in combat.

Bovidae family of ruminant herbivores that are primarily grazers. All have hollow permanent horns, not antlers. Includes sheep, cattle, antelopes and buffalo.

boxing technique of fighting used by deer of the same sex who are in dispute in a pecking order. Hinds often box one another. Stags do also, particularly when in velvet. Contestants rear up on their hind legs and approach each other with downward-kicking forelegs.

brocket Scottish name for a spiker.

browse eat the leaves of shrubs and trees.

brow tine first forward-facing tine at the base of each antler. Its function is to interlock with the opponent's antler in combat and to protect the eyes.

bulk feeder animal with a herbage diet of low nutrition and high bulk, primarily of grass and herbs.

canine teeth these teeth are non-functional in herbivores, but well developed in meat-eating animals. In the lower jaw of deer they are "disguised" as incisors. Absent in the upper jaw of hinds and non-functional "tushes" in stags. Often collected by hunters for sale (the Japanese buy them for jewellery).

calf Scottish name for a fawn.

calving bellow noise made by a hind at the moment of giving birth. Reminiscent of cattle lowing, only more high pitched.

catabatic wind light winds created by the warming and cooling effect of the ground upon its overlaying air. In the day the sun-warmed ground heats the air above, the air becomes less dense and rises as an up-hill and up-valley breeze. An opposite wind is created when the air is cooled by frosty ground, becomes heavier and rolls downhill.

Cervidae the deer family. They are ruminants and the males of most species have antlers. Most are browsers by preference, but some are equally able to graze.

Glossary

chin-up display manner of carriage of the head by stags in the roar. The head is held out in front of the body on a straight neck, with the chin held up so that the muzzle is on the same level as the eyes.

chivvying behaviour exhibited by stags in the roar towards a hind of the harem. Stag chases the hind to see if she will stand to be mounted.

clamping fawns do it. They lie still and concealed until mother returns.

cleaning removing of dead velvet from a stag's antlers. Also called fraying.

cleaves pair of major weight-bearing structures of a deer's foot. They create most of the print. Each has an outer horny coat and an inner spongy layer.

company *see* stag company.

concentrate feeder animal whose diet consists of low-bulk, high-energy vegetable matter such as leaf buds and fruits.

conformation manner in which a body is structured or shaped; the proportions of the various parts. It forms the basis for distinguishing young from old, fit from unfit, and so on.

coronet ring of pearled bone at the base of each antler.

cudding process by which ruminants regurgitate the contents of their rumen to chew it thoroughly and mix it with saliva before reswallowing it to the reticulum.

deer bed position repeatedly used by deer for sitting and cudding. These places often become slightly hollowed out.

dentine inner portion of a tooth, beneath the outer layer of enamel. In deer it becomes exposed by wear on the molar and premolar teeth, forming upstanding ridges which are used for cudding.

dew claws small pair of horny structures on the rear-facing surface of each lower leg, 3 to 5 centimetres above the upper limit of the cleaves. They are the vestigial remains of the index and fifth digits.

diaphragm thin sheet of grey muscle separating the belly cavity from the heart/lung (thoracic) cavity

dominant hind leader of a hind group. She will lead the group during its movement from place to place, often deciding where to go and what to browse. Constantly alert for danger, she occupies the position with the best overall view of the surroundings. She maintains her dominance even during the rut. Also called a lead hind.

enamel hard outer coating of teeth. With tooth wear it remains at the tooth edges as a thin upstanding strip on either side of the molars and premolars, which aids in cutting and grinding.

epiphyte any plant that depends on another for physical support. Sometimes the plant will completely smother the other as it grows. Literally means "growing on the outside of". Does not include plants that are parasitic on others.

fag younger stag in a company of two, usually a spiker. The fag takes the risks, in emerging first from cover, for example, but learns cunning from the older animal. (The term derives from the English public-school system in which a fag was employed by senior boys to do chores.)

fatiguing scientific term describing the gradual wearing off of the arousing effect of a continuing stimulus. For example, if you stay in a smelly room for half an hour your sense of that smell declines — it fatigues.

fawn young deer.
fewmets old term for deer droppings.
foil old term for the tracks of deer on grass.
fraying *see* cleaning.
fraying stock damage to vegetation caused by a stag cleaning off velvet. Deer favour thin-stemmed dense foliage for this, leaving small marks on small twigs. (*see also* rubbing)
full point special stance of a dog signalling that it has sighted game.
grazing eating grass and herbs.
gutters longitudinal grooves in the main beam of the antler.
harbour old name for the place a stag conceals himself.
hearst Scottish term for a 2-year-old hind.
heel rear portion of the cleave. It is the widest part of the cleave and contains the ball.
herding behaviour of a stag in the roar when holding hinds. The stag will run the perimeter of his harem in a chin-up display, chasing after any hinds that have strayed too far and running them back to the main group.
hind group band of female red deer living together to their mutual advantage. These groups have much more collective responsibility than stag companies, which is why biologists coined separate terms for each. Hind groups, especially smaller ones, are frequently matrilineal. (*see also* matrilineal hind groups; stag companies)
humidity amount of moisture contained in the air. The more humid, the more water.
hummel male deer that produces no antlers owing to a genetic defect in his pedicles. A lifelong condition.
hydatids infectious disease occurring in deer, communicable to man. The primary host of the disease is the dog which excretes the eggs of the adult worms in its faeces. Secondary hosts, e.g. deer, pick up the eggs by grazing. The eggs are activated in the deer's gut and migrate to various organs to form fluid-filled cysts. Man can become infected in the same way as deer, by ingesting eggs, or, more commonly, by ingesting the fluid content of cysts which contain infective larval forms.
incisors chisel-shaped teeth at the front of the mouth (three pairs in the lower jaw and none in the upper) that are used by deer to grasp, bite and nibble vegetation before swallowing into the rumen.
initiating behaviour of a stag in the roar when he lowers his head and invites engagement with an opponent.
lead hind *see* dominant hind.
licking during the roar stags lick the pre-orbital gland area of hinds in their harems. A stag can probably tell whether a hind is about to ovulate by this method.
locking stage after initiating (q.v.)when two stags in the roar interlock antlers.
luminosity term denoting the light-gathering power of a telescopic sight as distinct from its magnifying power. A valuable quality for hunters of the dusk and dawn. High-luminosity scopes have large front lenses and small eyepieces. Vari-power scopes give their maximum luminosity when turned to their lowest magnification.

matrilineal hind group hind group consisting solely of hinds that are related matrilineally — that is, great grandmother, her daughters, their daughters, and so on. (*see also* hind group)

molars back teeth. There are three pairs in both the upper and lower jaws (both sexes the same), which wear in a characteristic manner to form surfaces used for cudding. (*see also* premolars)

murderer deer with no tines on its antlers for locking an opponent stag in a pushing contest. The opponent is often fatally speared in the head or flank.

musk substance produced by scent glands, which acts as a chemical advertisement during the roar and in territory marking. Originally the term for the secretion of the musk gland of the primitive and nearly extinct musk deer, which was valuable to the perfume industry. Its use has now broadened to include other deer and other scent-gland secretions.

nursery site traditional calving ground to which hinds return every year.

oesophagus muscular tube that runs from the mouth to the rumen. Swallowed food travels down it to return later to be cudded.

offer small outward growth from the main beam of an antler. Larger than a snag but too small to count as a tine.

omasum third part of the stomach of ruminants.

ovulation time when a hind may become pregnant; she has produced an egg and is ready for servicing by a stag. Until she has ovulated she will not allow herself to be mounted.

parallel walk behaviour of stags in the roar by which, before combat, they eye up each other's body size.

pearling studded appearance of antlers owing to numbers of small bumps of antler material arranged in longitudinal rows.

pecking order order of superiority in a stag company or hind group. Also called ranking.

pedicles bony outgrowths from the skulls of stags on which are formed the antlers.

pellet individual deer dropping.

photoperiod period of time in a given 24-hour period in which there is daylight, that is, from sunrise to sunset.

pre-orbital glands scent glands situated just in front of each eye, comprising small forward-facing grooves filled with a waxy substance. Stags use their scent to mark territory in the rut, while the secretions from hind's pre-orbital glands may change with the onset of ovulation. They are named after their situation.

premolars teeth that, together with the molars (q.v.) in deer, form the grinding surface used for cudding. Red deer have three pairs of premolars in both their upper and lower jaws.

pricket Scottish name for a 3-year-old stag.

primitive deer deer species that closely resemble the ancient deer from which all deer evolved. Features suggesting primitiveness are: small size; males antler-less; non-harem forming; concentrate feeding; and deep-forest dwelling.

print as used in this text: the single mark left by a single deer foot, or the composite mark left by the registration of a back footprint on a front footprint.

quartering cutting the carcass of a deer up into its four component limbs. Also, the position of a deer standing in relation to a hunter, in which one of the animal's limbs obscures the hunter's view of the remaining parts of the animal.

ranking *see* pecking order.

registration as deer walk the back footprint is superimposed on the print left by the front foot.

relative humidity amount of water vapour held in the air expressed as a percentage of the maximum it could hold at that temperature (*see also* humidity).

reticulum second part of a ruminant's stomach. It accepts the chewed cud and holds it ready for transit to the omasum.

roar contest behaviour of stags in the rut when they stand at a close distance and roar at each other to ascertain each other's size.

roar noise made by a stag during the rutting season to attract hinds and signal his size to his rivals. Also, a synonym for the rut.

roaring rate number of roars emitted per unit of time. This, and not the volume or tone of the roar, is the signal to rival stags of the size of the roaring stag. Bigger stags have faster roaring rates.

roaring stand place from which stags in the rut prefer to roar. Often these stands make use of natural features that amplify the sound.

routes as used in this text: the composite trail made by many deer. Usually made by animals on journeys of longer distances travelling along traditional pathways, they typically adhere to the easiest and most sheltered terrain. They may, over the years, become deeply rutted.

royal stag bearing 12 points in the form; brow, bez, trez plus three surroyals on each antler. Traditionally, the surroyals should also be of sufficient length to surround and support a whisky glass.

rubbing damage to trees caused by a stag polishing his antlers. Deep gouge marks are left on the trunks and branches. (*see also* fraying stock)

rumen first part of a ruminant's stomach. It acts as a simple storage organ for freshly eaten material awaiting cudding.

ruminant any herbivorous animal capable of cudding (q.v.).

rut *see* roar.

scissor kick action of a deer striking forwards with the cleaves of the forefeet. Used by hinds to exert dominance.

semipoint special stance of a dog signalling that it has smelt, but not seen, deer. Usually the dog has a thin strip of hair standing up on the top of its spine. Sometimes the dog will change its head carriage and move slowly.

showing flehmen singular behaviour of stags in the roar. After sniffing or licking a hind, or a hind's urine, the stag will give a chin-up display and simultaneously curl the upper lip upwards and outwards.

slot mark made by the cleave of a deer's foot in soft ground.

snag small outgrowth of bone from the main antler.

snare collar device used by researchers for marking deer in the wild. Set in a special trap, a numbered collar is automatically attached to deer that walk through.

Glossary

sniffing during the roar stags sniff the anal area of a hind and her freshly passed urine. A stag can probably tell whether a hind is about to ovulate, by this activity.

soil patch patch of urine-sodden odoriferous underbelly fur surrounding the genitals of a stag; most pronounced during the roar.

spiker 2-year-old male carrying upright straight antlers.

splay passive separation of the cleaves caused by greater force on the foot. The resultant print has a "V" shaped appearance.

stag male red deer. In New Zealand, the term is strictly interpreted as an animal 4 years or older.

stag company group of male deer living together for mutual benefit. Group welfare considerations are not as evident as in hind groups, hence the different term. (*see also* hind groups)

staggart Scottish term for a 4-year-old stag.

step distance between one print on one side and the next print made by feet on the other side.

stereo pair two aerial photos of the same area taken from slightly different positions, which enables a three-dimensional view to be obtained.

stride distance between successive prints of the same foot. Said to be roughly equal to the height of the animal at the shoulder.

stripping damage to a tree caused by a deer gnawing its bark.

surroyals tines at the uppermost branching point of the beam (q.v.). Also called tops.

switch stag bearing no points above the brow tine (q.v.). A "clean switch" is one with no brow tines.

tail glands *see* anal glands.

thermal inversion atmospheric condition in which a layer of colder air is trapped in valleys under a layer of warmer air, often with a mist layer at the boundary.

tine significant outgrowth from the main beam of the antler.

toe front (and narrowest) part of the cleave.

trail as used in this text: the set of successive prints made by a single deer.

velvet soft brownish covering which develops from pedicles (q.v.). It overlies and nourishes the developing antlers. With the increasing development of the antlers it becomes thinner, changing from soft to hard velvet and finally dies and is frayed off by the stag on bushes and trees.

wallow shallow, water-filled pools used by stags in the roar as an aid to spreading their urine scent over themselves. Stags urinate into the water and then roll in it.

wiping stags in the roar mark their territories by wiping the secretions of their pre-orbital gland on to branches and upstanding twigs.

yeld hind barren hind in the spring. Common in Scotland because of poor feeding conditions, but rare in New Zealand.

Descriptive bibliography

A Guide to Hunting in New Zealand. Philip Holden. Hodder and Stoughton (1987).
A chapter by chapter guide to hunting all the important big-game animals in New Zealand. Has an introductory chapter with maps of Forest and National Parks, and Recreational Hunting Areas. Appendices list addresses of government agencies that issue hunting permits and sell maps, New Zealand Deerstalkers' Association branches, registered hunting guides, and taxidermists. Currently a textbook in the New Zealand Deerstalkers' Association HUNTS training programme.

A herd of red deer. F.F. Darling. Oxford University Press (1937). Reprinted by Lowe and Brydon Printers 1941, 1946.
One of the great books on deer. It contains a lifetime's first-hand observations of red deer herds in Scotland. Very enjoyable reading. The scientific deductions have mostly stood the test of time and have been confirmed by more recent studies.

A hunting guide to introduced wild animals of New Zealand. L.H. Harris. Wellington: Government Printer (1973).
A most accurate and succinct account of the behaviour of red deer and other species, from a New Zealand perspective. The maps of animal distribution are a little out of date, but otherwise this handbook contains a wealth of essential information.

Art of successful deer hunting. Francis E. Sell. Stackpole Books (1971).
A relatively cheap paperback written for North American hunting, particularly of Columbia blacktail, mule and whitetail deer. However, there are good sections on the recovery of wounded deer, reading deer sign, snap shooting and other useful information for New Zealand hunters.

British deer and their horns. J.G. Millais. Henry Southeran and Co (1897).
A rare and fascinating big format book. Superb lithographic illustrations and early photographic prints. A very expensive collector's piece, but the National Library has a copy (unfortunately, in a bad state of repair). The text contains some interesting observations on the habits of red and other deer.

Deer. R.E. Chaplin. Blandford Press (1977).
Deer are examined from a zoological point of view. A jewel of a book, the colour photographs are superb, the text easily read and the section on antler growth particularly fascinating.

Deer farming in New Zealand. David Yerex. Deer Farming Service Division of Agricultural Promotion Associates (1979).
Written for deer farmers, but contains much information useful to the deerstalker.

Field guide to British deer. F.J. Taylor Page. British Deer Society Publication (1970).
A small easy-to-read handbook containing the basic elements of sign recognition plus information on seasonal variation of behaviour.

Descriptive bibliography 189

Highland year. L. MacNally. Phoenix Press (1968).
An easy-to-read account of herd behaviour in the Scottish Highlands. Exceptional photos of red deer in the wild.

Introduced mammals of New Zealand. K. A. Wodzicki. Wellington: DSIR (1950).
An account of the introduction and spread of red deer and other species in New Zealand. Has a section on the preferred browse of red deer, but otherwise of little relevance to the modern deerstalker.

Red deer. P. Delap. British Red Deer Society Publication (1970).
A small easy-to-read handbook of basic information on the British and Scottish red deer herds.

Red deer: behaviour and ecology of the two sexes. T.H. Clutton-Brock, Edinburgh University Press (1982).
A detailed scientific study of the behaviour of the red deer on the island of Rhum in Scotland. There is extensive statistical analysis of many painstaking and thorough scientific observations. Not a book for those unused to scientific terminology and shy of statistical mathematics.

Red deer farming in New Zealand. E. H. Dixon. Millwood Press (1975).
A small book written for deer farmers, but the sections on feeding preferences and the seasonal variations of behaviour are useful to the deerstalker.

Red deer stalking in New Zealand. T. E. Donne. First published Constable and Company Ltd (1924); reprinted Halcyon Press (1984) (limited edition).
Perhaps *the* "classical" book of New Zealand deerstalking. Recent scientific findings have made some of the information out of date, but some of the information has always been wrong, for example, the photo showing the aim points of the stag — with the sole exception of the headshot, the points shown are not killing shots. Nonetheless, an excellent book, giving some basic knowledge in deerstalking techniques, plus a feel of what it was like hunting in the early twentieth century in New Zealand.

Teeth as indicators of age with special reference to red deer of known age from Rhum. V.P.W. Lowe. *Journal Zoological Society,* London, 152, 137-153 (1967).
A scientific reference, but it is the only English language study of the method of dating the age of red deer from their teeth and therefore is essential reading for anyone wanting to accurately estimate age.

The microflora of the rumen. P.N. Hobson. Medowfield press.
A text for the scientific deerstalker. Describes in detail those organisms that live in the stomachs of Bovidae and Cervidae and whose job it is to break up cudded food.

The native trees of New Zealand, J.T. Salmon. Reed Methuen (1980), plus the companion volume *A field guide to the native trees of New Zealand,* J.T. Salmon, Reed Methuen (1986).
For the deerstalker who is serious about understanding the plants the quarry eats. Expensive but extremely useful. The small field guide is full of excellent photographs of the more common trees and is easily carried in a backpack.

The natural history of deer. Rory Putman. London: Christopher Helm Publisher (1988).

An analysis of the currently available scientific information on deer in general. Some knowledge of scientific terminology is required to understand this book.

The natural history of New Zealand, an ecological survey. Gordon Williams. Reed (1973).

Contains some information relevant to the deerstalker, especially the results of the Cupola Basin studies.

The sharp shooter. M. & B. Grant. Reed (1972).

Undoubtedly the best book available on ballistics for deerstalking in New Zealand conditions. An interesting section on efficient game killing complements the shooting section of our book.

The Young Hunter. Graeme Marshall. Halcyon Press (1987).

A good beginner's guide to hunting in New Zealand, covering many basic things not included in our book. For example, there are chapters on buying a rifle, sighting in, firearm safety, planning a trip, and reloading. Currently a textbook in the New Zealand Deerstalkers' Association's HUNTS training programme.

Vegetative cover of New Zealand. P.F.J. Newsome. National Water and Soil Conservation Authority.

An essential for the serious New Zealand deerstalker. Describes vegetation in all areas of New Zealand with detailed maps covering the whole country. Invaluable for planning a trip to a new area with which you are not familiar.

Wild deer. A. J. de Nahlick. Faber & Faber (1959).

Written for British and European conditions, but contains much information useful to the New Zealand hunter. Has a good section on deer recognition and the behaviour of deer when shot.

Index

Aerial photographs 90
Age estimation 163 168-9 171
Altitude 53
Antlers 18 166 168 176 178
    cleaning 18
    nomenclature 168 183
    rubbing 18
    shedding 24
    table 166
    velvet 18 166
    why deer have 176-8

Ball 6 11
Barking 25
Barometer 65
Beech 47
Bile 16
Boning out 156
Bovidae 176
Bringsel 119
Broadleaf forest 48 53
    species 45 47-50
Brocket 168
Browsing 18 19 51
Bulk feeders 176
Butchering 135
    boning out 156
    first observations 135
    gutting 137 139
    hanging 135
    quartering 148
    skinning 148

Calcium 34
Calving bellow 25 78
carrying a carcass 145
Chivvying 83
Clamping 79
Cleaning 18
Cleaves 6 13 73
Clothing for hunting 35 98
Coat 80
Conformation 161 163
Coprosma 41 47-8
Cross-breeding 178
Cudding 70
Cupola Basin 75

Deer
    beds 23-4 70 72
    dental formula 171

Irish elk 176
    noises 24
    reindeer 176
    sambar 178
    sika 178
    wapiti 178
    water deer 176
Dew claws 6 9 11
Dogs 113-9
Dominance 73 79
Droppings 16 18

Evolution 174 176

Fag 79
Fast sign 6
Fawn 25
Feeding 18
Fire 32
Fivefinger 41 47-50
Flehmen 83
Flushing 50
Food preference 39-51
Forest types 45 47
Fraying 18

German Short-haired Pointer 113-4
Grazing 18
Ground scenting 32
Gutting 137 139

Hair 24
Harems 176 178
Headskin hair 163 166
Hearing, sense of 33-4
Hearst 168
Helicopters 106
Herbivore 174
Herds, social structure 73
    in rut 82
Hilar kill zone 123 127
Hind groups 73 77-8
Hot spot 77
Humidity 34
Hummels 166
Hungarian Vizsla 113-4
Hunting methods 94
    alpine bushline 95
    bush stalking 95
    fixed position 94
    helicopter 106

hunting platform 35
in pairs 99
in roar 101-3
on farmland 104
on slips 105
putting out food 106
river beds & flats 94
stalking into roars 103
with dogs 106
Hunting pressure, effect on deer 92
Hydatids 143-4
Hygiene, importance of 136
Hygrometer 64

Initiating in rut 83
Intestines 137-9

Karamu 41

Leptospirosis 137
Licking, in rut 83
Locking of antlers 83
Luminosity of scope sights 160 184

Maps 45 90
Matrilineal 73 77
Maximum and minimum thermometer 64
Mixed forest types 50
Moonlight 63
Mouse deer 176
Mucus 16
Musk deer 174 176
Musk glands 33

Neck shot 128

Ovulation 33 79

Parallel walk 83
Pedicles 166
Photoperiod 57
Planning trips 92
Pointing 113
Post mortem 141 143-5
Pre-orbital glands 33 82
Prickett 168
Prints 5 9-11
Protein 39
Protozoa 39
Pulley block 136

Quartering 148

Registration 11 13
Reticulum 39
Roaring 25 82-3
Routes of travel 15

Rubbing, antler 19
Rumen 39 71
Rut 81

Scenting 32
Semi-pointing 113
Senses 30-8
Skinning 148
Smell, sense of 32
Snare collar 75
Sniffing, in rut 83
Social structure of herds 73
Soil patch 33
Sound 33-4
Spiker 168
Stag nomenclature 168
Staggart 168
Step 11
Stereoscopic photograph 91
Stride 11
Sunlight 57

Target practice 126
Teeth 169 171
Territory 175 180
Testosterone 166
Thermal inversion 59
Timing of roar 57 84
Topographical maps 90
Toxins 39 51
Tracking wounded deer 128 130-1
Trail 11 13
Tuberculosis 141 143

Vegetative cover maps 47 90
Vision, sense of 34-5
Vital points 123

Wallows 20 23
Weather effects 57
autumn 78 81
catabatic winds 58-9
fatiguing of senses 61
frost 59 61
humidity 60-1
rain 62
snow 63
spring 77 80
wind 58
winter 77 80
Weimaraner 113-4
Whiteywood 45
Wind 58

Yarding up 77 80
Yersinea enterocolitica 137